I0148359

IT STARTED
IN THE GARDEN

*A Biblical journey back to the Garden of Eden
to discover God's plan for marriage*

Tim and Mary Lou Tiner

innovo
PUBLISHING

Published by
Innovo Publishing LLC
www.innovopublishing.com
1-888-546-2111

Providing Full-Service Publishing Services for
Christian Authors, Artists & Organizations: Hardbacks, Paperbacks,
eBooks, Audiobooks, Music & Videos

It Started in the Garden
Copyright © 2012 by Tim and Mary Lou Tiner
All rights reserved.

No part of this publication may be reproduced, stored in a retrieval system, or
transmitted in any form or by any means electronic, mechanical, photocopying,
recording, or otherwise, without the prior written permission of the author.

Unless otherwise indicated, Biblical quotes are from The New King James
version of the Bible © 1982, Thomas Nelson, Inc.

ISBN 978-1-61314-045-1

Cover Design & Interior Layout: Innovo Publishing LLC

Printed in the United States of America

U.S. Printing History
First Edition: 2012

DEDICATION

We dedicate this book to our five children,
their wonderful spouses,
and our amazing grandchildren.

We thank the Lord for each of you
and pray your marriages will always be
a beautiful reflection of Jesus' love.

We dedicate this book to Jesus,
to be used as He chooses.

Without Jesus, the pages of this book
would be empty, as would our lives.

CONTENTS

ACKNOWLEDGMENTS

Special thanks to Kelly Stern for the wonderful,
professional service she offered in editing the text for us.
Thank you for donating your time and talents
to making this book what it is today.
We couldn't have done it without you!

Thank you, Steve and Gail Felker, for your insights, wisdom,
honesty, and faithfulness in proofreading each chapter
and challenging us to think more deeply.

Thank you, Mel Davis, for coming to our rescue and formatting
our book. Your keen eye and designing skills are amazing!

Thank you to many of our dearest friends, who have prayed
for this project and encouraged us to keep going.

To our children and their spouses: thank you!
You have believed in us and shared in
our excitement over this project.
Thank you for writing the foreword for the book.
Most of all, thank you for being examples
of the truth contained herein.

Thank you, Jesus, for healing our marriage,
for giving us the amazing relationship we have today,
and for allowing us the privilege of sharing
Your truth and hope.

FOREWORD

When I was asked to contribute to the foreword for this book, I was humbled and delighted to do so. However, after being informed that I didn't need to write a book myself for this foreword, I was less enthusiastic. The question arose almost instantly: "How could I condense thirty-plus years of gratitude into a few words?" Gratitude? Yes! That is the word I would choose to use to thank my parents for the countless hours of wisdom that they poured into my life in preparation for marriage.

Take this advice from the oldest child of the Tiner tribe: Listen to the wisdom that is conveyed in this book, and act on it. I benefited from years of input as my parents poured this information into my heart. Today, because of what Mom and Dad taught us as a couple, my husband Stephen and I have a dynamic and vibrant relationship based on the Lordship of Jesus Christ and the wise counsel of Scripture.

Both Mom and Dad have spent decades counseling couples and individuals, pouring the truth of God's Word into their lives and asking God to bring transformation to these hurting people. My husband and I are a testimony to the wisdom and accuracy of the counsel that they give. All of what you will learn in this book needs to be revisited at regular intervals in order to keep a healthy marriage relationship. Don't wait until there are problems to learn what the solutions are! Be proactive in your marriage by seeking wisdom. Keep your focus on Jesus and His Word, and allow this book to give you greater insight into how to translate the truth of Scripture into your marriage.

Thank you, Mom and Dad, for caring so much about me and my future family. Thank you for equipping me with the tools I would need even *before* I was looking for a husband. My heart was *(and still is)* ready to be guided by the Lord because of how you shepherded me.

Thank you,

Julianne Bounds

(Julianne is the oldest of the five Tiner children. Julianne and her husband Stephen are currently living in Illinois, where Stephen serves as associate pastor. Julianne is actively involved in ministry alongside Stephen. They have been married since 1997 and have five children.)

I recently ran an Internet search on "books on marriage" and in less than one second, I had 272 million results! You could attend marriage seminars and conferences year-round. The good, the bad, and the ugly marriage resources are in abundance (and yes…there is an app for that!). It is easy to get marriage advice on the radio, television, and Internet as well as from magazines, self-help books, doctors, parents, and pastors…but even with such a myriad of tools and "wisdom" at our disposal, marriages are still falling apart. Why? Our society quickly turns to those who have a popular opinion or "flavor of the week" idea about marriage. In so doing, we have neglected the Designer and Creator of marriage. Is it any wonder that marriages are falling apart?

I have truly lived a blessed life, for my parents did not just study God's design for marriage but lived it out on a daily basis. I was their ever-watching student. I have read this book cover to cover many times—not the words, per se, but the living out of their truth: I have watched my parents loving each other, working out disagreements, being patient with each other, and being humble toward each other. I have seen this book lived out. My parents' investment in their marriage by living out God's design continues to reap massive dividends not only in their marriage but also in mine and countless others'.

I encourage you to seek to live out for yourself God's design for marriage. In fact, I urge you to seek not merely the design, but most important, seek the Designer Himself. Not only does God have a perfect design for our marriages, but He also has a perfect design for our lives. God will help each of us live out that design if we only ask Him to. Ask Him and seek Him, and you will experience blessing in your marriage and in your life—beyond your wildest imagination.

Joshua Tiner

(Joshua is the second born Tiner. Joshua lives with his wife Mindy in Alaska – and absolutely loves it there! Joshua serves as Children's Pastor at The Crossing Church. Josh and Mindy were married in 2000 and have three children.)

Writing a foreword is a HUGE responsibility! It may be the only thing a person reads to determine whether a book is worth his time and money. So allow me to make this easy for you: If you are looking for a quick fix to your marriage, then put this book down! Seriously! Marriage takes a lot of work! But if you are up to the challenge, then this book needs to be on your "Top 10 Must-Read" booklist this year. This book is filled with more wisdom, truth, and "ah-ha" moments than I can count!

My mom and dad are exceptional writers, lovers, and parents. They capture the very essence of what marriage is all about. Growing up, I had a "front row seat" in their marriage. I saw this book lived out on a day-to-day basis long before my mom and dad sought to put its truths on paper. I am so blessed to call Tim & Mary Lou my parents, and I pray that the godly principles articulated in this book will transform your life as they have my husband's and mine.

Janna Clark

(Janna is the third child in the Tiner line-up. Janna and her husband Todd will be moving to Alaska with their three children in the summer of 2012. Todd will serve as principal of Birchwood Christian School and Janna will work as Assistant Director of Children's Ministry at The Crossing Church. They were married in 2004.)

When my parents asked my wife and me to write a short foreword for their book, I started to think about what I could say. I have to be honest and tell you that I really didn't know what to write! The reason? It is like trying to describe a pepperoni pizza to someone who has neither eaten one nor even seen a picture of one. How would you begin to describe the most delicious thing ever?

Then I thought that the best thing I could say is that my parents have always been an outstanding example for me, and a great source of information, both Biblical and practical. This has been a great help to me in the circumstances of my everyday life. Without my parents by my side, I would not be the man I am today. As the fourth of five kids in the Tiner family, I know I've had my fair share of ups and downs. But even though life is sometimes a rollercoaster, I have seen that God and my parents have always been there—not only as an example for me but also for many others.

Love you, Mom and Dad!

Josiah and Elke Tiner

(Josiah is the fourth sibling. Josiah and his wife, Elke, live in Knittelfeld, Austria. Together they serve as worship leaders in their church. Josiah completed training as a Master Coffee Roaster and started his own coffee roasting business in 2012. They were married in 2008 and are currently expecting the arrival of their first child in September, 2012.)

I have to admit that I thought it was a bit funny when my parents asked me to contribute to the foreword of their book; after all, I'm the only one in our family who is still unmarried! Nevertheless, I have seen firsthand what a healthy marriage looks like. And as a result of watching my parents, I can't wait to be married myself. Every day I've had the privilege of seeing my parents grow even more in love with each other.

I cannot think of anyone else who is better qualified than my parents to write a book about marriage. This book is not merely a bunch of words in a fancy cover; rather, it is God-given wisdom and experience that my parents want to share with you. So even though I may seem unqualified to recommend this book, believe me when I say that it may well be God's way of bringing you and your spouse closer to each other—provided you allow God to work.

Thank you, Mom, for caring and loving me every minute of my life. And Dad, thank you for preparing me for life and being a godly example to me.

Josef Tiner

(Josef is the youngest of the Tiner's children. Josef graduated from high school in 2012 and will begin attending Bible College in the Fall.)

HOW TO USE THIS BOOK

This book is a tool, not a magic wand. It has no secret power to heal a broken marriage, restore a lukewarm relationship, or prevent a healthy marriage from becoming sick. But it does present God's "instruction manual" for marriage as it is communicated in the Bible. If you are willing to apply God's principles to your relationship with your spouse, you will be amazed by the miracle God will produce in your life.

God wants to give you life in abundance! John 10:10 says, "The thief does not come except to steal, and to kill, and to destroy. I [Jesus] have come that they may have life, and that they may have it more abundantly." Many "thieves" creep into the garden of marriage intent on stealing, killing, and destroying the unity, joy, and love that God intends for us to experience in marriage. But Jesus has come to bring life in abundance.

This book communicates the truth about God's plan for marriage as set forth in the Bible. But you must do more than acknowledge or even agree with it on an intellectual level. As is often said, "A good marriage takes work; a great marriage takes even more!" You must decide: Is your marriage worth working to improve? Are you willing to do all it may take to bring healing and restoration?

Who should use this book?
- Couples who are engaged.
- Couples who have healthy marriages and want to keep them that way.
- Couples whose marriages seem dry and desert-like.
- Couples whose marriages seem overgrown with weeds and overrun with enemies.
- Couples who believe their marriages are dead.

- Counselors, pastors, teachers, and individuals seeking a Biblical resource on marriage.

In what context should this book be used?
- Personal study.
- Small groups.
- Sunday School classes.
- Marriage seminars.

This book includes an introduction, which provides an important foundation for this study, followed by fourteen chapters of teaching material, and one chapter of resources. At the end of each chapter is a study guide designed to help readers make personal applications to their marriage. We encourage you to take your time to work through this book. We suggest allowing a week for each chapter. Be willing to invest fully in this study—and prepare to be amazed by the blessing you will reap. Make a commitment to complete the entire book. Most important, make it a priority to pray for your spouse and for yourself—that the Lord will speak to you as you allow His Word to saturate your marriage.

If you are reading this book as a couple, we suggest that you first read each chapter and complete the study guide individually. (It is best not to answer the study guide questions with your spouse. Many of the questions encourage husband and wife to take inventory of attitudes and actions they might need to change. So carefully think through your response to each question, and record your answers—perhaps in a notebook rather than in the book itself. You also may wish to record additional notes, insights, questions, and/or action plans.) Then read the chapter a second time, together. Discuss insights you gained or questions you have. Then share your responses to the study guide questions.

If you are using this book in a small group or Sunday school class, we suggest a similar schedule: one week per chapter. Remember that many of the questions in the study guide are not designed to be answered in a group setting; rather, answers should be shared by the couples, privately. If possible, allocate time at the end of each study for couples to share their answers privately with each other.

Prayer is critical in a study of this nature. We strongly suggest assigning prayer partners for each couple for the duration of the study. The prayer partners do not need to attend the study but should be willing to pray faithfully for and even with their assigned couple. It is preferable for the prayer partners to be other married couples.

If you are a leader or teacher, you will want to familiarize yourself with additional resources. Many of the issues discussed in this book—to include pornography, adultery, past hurts, etc. —are not easily resolved and may require Biblical counseling. Perhaps an accountability partner or a mentor is needed. Prayerfully consider who that person(s) might be.

You may wish to consider a weekend kick-off for your study, perhaps at your church or at a hotel. Chapters one through four could be covered during a two-day retreat. (Be sure to allow sufficient free time for each couple to process together what they are learning.) For many couples, just having time away from everyday activities allows for realignment and refocusing.

We are available to lead marriage seminars for your church or home group. We do not charge a fee for the seminars we lead. It is our desire, passion, and joy to serve the Body of Christ freely. Please contact us to schedule a seminar. Seminars typically are two to three days in length but can be adapted to meet your needs.

Contact: ttiner@mac.com
tiner@tinerfamily.com

*May God bless you as you seek to align your marriage
with His purposes!*

IT STARTED IN THE GARDEN

"Therefore a man shall leave his father and mother and be joined to his wife, and they shall become one flesh." As these words echoed around the great marble hall of the ancient cathedral, the awed look on the faces of those attending the wedding ceremony in this small French village could not be missed. It was not the bride or the solemn beauty of the cathedral that held their gaze; it was the words that were being spoken.

As I stood behind the pulpit facing the bride and groom, I continued preaching. I was using the Bible as the foremost instruction manual on marriage. I explained how it all started in the Garden of Eden. The majority of those present had attended church only rarely—and for similar occasions. After the ceremony, as the bride and groom were being photographed, many of the guests approached me with comments such as, "I never knew God had so much to say about marriage!" and "Is all that *really* in the Bible?" I was amazed that so many people in that church were unaware that marriage is God's idea and that He has a lot to say about it.

For many years, my wife and I have been asked to write a book based on the material we use in the marriage seminars we lead. With so many books already written on this subject, what makes us qualified to write yet another? Are we qualified because of the studies we did on this subject in Bible college and seminary? Does our qualification rely on the numerous marriage seminars we've led or the many hours of marriage counseling we've performed? Or are we qualified because we've been married since 1973?

While these qualifications may impress you, we choose instead to point to our testimony: We are a couple whose marriage has been saved and renewed by applying God's Word to our lives. We can speak from personal experience that God's plan works!

In 1973, shortly before we married, we chose Proverbs 3:5–6 as our life verse: "Trust in the Lord with all your heart, and lean not on your own understanding. In all your ways acknowledge Him, and He shall direct your paths." Whenever we have tried to lean on our own understanding, we have fallen flat on our faces! In those times, when we've been groveling around on the ground, we've learned that only by acknowledging Him and His perfect plan can we get on the right path and avoid some nasty bruises!

The purpose of this book is to open God's Word to you and to help you discover, as we have, God's perfect plan for marriage. We believe God is the ultimate authority on marriage and on the amazing plan He started in the Garden of Eden.

The Purpose: to open God's Word to you and help you discover God's perfect plan for marriage.

Like many of the guests attending that wedding in France, countless couples today believe the Bible is irrelevant to the institution of marriage. Many claim that we cannot apply the various cultural and historical situations of the Bible to our world today. Others would rather trust in the wisdom of man and modern psychology, believing that therein lie the answers to the numerous problems plaguing marriages today. Some may even declare that it is old fashioned, uneducated, and naïve to use the Bible as a complete guide for marriage.

However, we make no apology for what we believe. Our core belief is this: God's Word, the Bible, is the absolute authority. We believe the Bible speaks truth that will transform the lives and relationships of those who choose to embrace it. Our belief in the authority of God's Word is not simply wishful thinking. We have experienced firsthand the power of God's Word in our lives and in the lives of others. Psalm 18:30 tells us, "As for God, His way is perfect; the Word of the Lord is proven; He is a shield to all who trust in Him." God's Word has been proven in our lives. His way *is* perfect!

In Isaiah 55:8–9, we read, "'For My thoughts are not your thoughts, nor are your ways My ways,' says the Lord. 'For as the heavens are higher than the earth, so are My ways higher than your ways and My thoughts than your thoughts.'" We invite you to consider with us what may be a startling idea for you: God's ways are not the same as your ways! God has a perfect plan for marriage, and His plan is very different from what culture, psychology, or even tradition suggests.

Read further in Isaiah 55:10–11a: "For as the rain comes down and the snow from heaven and do not return there but water the earth and make it bring forth and bud, that it may give seed to the sower and bread to the eater, so shall My Word be that goes forth from My mouth; it shall not return to Me void." Isn't it interesting that many people describe their marriages as being void or empty? What is it that they are missing? Are they expecting their partners to fill this emptiness in their lives, only to be bitterly disappointed? Could it be that they are choosing their own ways and rejecting God's?

"But it [My Word] shall accomplish what I please, and it shall prosper in the thing for which I sent it" (Isaiah 55:11b). God gives us a promise: His Word will bring fullness of life, not emptiness. Just as the rain causes the seed to grow and produce, so His Word brings forth new life in us. Can your marriage really prosper without God's Word? No! Only when we allow His Word to permeate our lives and relationships can we stand on His promise that He will bring a prosperous result.

Keep reading in Isaiah: "For you shall go out with joy and be led out with peace…" (Isaiah 55:12a). This is a promise for those who have allowed God's Word into their lives. Would you describe your marriage as a peaceful and joy-filled union? Is this the longing of your heart?

Isaiah continues: "The mountains and the hills shall break forth into singing before you, and all the trees of the field shall clap their hands" (Isaiah 55:12b). Does your marriage make your heart sing, not just when you are standing on the mountaintop but even when you are climbing up those jagged slopes? Or perhaps you feel as if the mountains and the hills are falling down on top of you.

We particularly love what Isaiah says next: "Instead of the thorn shall come up the cypress tree, and instead of the brier shall come up the myrtle tree; and it shall be to the Lord for a name, for an everlasting sign that shall not be cut off" (Isaiah 55:13). Are you tired of living among the thorns? The Lord desires to create something of beauty in your marriage, something He can write His name on and take credit for. When an artist has created a masterpiece, he writes his name in the corner. In the same way, God wants to write His name on your marriage as He creates a masterpiece in your life! We encourage you to allow God's Word to become the ultimate authority in your life and marriage. Your marriage can become a work of art.

Are you tired of living among the thorns?

What about you? If you could compare your marriage to a painting, what would your marriage look like? Has God just set the canvas on the easel and only now is mixing the colors? Some of you may not yet be married. We are thrilled that you are reading this book! We love working with couples before they are married and helping them lay the best foundation. It is much easier to begin with an empty canvas. Our prayer for you is that the Lord will use this book in your life to help you start fresh and clean, without any smudges.

Perhaps you already are married, and you feel as though your marriage has faded and lost the vibrancy it once had. No problem! The Lord is masterful at retouching, restoring, and renewing.

Some of you may be thinking, "Our marriage is so messed up, there is no hope. All our attempts to create something of beauty have failed, and we are ready to throw the whole thing out." *Stop! Don't do that!* It is never too late to start anew. Allow the Lord to take over, and you will be amazed at the masterpiece only He can create.

So join us as we go back to the beginning....
After all, it started in the garden!
Tim and Mary Lou Tiner

Author's note: Whenever brackets [ ] are used within a Bible passage, the comment or explanation is ours, provided for the sake of clarity.

Throughout this book, we relate stories of various couples we have known and counseled over the years. In order to respect the privacy of these couples, names and some identifying details have been changed.

INTRODUCTION

Read Psalm 18:30 and Isaiah 55:8–13

The purpose of this study is to help you discover God's perfect plan for your marriage. We believe God is the Creator of all things, including marriage. God is the One who placed in motion the amazing plan He started in the Garden of Eden. Our core belief is this: God's Word, the Bible, is the absolute authority. Because marriage is God's idea, there is no better place to go for guidance, instruction, correction, or help than "THE SOURCE": God's Word.

Throughout this study, we use God's Word as our instruction manual. We believe the Bible speaks truth that will transform the lives and relationships of those who choose to embrace it. Our belief in the authority of God's Word is not simply wishful thinking. Rather, we have experienced first-hand the power of God's Word in our lives and in the lives of others. Our prayer for you is that your marriage will be enriched and transformed by the power of God's Word.

DIGGING DEEPER

1. Read Psalm 18:30: "As for God, His way is perfect; the Word of the Lord is proven; He is a shield to all who trust in Him."

   a. List three key words from this text:
   1. God's way is:
   2. God's Word is:
   3. God is a:

    b. What must we do? (read the end of the verse):

    c. How has God's Word been proven to you in the past?

2. Read Isaiah 55:8–9: "'For My thoughts are not your thoughts, nor are your ways My ways,' says the Lord. 'For as the heavens are higher than the earth, so are My ways higher than your ways and My thoughts than your thoughts.'"

    a. How can we apply this verse to marriage? What "ways" of man could be included here?

3. Read Isaiah 55:10–11: "For as the rain comes down and the snow from heaven and do not return there but water the earth and make it bring forth and bud, that it may give seed to the sower and bread to the eater, so shall My Word be that goes forth from My mouth; it shall not return to Me void but it [My Word] shall accomplish what I please, and it shall prosper in the thing for which I sent it."

    a. What promise do we find here about God's Word?

    b. What do you think God wants to accomplish in your marriage?

    c. Can your marriage prosper without God's Word?

4. "For you shall go out with joy and be led out with peace; the mountains and the hills shall break forth into singing before you, and all the trees of the field shall clap their hands. Instead of the thorn shall come up the cypress tree, and instead of the brier shall come up the myrtle tree; and it shall be to the Lord for a name, for an everlasting sign that shall not be cut off." Isaiah 55:12–13

   a. Circle the words in the text above that describe your marriage.

   b. Underline the words that do not describe your marriage.

   c. The Lord wants to write His name on your marriage. Does your marriage reflect His glory, or does it reflect something else?

   d. What other words would you use to describe your marriage?

5. Compare your marriage to a painting. The Lord wants to create a masterpiece on the canvas of your marriage that will bring Him glory. The world should be able to see His signature in the corner. Using this analogy, at what stage is your marriage? (check whatever applies)

   ☐ God has placed a blank canvas on the easel and is just beginning to paint.
   ☐ The colors in your painting have faded. You need to be refreshed and restored.
   ☐ Your painting has been damaged. You have tried to create this painting without God's help, and you have made a mess.
   ☐ You are ready to throw the whole painting away. It seems beyond repair.
   ☐ You blame God for how your painting looks.
   ☐ Other people can see the Lord's name written in the corner.

CHAPTER ONE

ALONE IN THE GARDEN

An Imaginative Paraphrase of Genesis 2

A gentle mist had settled over the garden, and the air was delightfully cool. Sunlight cascaded through the branches of fruit-laden trees, causing the blades of grass to glisten and glimmer like diamonds. The garden was alive with brilliant, luminous colors. Every plant was in full bloom, filling the air with a sweet, glorious fragrance. Every tree was beautiful to look at and filled with the very best of fruits.

The ground was covered with the softest turf. There were no thorns or troublesome weeds. Nuggets of gold and other precious gems could be seen reflecting from the bottom of the crystal clear river that flowed through the garden.

This was no ordinary garden. The Maker Himself had planted it. He had chosen the most beautiful trees, the most perfect bushes, and the most unique plants from all His creation. He had laid it out with perfect care, arranging and combining the plants, bushes, and trees to provide the best growing conditions and the most luxurious setting.

There were shady spots where the lacy moss of the trees hung down like a curtain around an especially soft patch of grass; tiny hills with low bushes overflowing with the sweetest, juiciest berries; and ferns and water lilies gracing the river banks. Rose bushes replete with colorful blooms stood gracefully between the vines and trees of the orchard.

Into this perfect garden home, the Maker brought the man to live. Together, the man and the Maker walked along grass-covered paths. The

Maker pointed to this plant or that tree and explained why He had created it and what it was good for.

The man enjoyed the most amazing food. There was always some new fruit or vegetable to taste, and he was never bored. The river was so clear and pure that even the smallest sip satisfied completely. What more could a man ask for?

The man, Adam, loved his garden home and the jobs the Maker had given him to do. Not only was he to cultivate the garden, but Adam also had the task of giving names to the animals. Mooing or neighing, grunting or purring, the animals were brought to Adam, and Adam gave them their names.

The Maker smiled as Adam walked up to the first creature and gently stroked its head. Adam looked him over thoughtfully and then announced, "Lion. Yes, it shall be called a lion. Oh, wait! There is another one. That is also a lion." Adam noticed a small, furry creature scurrying past the feet of the lion, and he said, "Hmm. How about calling this little fellow a hamster? And there goes another one!" The Maker pointed to another group of animals. Adam continued, "You two are kangaroos. I'll call you llamas; you look like camels; and you big creatures are yaks."

Slowly, something began to occur to Adam. He mentioned it to the Maker during one of their walks. "I have noticed You have created two of every kind of animal. There are some differences, but it is clear they belong together, and they seem to take pleasure being with their mate."

Adam continued giving names to the creatures, and as he did, he became more and more aware of this pattern: There were two of everything—Mr. and Mrs. Elephant, Mr. and Mrs. Zebra, Mr. and Mrs. Panda Bear—but only one of him. He finally came to the realization: "I have found no one like me. I AM ALONE!"

"Finally!" thought the Maker. "He gets it!"

A CLOSER LOOK

Most of you are familiar with the story of creation. (If you missed this story in Sunday school, please take a moment to read Genesis chapters one and two now.) Have you ever asked yourself why God created things the way He did? There are three questions that jump out at us from this passage:

1. Why did God make Adam (the man) before Eve (the woman)?
2. Why did God make Adam wait before He created Eve?
3. Why did God give Adam the job of naming the animals?

The first question emerges as we examine the account of creation. We see absolute perfection in the order of God's plan. God waited until the sixth day to create man because man certainly could not have survived had he been created on the first or second day—not unless he could have treaded water for a long time! (Just in case you forgot: water covered the earth until day three of creation, when dry land appeared.) We can easily discern that God is a God of order and purpose. In chapter two, we see that God created man and then, some time later, God created woman. Why did God create man first? Why not create them simultaneously? Was God trying to indicate that man was more valuable than woman? Is that why He created man first? No! This is not what God's Word teaches. (See Galatians 3:28.) God had a purpose in creating man first, but it was not to indicate gender preference. Before we answer this first question, let's consider the other two questions.

The second question arises as we look at Genesis 2:18–20. God said, "It is not good that man should be alone." And yet, God did make man alone. Did God make a mistake, or did He come to this realization only after He had created man? Obviously not! God does not make mistakes, and He is all-knowing. Adam's aloneness did not come as a surprise to God. There must be another explanation.

We read in the rest of verse 18 that God was planning to "make him [Adam] an help meet for him" (KJV). God recognized Adam's need and planned to create Eve; yet we see that God didn't create Eve immediately. In verses 19 and 20, God assigned Adam a task to do first. Since God knew it wasn't good for Adam to be alone, why did God make him wait? Why not bring this wonderful gift to Adam right away? Why give him a job to do first?

Finally, the third question: Why did the Maker give Adam this particular job of naming the animals? Did God really need Adam to come up with names because He couldn't think of any Himself? Clearly, the Lord of all creation doesn't need help coming up with original ideas! Was He trying to give Adam some sense of worth or purpose by giving him this task to do? No. If God only wanted to keep Adam busy, then just cultivating the garden would have fulfilled that need—especially if God permitted a few weeds to grow!

So we return to our three questions: Why did God create Adam first? Why did God make Adam wait before He created Eve? Why did God give Adam the job of naming the animals? There is one answer to all three questions: God wanted Adam to discover for himself that something was missing. Adam needed to see he was alone and that it was not good. This understanding would lead Adam to appreciate the wonderful gift of woman!

The Maker had a purpose in giving Adam the job of naming the animals. In bringing the animals to Adam, God allowed him to discover his human uniqueness as well as his human need. At some point in the naming process, Adam must have discovered a pattern in God's creation: there were males and females. We read in Genesis 2:20 that Adam did not find another creature like himself; Adam discovered he didn't have a counterpart.

We don't know how much time passed as Adam went about the task of naming the animals. We don't know how long it took before Adam finally realized, "Hey, I am alone! There is no one like me!" But we do know this: Adam finally acknowledged his need, and God was ready to respond.

This brings us to our first lesson from the garden: It is not good for man to be alone. God never intended for man to be a self-sufficient, solitary being. God's design from the beginning of time was for man to have a "help-meet." Taking a quick look at this word, we discover two important things: first, man needs help! Second, he needs help that is "meet" for him—that is, help that is suitable, appropriate, fitting, complementary, satisfying, or completing.

God never intended for man to be a solitary being.

Unfortunately, too many men today have not learned this first lesson. They may be married, but they live very solitary lives, particularly in the way they relate to their wives. These men don't realize they need their wives, and therefore they fail to appreciate them.

Some men today have segregated their marriages from other areas of their lives. This kind of man lives in his own world. He has his career, his interests, his friends, and his possessions. He doesn't relate to his wife on any real, deep, or personal level. While he coexists in the same house with his wife, they don't truly live together. He doesn't think he needs her. He doesn't realize that he is alone and that it is not good.

Let me introduce you to a man named Carl. Carl dashes out the door each morning before the sun comes up, with a cup of coffee in his hand. He works at least 12 hours a day, often longer. After work he heads to the gym to work off the stress of the day or out for drinks with co-workers. By the time he arrives home, his children have finished their dinner and are already in bed. He takes his dinner out of the oven and plops down in front of the TV to watch the news. He is vaguely aware that his wife is talking to him and gives her an occasional nod between mouthfuls. After dinner he heads to the computer to finish some work he brought home with him. Around midnight, he falls into bed, exhausted.

Carl thinks he is a good husband. He has never been unfaithful to his wife. He works hard and has provided his family a nicely furnished home. He even goes to church with his family each Sunday. Carl thinks he doesn't need anything. But Carl is wrong. Carl is alone, and it is not good. What he is experiencing is not God's plan for marriage.

Other men view their wives as a possession or status symbol, not something they need but rather something they own. Let me introduce you to another man. Patrick met his wife in college and was especially drawn to her beauty and sweet personality. She was quite popular, and Patrick felt like the king of the campus when she walked beside him. Soon after he graduated, they were married.

Patrick, who is highly educated, regards his wife as intellectually inferior. He is proud of how beautiful she is and often brags about having such a lovely wife. But he also makes cruel jokes about how there isn't much inside his wife's lovely little head. He often belittles her in public, interrupting her when she makes a comment and correcting her in a patronizing manner. Patrick often recounts the sacrifices he makes, particularly in putting up with the foolish things his wife does.

Like Carl, Patrick thinks he is a good husband. After all, he never misses an opportunity to correct his wife and instruct her. He thinks his wife should be thankful to have a man like him taking care of her. Patrick doesn't think he needs anything. But Patrick is wrong. Patrick is alone, and it is not good. What he is experiencing is not God's plan for marriage.

Both Carl and Patrick have failed to learn this simple truth: "Hey! You are alone! IT IS NOT GOOD! You need your wife!"

Frequently in counseling situations, the wife will share how very alone she feels in her marriage: "My husband has created his own self-sufficient world. He has his career and his colleagues. Hobbies, sports, and entertainment occupy his free time. He has no time for me. He wants me to fulfill his physical needs, but sometimes I think that is all I am good for."

"What does she want from me?" the husband retorts. "I bring home a good salary. I even help with the chores around the house. Why is my wife so needy?" Not only is this husband alone, but neither does he see how very alone his wife is!

It is interesting to consider why God didn't take Eve through the same learning process as He did Adam. Did Eve need to be shown that she was alone and that it was not good? Or is it possible that God created her differently? God could have created Adam and Eve simultaneously, placed them in separate gardens, and allowed them both to discover their need for each other. But this is not what He did. Is it possible that God knew it would be Adam, not Eve, who needed to learn this lesson?

It has been our experience in counseling situations that it is usually the wife who first seeks help for a troubled marriage. Most women seem to have an instinctive ability to discern their need for relationship as well as to determine when something is lacking. The husband is often clueless that anything is wrong. Like Adam, he is alone and hasn't quite figured out that something is missing!

Men: As we look more closely at this passage, we challenge you to prayerfully consider your relationship with your wife. The focus of this next section is directed primarily at you. After all, God started with you in the Garden of Eden.

Women: Don't stop reading! Although we are zeroing in on your husbands, there are some important truths here for you. Do not underline all the passages in this book that your husband really must read! Rather, let the Lord speak to him! And open your heart to hear what the Lord would say to you.

We want to consider three foundational points from Genesis chapter two:

- Man must realize he has a need.
- Man must receive God's provision to meet the need.
- Man must rejoice in the provision he has received.

REALIZE THE NEED
Tim's Story

We have already discussed how God allowed Adam to realize he was alone. Let me tell you a bit of my story. When I was a young man in college, it became more and more obvious to me that I needed a wife. Well, to be more accurate, I probably didn't realize just how much I needed a wife, but I sure wanted one!

Like most men my age, I was on the "hunt!" In my immaturity, I'm sure I operated under many misconceptions and expectations. I wasn't fully aware of what I really needed. On the surface, I was searching for companionship—someone to work alongside me in ministry, someone who would love me and appreciate me.

When I found Mary Lou, I knew my hunt was over. After our first date, I knew I was going to marry her. We had spent hours together sharing our dreams. We had everything in common: the same faith, goals, and commitment to Christ. Besides all that, she was beautiful! Truly this would be a marriage made in heaven!

We enjoyed the first years of our marriage—the so-called honeymoon phase. It was fun simply being together. But as time passed, a subtle change occurred. Gradually, I became self-sufficient. I was serving as associate pastor in a vibrant new church. Many people looked up to me as an authority figure, and I had many responsibilities. The Lord had blessed us with children, so Mary Lou was busy changing diapers and chasing toddlers. No longer did I view her as someone I needed or even really valued. She wasn't quite on my level anymore. I wasn't even sure that her opinion was all that valid.

Slowly, we grew apart. Oh, I did love her, in my own way. But I didn't think I needed her. God had to do some painful chiseling in my life to finally bring me to the realization that, like Adam, I was alone! Into the ashes of our marriage, the Lord breathed new life. He healed what was broken and helped me realize what an amazing gift my wife is and how I had taken her for granted.

More than anyone else, Mary Lou has helped me grow in my faith, ministry, character, and abilities. Time and again God has used her in my life to speak truth to me. She has tremendous strengths, insights, and gifts that I don't have. She truly is my help and my completion. Learning to be a husband to her has produced more growth in my life than all my years of Bible college and seminary combined.

In letting you see a bit into the cracks of our marriage, we hope you will pause and ask yourself if you have taken your wife for granted. Do you realize how much you need her? Not for the cooking or cleaning but to provide nourishment and cleansing for your soul. MEN: you need your wives! She is a great gift to you. Do you realize how incomplete you are without her? God never intended for you to be self-sufficient. Do you realize you will never be the complete man the Lord intended you to be until you learn to appreciate this gift of your wife? It is not a sign of weakness to admit your need. Adam was not revealing some flaw in his character when he realized he was alone. At the point that Adam discovered he was alone, Adam had not yet sinned. It was not his sinful nature that caused him to feel alone or incomplete. Rather, Adam came to understand that the Creator of the universe had a unique design and plan for his life and wanted to give him an amazing gift.

> *Adam was not revealing some flaw in his character when he realized he was alone.*

RECEIVE GOD'S PROVISION

In Genesis chapter two we see God the Creator proactively involved in Adam's life. First, in verse 7, we see that God Himself formed man and breathed into him the breath of life. Man is unique among all God's creatures: He alone was created with the capacity to know God and to enter into relationship with Him.

Looking back in chapter one, we see that God made man in His own image or likeness. In Genesis 1:26 we read, "Then God said: Let US make man in OUR image." These two pronouns—"us" and "our"—reveal much about God. He was not alone when He created the world. God the

Father, God the Son, and God the Holy Spirit were all present during creation. God is triune—three in one. The trinity demonstrates that God is a God of relationships.

Jesus also refers to the relational quality of God. As He was praying for His disciples, Jesus spoke of His relationship with the Father, saying, "That they [His followers] may be one, as You, Father, are in Me and I in You, that they also may be one in Us" (John 17:21a). We won't take time here to discuss the theology of the triune God, but allow us to reiterate: God is a God of relationships. Because we are made in His image, we, too, are made to have and enjoy relationships. God's design was for man to be in relationship with Him. In the same way, God's design is for a man to be in relationship with his wife: "So God created man in His own image, in the image of God created He him; male and female He created them" (Gen. 1:27).

> *God is a God of relationships. We are made to have and enjoy relationships.*

We continue to see God actively involved in Adam's life: "The Lord God planted a garden eastward in Eden: and there He put the man whom He had formed" (Gen. 2:8). This was a perfect place God had prepared for Adam. The name "Eden" literally means "delight" in Hebrew. It truly was a "Garden of Delight." We can only imagine what this garden must have looked like! Surely any garden that God Himself planted would be filled with the most beautiful trees and plants. Every tree was good for food. All Adam could ever need was in the garden. Or was it?

Time and again we have heard couples say, "If only we could purchase our own home, then our problems would be solved." Or, "When I get that promotion, I'll have the money to really provide for my family. I know we can be happy then." Many couples live in the world of "if only." Unfortunately, even when they do realize their dreams, they don't find what they really need. Like Adam, they can live in Paradise and still be missing something. God allowed Adam to discover that even in Paradise, he wouldn't find all he needed.

"Out of the ground the Lord God formed every beast of the field and every bird of the air and brought them to Adam to see what he would call them. And whatever Adam called each living creature, that was its name"

(Gen. 2:19). Here we see the Lord bringing work to Adam and using it to teach Adam an important truth. God often brings a variety of situations into our lives to help us learn valuable lessons.

What about you? How many times has the Lord brought things into your marriage to teach you that you are alone—and that being alone isn't a good thing?

But here comes the good part: "And the Lord God caused a deep sleep to fall on Adam, and he slept; and He took one of his ribs and closed up the flesh in its place. Then the rib which the Lord God had taken from man He made into a woman, and brought her to the man" (Gen. 2:21–22).

Dr. Matthew Henry said it well: "The woman was made of a rib out of the side of Adam; not made out of his head to rule over him, nor out of his feet to be trampled upon by him, but out of his side to be equal with him, under his arm to be protected, and near his heart to be beloved."[1] Woman was to be the completion of man. Perhaps this is where the expression "She's my better half" comes from.

Here again we see God being proactive in Adam's life: "And [God] brought her to the man." God had provided a perfect gift for man—exactly what he needed. Adam had realized his need and was ready to receive God's provision. Men, have you ever really considered that your wife is a personal gift from the Lord to you?

Imagine that one afternoon you hear a knock at your door. There before you stands a delivery man with a small envelope in his hand. You look curiously at the envelope, studying the return address. You are startled to read the name handwritten with golden letters in the corner: From Her Royal Majesty Queen Elizabeth II of the United Kingdom. The royal seal is on the envelope.

You are astonished beyond words. With trembling hands, you carefully open the envelope. Inside you discover a set of keys to a brand-new Mercedes. The enclosed card reads,

It pleases her Royal Highness to bestow this gift on you.
May it bring you much pleasure.
With regards,
Her Majesty, Queen Elizabeth II

You stand in utter shock. When you finally stop re-reading the note, you look up and see a beautiful jet-black Mercedes parked in front of your house. Needless to say, this car would become a priceless treasure. Certainly you would show it to all your friends and treat it with the greatest care.

Don't you see? The King of the universe has sent you the gift of your wife! Believe it or not, she is even better than a Mercedes! How have you responded to this gift He has given you? Do you take her for granted? Do you mistreat her? Do you give her the honor she is due? Do you criticize or belittle her? You cannot value something you are constantly tearing apart.

You might understand exactly what we are talking about if you could meet Matt and Sherry. It is hard to feel comfortable when you are with this couple. Matt constantly ridicules his wife. He criticizes her openly and belittles everything she says or does. You can see her jaw tighten as she attempts to brush aside his cruelty with an awkward laugh.

Matt does not see Sherry as a gift. He clearly does not value or respect her. Yet Sherry is a very capable woman who is respected by many people in her workplace. She has many abilities that Matt does not have and that he really needs. When Matt looks at his wife, he sees only someone who is very different from himself, and he views these differences as being wrong.

We could speculate as to the deeper reasons why Matt treats his wife the way he does. Perhaps in his childhood he was treated with disrespect. Perhaps he is very insecure and seeks to build himself up by tearing his wife down. Whatever the underlying reasons for his behavior, one thing remains true: he does not value his wife as he should. And this behavior is wrong.

Not only is Matt rejecting this gift of his wife, but his actions and attitudes indicate that he is also rejecting the Giver of this gift. He is refusing God's design and plan for his life. Matt's attitudes and actions are egotistical, arrogant, and self-sufficient. The truth is that Matt is refusing to see the significant flaws in his own character. God has given him the gift of his wife; if Matt were willing, God could use her in powerful ways to help him grow.

But how can a man like Matt change? He must start by acknowledging that God's Word teaches that it is not good for man to be alone. He must admit that he is living a self-sufficient, self-centered life, rejecting the gift God has given him. Matt must change the way he views his wife. He must begin to see her as a highly valued gift—as someone the Lord made just for him, as someone he desperately needs. Matt must begin to listen to his wife, to ask for her opinion, to seek her insights. He must be willing to ask her to point out his weaknesses and then believe what she says. (At the end of this chapter, we provide some exercises designed to help individuals apply this truth.)

Does this mean Matt's wife is perfect? Are we saying his wife has never made a bad decision or held a foolish opinion? No. That is not what we are saying. Certainly his wife has her share of weaknesses, and her actions are not always correct. But God can use even the weaknesses in her life to help him grow. We must return to the garden, to God's original design: Man and woman are made to complete each other. Man needs woman's strengths and her weaknesses.

Consider another example from our marriage. I, Mary Lou, can often see things that Tim can't. Often he is too close to a situation to have much insight into it. As a young pastor, Tim didn't always pick up on the emotional state of the people to whom he was ministering. One day after church, I took Tim aside and whispered, "Honey, something is really bothering Thomas." "Really?" came his puzzled reply. "I hadn't noticed. How do you know?" Call it women's intuition; call it a spiritual gift; call it whatever you like. I knew.

Tim tested what I said. As he called Thomas into his office and asked how he was doing, Thomas's eyes filled with tears. Thomas was struggling with some very serious problems. Hours later, as their conversation came to an end, Thomas remarked, "Wow, Pastor, you are such a sensitive man. No one else even knew about this problem. I don't know how you knew. But thanks for taking the time to ask me how I was doing."

It didn't take Tim long to learn: I possessed strengths he didn't have. Tim learned that I am a gift to him, to help complete him.

Tim has also grown through my weaknesses. I tend to be a perfectionist. Often, my perfectionism results in unreasonable stress. Tim has learned how to calm his frenzied wife. He has an amazing ability to bring stability into the chaos I create in my quest for perfection. As he has discovered how to help me grow in this area, he has also gained great skills as a counselor and advisor to others.

It has taken us many years to learn how to appreciate each other's strengths and to incorporate them into our lives. The result of this process has yielded a precious blessing for both of us. We have discovered how much we truly need each other. We function so much better as a team!

A word here to women: If you realize that you are a precious gift to your husband, then you should live in a manner worthy of this calling. Do you only see yourself through the eyes of culture or society? Do you try to measure up to some worldly ideal of external beauty or success? Women, you are of great worth! There is an erroneous belief that Christianity and the Bible do not value women. Nothing could be further from the truth. The first four books of the New Testament reveal how Jesus valued and cherished women. Even in Genesis—in the very beginning—we read that God Himself prepared the amazing gift of woman and brought her to man. Never forget that you have great value in God's eyes! Let your life be a reflection of the amazing gift you are!

REJOICE IN THE PROVISION

"And Adam said: This is now bone of my bones and flesh of my flesh; she shall be called Woman, because she was taken out of Man" (Gen. 2:23). A more accurate translation of this verse might be: "And Adam said, 'WOW!'"

Adam was thrilled with what God had created! Do you read any hesitation in his voice? Did he have to think about whether he wanted to accept this gift? Did he look around to see if there was anything better? No way! He claimed her immediately and called her his own. Adam rejoiced in this gift from the Maker.

One of the most effectual cures for an ailing marriage is to express gratitude and appreciation for each other.

What about you? Do you rejoice over the gift of your wife? Proverbs 5:18 exhorts men, "Let your fountain be blessed, and rejoice with the wife of your youth." One of the most effectual cures for an ailing marriage is to express gratitude and appreciation for each other. Start by expressing your gratitude to your Maker for this gift He has given you. When was the last time you truly thanked God for your spouse? Why not stop and do that right now?

Next, learn to communicate your appreciation to your partner. Identify specific things for which you are thankful. Make a list. Be sure that your list includes qualities and strengths that your partner possesses and not just a list of things she does. Your partner should feel she is a precious, invaluable gift to you. Don't assume that your wife knows that you value her. Chances are, she doesn't. You need to tell her and show her. (Women, the same goes for you: You, too, must learn to express your appreciation for your husband.)

We will never forget a conversation we had with a young man many years ago. He was working alongside us in ministry, and we had expressed our appreciation to him for the great job he was doing. At first, as he shrank from our gratitude, we thought his response was one of humility. But with more discussion, we learned otherwise.

This young man believed that a person should not be thanked or appreciated. He claimed that he was doing what he did for the Lord and that was enough. He felt that any words of praise from us would take away from his eternal reward. Not only did he refuse any words of appreciation for himself, but he also failed to acknowledge and appreciate the people around him.

Is this truly what the Bible teaches? Obviously, the ultimate One who deserves all thanks and praise is our Lord. But does this mean we should never say a word of thanks or appreciation to one another? Throughout the Bible we read about the importance of our words—not just the negative ones, but also the positive ones, those that build up. 1 Thessalonians 5:11 is just one example: "Therefore, comfort each other and edify one another, just as you also are doing." What better way to build up another person than by expressing heartfelt, sincere words of appreciation?

REFLECTIONS

Allow us to take a brief detour: Although this is a book about marriage, we cannot miss the opportunity to draw an important analogy. Ephesians 5:22–33 reveals that marriage is a picture of Jesus' relationship with His Bride, the Church. In verses 23 and 25 we read, "For the husband is head of the wife, as also Christ is head of the church; and

He is the Saviour of the body. Husbands, love your wives, just as Christ also loved the church and gave Himself for her." As we examine marriage using the ultimate guidebook of God's Word, we discover many comparisons between our earthly marriage and our relationship to God.

In this chapter, we have considered three foundational truths:

- Man must realize he has a need.
- Man must receive God's provision to meet the need.
- Man must rejoice in the provision he has received.

Just as Adam had to realize that he was alone and that something was missing from his life, so you, too, must realize that you are alone and that something is missing from your life. You were created to be in relationship with God. There is a God-shaped hole in your heart that only He can fill. Like Adam, you may be living in Paradise but still feel alone.

Are you living in Paradise, but still feel void and empty?

God has tried repeatedly to get your attention; He continues to wait for you to finally get the point: You are alone! But God never intended for you to remain alone. He has made a provision for you: "For God so loved the world that He gave His only begotten Son, that whoever believes in Him should not perish, but have everlasting life" (John 3:16). God gave the best He had: His Son. Jesus came and walked this earth to reveal God's love and to show that you don't need to remain alone. Your sins cut you off from Him, but through Jesus' death on the cross and His resurrection from the dead, God has provided exactly what you need.

When you receive God's provision, He fills the emptiness in your life and brings you into a beautiful relationship with Himself. Only then is your heart truly filled with rejoicing!

But how can you receive God's provision? Perhaps you are reading these words and thinking, "That's me. I am alone. I know it. I've tried to fill this emptiness with so much stuff, and still I remain alone and empty."

First, admit that you are separated from God because of your sin. Romans 3:23 says, "For all have sinned and fall short of the glory of God." You might be thinking that you are not as bad or as sinful as someone else. This is not a contest. It doesn't matter if you have sinned ten times or a hundred times today. All it takes is ONE sin to separate you from God. Romans 3:10 reminds us: "There is none righteous, no not one." A few chapters later, in Romans 6:23, we read, "The wages of sin is death, but the gift of God is eternal life in Christ Jesus our Lord." In other words, the result of my sin is death, which means separation from God. But the free gift of God is eternal life through Jesus Christ our Lord.

Second, receive God's provision: Jesus Christ. Jesus died to pay the price for your sin. "But God demonstrates His own love toward us in that while we were still sinners, Christ died for us" (Romans 5:8). "And He Himself [Jesus] is the propitiation for our sins, and not for ours only but also for the whole world" (1 John 2:2). Propitiation means payment. The payment for my sins is paid in full because of Jesus! We must receive this gift of Jesus in the same way we would receive a gift of a new Mercedes: we take the keys! "But as many as received Him, to them He gave the right to become the children of God, to those who believe in His name" (John 1:12). Part of receiving God's provision involves believing. You must believe that Jesus is the Son of God, who died for your sins and came to life again, and believe in His promise of new life for all who receive Him. "If you confess with your mouth the Lord Jesus and believe in your heart that God has raised Him from the dead, you will be saved" (Romans 10:9).

Receive God's provision and allow Him to fill the emptiness in your life.

You can do this right now by talking to God. That's what prayer really is: talking to God. Tell God that you know you are a sinner and that your sins have separated you from Him. Tell God that you realize you are alone and that it is not good! Tell God that you need a relationship with Him and that you are ready to receive His provision: Jesus, God's Son, who died and rose for you. Ask Jesus to come into your life and make you new.

Now comes the great part when you can say—as Adam did—"WOW! Look what God has given me!" We read in 2 Corinthians 5:17, "If anyone is in Christ, he is a new creation; old things have passed away; behold all things have become new." If you have made this decision for Jesus, then a new life has just begun. We are so excited for you! WOW! In chapter fifteen you will find our contact information. Please write and tell us of your decision. We would love to send you some information about how you can grow in your faith and know Jesus better.

If you have made this decision for Jesus,
your new life has just begun…
WOW!

STUDY GUIDE

Read Genesis 2:7–23

As you read through this passage in Genesis, put yourself in Adam's place. You have been given a perfect place to live, a significant and fascinating vocation with good job security, an amazing garden to tend, not to mention a terrific "boss" who enjoys spending time with you. What more could you want? You soon will discover that something *is* missing.

God Himself mentions it in verse 18: "It is not good for man to be alone." Doesn't it strike you as interesting that although God makes this statement in verse 18, He doesn't act on solving the problem until verse 21? God has something He wants Adam to learn first. So God gives him another job: naming the animals. Does God really need Adam's help to come up with creative animal names? Surely, the God who created the entire universe could handle the task of naming His creation! If God simply wanted to accomplish the job of naming the animals, wouldn't it have made more sense for Him to create woman *before* He gave Adam this task? *(After all, we know how talkative women can be, and Eve certainly would have had plenty of suggestions for animal names!)* But God did not make a mistake. In fact, He had a very specific plan. The answer lies in verse 20. Adam discovers a pattern in God's creation. He recognizes that God has made two of each kind of animal, male and female. But Adam also realizes that there is no one like him. He is alone. Let's dig a little deeper.

DIGGING DEEPER

1. Why did God give Adam the job of naming the animals?

2. Was it good for man to be alone? Why or why not?

3. Name at least three things that God provided for Adam in this passage.

4. Because we are created in God's image, what similar characteristics do we possess?

5. What were the three foundational points from this chapter?

6. Of these three foundational points, which one is the hardest for you to apply to your marriage?

7. How would you summarize chapter one in one sentence?

8. **Husbands**: How would you categorize the way you relate to your wife? (Check as many as apply.)
   ☐ You view her as a possession.
   ☐ You view her as a liability.
   ☐ You live separate lives.
   ☐ You don't think you need her.

☐ You need her sometimes.

☐ You know beyond a doubt that you need her.

☐ You tolerate her weaknesses but do not appreciate her strengths.

☐ You don't think she has any strengths.

☐ You can easily name five strengths your wife has that you do not have.

☐ You don't remember when you last told her thank you for anything.

☐ You think she knows how much you appreciate her.

☐ You highly value and appreciate her.

☐ You often tell her that you value and appreciate her.

Once you have marked the statements that apply, share your list with your wife. Ask her whether she agrees with your assessment.

9. **Husbands**: What experience(s) have you had that caused you to realize you can't make it alone? You may include experiences in your marriage as well as in your personal life.

10. **Husbands:** Make a list of the things about your wife for which you are thankful. What qualities initially attracted you to her? Be sure to list character traits, qualities, strengths, and talents—that is, not just the work she does but also who she is. Share this list with your wife. *(Use a separate sheet of paper if you need more space.)*

11. **Husbands:** Ask your wife to tell you several practical things you could do which would help her feel more valued. Write down one or two of these suggestions that you intend to work on in the next week.

12. **Husbands and wives:** Write a prayer of thanksgiving for your spouse. We provide two examples to guide your thinking, but please write your own prayers. After you have finished, take time to pray this together (or give it to your spouse to read).

"Lord Jesus, I want to thank you for my wife. She has so many amazing qualities I don't have. She is creative and sensitive. You have also given her incredible instincts. She is the one who brings life and joy into our home. Thank you for giving me such a perfect gift. You knew just what I needed, even when I was too full of pride to see it. Thank You, Jesus, for my wife."

"Jesus, thank you for the husband you have given me. He is exactly what I need. He provides leadership and stability for our family. You have given him many strengths that I don't have. He works hard to provide for me. He has great wisdom and understanding. I am thankful for the little things he does daily to show me his love. Thank You, Jesus, for my husband."

CHAPTER TWO

ROOTS

One Saturday Morning...Marriage Seminar
Session One

Looking out across the auditorium, we wondered how—in just one morning session—we were supposed to fix the multitude of problems besetting the crowd that stared back at us. On the right sat an older man obviously in need of a second cup of coffee. Next to him (only in the most literal sense of the phrase) sat his wife, arms folded, tight-lipped, never looking at him. Behind them sat a woman with unspoken sorrow etched across her brow. She sat alone. On the left was a young couple: She sat on the edge of her seat, with a desperate look in her eyes; he was slumped in his chair and wore an expression that seemed to moan, "Why did you drag me here?"

There we stood, behind the podium, the "experts" on marriage. We had been invited to speak to this diverse group about the "basics" of marriage. We felt the crowd sizing us up. Because the schedule was full, our time was limited. We knew it was totally unrealistic to expect that deeply rooted marriage problems could be solved in a few hours of teaching.

However, we also knew from personal experience that the Creator of marriage has given us a Guidebook that contains absolute truth with the power to heal, restore, and renew broken relationships. We would not waste our time discussing some new psychological finding or therapy technique. Our Bible made a loud thud as we set it down firmly on the podium. The old man gave us a startled look; perhaps he had already dozed off. "Open your Bibles to Genesis 2," we began.

RIDICULOUS RULES?

"Therefore a man shall leave his father and mother and shall cleave unto his wife, and they shall become one flesh" (Genesis 2:24). To set the stage for you, we are back in the Garden of Eden. God has just introduced Eve to Adam, and as soon as Adam stops jumping for joy, God issues these rules. But wait! These rules don't make sense! God is talking to Adam and Eve. And neither of them had a father or mother. Who were they supposed to "leave"? Adam and Eve likely had no idea what a "father and mother" even were!

Marriage was God's idea, and He has made the rules!

Eve was the only woman in the Garden. It must have seemed pretty obvious that Adam would be joined to her. As soon as Adam saw Eve, he instantly claimed her as his own. In the verse just prior to this one, Adam himself acknowledged that they were one flesh. So why did God give Adam and Eve these seemingly ridiculous rules?

From the beginning of time, God wanted to make it clear that marriage was His idea and that He was making the rules. These instructions were not just for Adam and Eve. Throughout the ages, these simple rules have provided God's foundation for marriage.

We often meet people who claim that the Old Testament is not relevant today. They assert that any rules from Genesis are not really worth considering. We could spend hours debating the foolishness of that claim. (Often, these people are the same ones who rarely even open their Bibles.) But allow us to indulge their foolishness for just a moment.

Any good investigative reporter looks for not just one, but for several corroborating sources to establish the truth. Applying this same principle, we too will look for several sources to determine whether Old Testament teaching is relevant. I can think of no better source than Jesus Himself. Jesus, the Son of God, would not quote a passage from the Old Testament if it were not important and valid.

In Matthew 19, Jesus was in a discussion with the religious leaders of His day. These leaders, the Pharisees, were attempting to trick Jesus, hoping He might contradict the teaching of the Jewish law regarding marriage. Jesus confounded these leaders and established the validity of this passage from Genesis, saying, "Have you not read that He who made them at the beginning made them male and female, and said, 'For this reason a man shall leave his father and mother and be joined to his wife, and the two shall become one flesh?'" (Matthew 19:4–5). Jesus quoted these foundational rules from Genesis and reminded the hypocritical leaders of the truth the rules contained. (Read another account of this event in Mark 10:2–7.)

Our second source comes from the Apostle Paul, who quotes Genesis in his letter to the church at Ephesus: "'For this reason a man shall leave his father and mother and be joined to his wife, and the two shall become one flesh'" (Ephesians 5:31). Not only was Paul familiar with this passage from the Old Testament, but he also declared it to be relevant teaching for the New Testament church.

Genesis 2:24 is not some outdated Old Testament nonsense. Rather, it embodies living truth, as valid today as it was in the Garden. Many have tossed this verse around like a worn-out cliché, missing its power. We are convinced that this verse can provide a solid foundation for every marriage. We also are convinced of the disastrous results that occur when even a part of this verse is violated.

Contained in this single verse are three basic rules for marriage:

- LEAVE
- CLEAVE
- BECOME ONE

Note: Some translations use the word "join" but we prefer to use the word "cleave" from the King James Version because it paints a stronger and more accurate picture. We will discuss this in more detail as we look at this second rule.

RULES?

Why do we call them rules? There is a word that bears mentioning here: It is the word *"shall."* This word is used in the Bible more than 9,000 times! Exodus 20, where we find the Ten Commandments, uses the word *shall* repeatedly. *Shall* is an imperative, a command.

Through its repeated use of the word "shall," the King James Version sheds light on the fact that Genesis 2:24 contains three distinct rules: "Therefore a man *shall* leave his father and mother and *shall* cleave unto his wife, and they *shall* become one flesh." We read not one rule but three, each with the imperative *shall*. We live in a culture that bristles at the idea of being told what to do. We like our freedom, our power of self-determination. Even in the church, we shy away from sermons that focus on rules and "thou shall nots." We don't want our pastors to tell us what to do because that makes us feel uncomfortable. Obedience is not a word we like to talk about. We'd much rather sing "Amazing Grace" than "I Surrender All."

> *We'd rather sing "Amazing Grace" than "I Surrender All."*

It is true that we are saved by grace alone and that adhering to the Law will never bring salvation (Romans 3:20, 28). But it is also true that God has given us laws and rules for our own good, and these laws remain valid today (see Matthew 5:17–18; Romans 3:31; and Romans 7:12).

Consider the following analogy: When you got your car, you were given an instruction manual that was replete with rules about how to care for your car: The tires require a specific amount of air pressure; the car uses only a certain type of fuel; periodic services must be provided. The list goes on. But that car belongs to you! You can choose to ignore those rules! But you'll soon discover what happens if you do. You may burn up your engine, ruin your tires, or cause an accident. These rules are actually for your own good. Obey them and your car will keep running, and you will be kept safe.

So it is with the rules God has given for marriage: He gave you these rules to help, bless, protect, and encourage you.

Ridiculous? We don't think so. Let's take a closer look at God's rules for marriage, starting with rule one.

RULE ONE: LEAVE
A Closer Look At The Roots

To help us understand this first rule—*leave*—we invite you to consider another analogy, this time from nature. Think about the roots of a plant. As we explore the relationship between the root and the plant, some great lessons emerge that can be applied to marriage.

Wikipedia describes the function of roots as follows: "The two major functions of roots are (1) absorption of water and inorganic nutrients and (2) anchoring of the plant body to the ground. In response to the concentration of nutrients, roots also synthesize cytokine, which acts as a signal as to how fast the shoots can grow. Roots often function in storage of food and nutrients."[2]

Roots allow water and nutrients to flow into the stem, which supports the leaves, fruits, and, eventually, seeds. Roots keep plants anchored to the ground. But is that all a plant is created for, to remain stuck in the ground? We know that the greater purpose for a plant is to reproduce. *(Please forgive this very simplified science lesson. A botanist I am not!)*

When the seed begins to germinate, what is usually the first thing that appears? A tiny root! This root breaks out of the seed and begins to grow into the earth. Soon thereafter, a small stem starts to grow from the seed, reaching toward the light. The root continues to grow deeper, providing stability and nourishment for the young plant. As time passes, the plant grows. Soon the time comes for the plant to reproduce, most often by producing seeds. Note that the seeds leave the parent plant in order to start the cycle over again.

When the seeds leave, they take with them the genetic material from the parent plant. A tomato seed will produce a tomato plant; a watermelon seed will yield watermelons. Although the new plant and the parent plant may look alike, they are not the same; each plant has its own roots, stem, leaves, fruit, and seeds.

What happens when seeds are planted too closely together? Let's look at corn for example. Planting corn too closely adversely affects root growth. It also has harmful effects on the shoots. In order for corn to grow, it must have enough room to develop an adequate root system to anchor and nourish the plant. When air, light, and water are circulated inadequately because of too close sowing, the plants are subject to disease. Further, disease and pests can spread easily when corn is planted too closely.

So it is with our marriages: God has given this incredible first rule, "Leave father and mother," not as a punishment upon the children or upon the parents but rather as a blessing, to allow for the growth of something new and beautiful. The "roots" (father and mother) provide years of stability and nourishment to the plant (the family). Then comes time for the seeds (the children) to leave the roots and the plant so something new can grow.

> *God has given us this first rule not as a punishment but rather as a blessing.*

Some of these roots might have been wonderful, healthy, nourishing; some might have been diseased, weak or even destructive. While we won't take time here to discuss the implications of the kind of roots we experienced in our families, one fact is clear: Even though we were connected to those roots for many years, we must learn to leave them behind.

Violating this rule reaps the same result as planting seeds too close together. Roots can't grow properly, disease can spread, and nourishment is inadequate. The young plant may sicken and even die. The situation is the same when a young couple refuses to leave their parents—and, for that matter, when parents have difficulty allowing their married children to leave. We have seen young marriages die on the vine because the couples failed to obey this first rule.

A word for parents: You have had an important job. For the past eighteen years or so, as your son or daughter grew, you provided stability and nourishment. Just because God is telling your married children that it is time to leave you does not mean that you are now worthless or obsolete. Rather, it is time for you to discover a new, richer, and more fulfilling relationship with your married children. Stop trying to cling to them like a withered old root!

> *Let them go!*
> *Let them grow!*
> *Let them become all God wants them to be.*
> *Sit back and behold the new, beautiful plants*
> *they are becoming.*

LEAVE!

I (Tim) smiled as I looked across at the newly engaged young couple in my office. Too often I had counseled couples whose marriages were in ruins, and it was refreshing to observe this young love. They never stopped holding hands as they told their bubbly tale of courtship. No one could deny they were in love.

I sat behind my old, oak desk and listened patiently. Finally, when they paused for a breath, I asked them a few questions about their plans. I have always required pre-marriage counseling for every couple that asks me to perform their wedding ceremony. During the first session, I usually try to get background information. This helps me determine how to shape our subsequent meetings.

"Where will you live after you marry?" I asked. "We don't have enough money to get our own place," answered the young man, "so we plan to live with her parents. It's great! We can live there for free. We can eat with them, and we won't have to worry about money or getting a job." Slowly I closed my Bible and said, "I'm sorry. I can't perform your wedding unless you are willing to make some changes in your plans. You already are breaking the first rule of marriage." I spent the next few minutes explaining God's rules for marriage, focusing on the part that says, "Leave father and mother," and suggesting they rethink their plans. They left my office clearly annoyed with me and determined to find another pastor to perform their marriage ceremony.

I anticipated some repercussions, as her parents were key members of our church. Sure enough, the phone rang about an hour after the couple had left. "Pastor Tim," said the familiar voice. "I understand you just met with our daughter and her fiancé. Is it true you told them you refused to do their wedding ceremony?"

I braced myself for the scolding I was sure would ensue. Somewhat timidly I answered, "Yes." What I heard next caught me completely off guard. "Thank you, thank you, thank you!" the father exclaimed. "We had been telling them they weren't ready to marry and we didn't want them living here with us. Thank you for being willing to tell them the truth!"

It was simple to see that this young couple was not ready to leave father and mother, even in the literal sense. They both were reliant on their parents and were unwilling to take responsibility to form a new family. Both were deeply rooted to their parents; they were still behaving like children. They had not learned what it means to leave the "old" roots behind and plant something new. Within a short time after that meeting, this couple broke off their engagement. They did not get married.

CULTURAL CONSIDERATIONS

In our years of ministry, we have traveled often to the Middle East, Europe, Russia, and America, teaching and leading marriage seminars. We recognize the existence of many cultural differences as well as cultural considerations. So before we go any further, allow us to make a clarifying statement: We do understand that in many cultures, several generations within one family will live together in the family home or on the family property. For example, we have often seen this situation in Egypt. The parents live on the bottom floor of a large home; the elder son and his family build their apartment on the middle floor; and the younger son remodels the top floor with plans to move in once he marries. Not only do we understand this tradition but we also understand the financial need that often necessitates this practice. Many Egyptian couples would never be able to afford a home of their own without such assistance from their parents.

Thus, we are not saying that the couple that shares a family home with their parents automatically violates this first rule, of leaving father and mother. Rather, the real issue is that the newly married couple must become a new family unit. This is primarily an issue of responsibility and authority. Even if a couple lives in the same building as their parents, the new husband must be the head of his wife. No longer is he under the authority and control of his father and mother. Rather, he is now fully responsible to meet the needs of his new family. In the example we gave of this young couple that was planning to live at home, it is important to note that this couple was unwilling to stand on their own. They were content to allow their parents to continue to provide for all their needs, as they had when they were children. They had no intention of becoming their own new family unit. They were not yet ready to grow up.

This is an issue of responsibility and authority.

We have seen this same situation in Austria. Often, an Austrian family will own a large piece of property with enough acreage for the children to build a home adjacent or connected to the parents'. While choosing to live next door to mom and dad does not necessarily violate the "leave father and mother" rule, the real question is whether the new couple has truly become an independent, self-sufficient, uniquely new family unit that is no longer reliant on mommy and daddy. "Leaving father and mother" requires both the willingness and the ability to stand on one's own.

When married children do live in the same home or on the same property as their parents, some challenges and struggles must be addressed to ensure that the "leaving" rule is not being violated. Clear lines must be drawn so that there is no question of responsibility and authority.

This first rule may be very difficult for people from certain cultures to understand. Allow us to say something further about culture: This rule was given at a time when strong family clans constituted the core of the culture. Grown children remained within the family clan as grandparents, parents, and children worked and lived together. Nevertheless, it is important that we do not allow culture to interpret God's Word; rather, God's Word must take precedence over culture. God's Word transcends culture. Leaving father and mother is not a westernized teaching. It is not our idea. It is God's rule for marriage. Why do we allow our culture—whatever it may be—to define God's Word? Instead, we must allow God's Word to define our culture.

LEAVING – PHYSICALLY

Let us introduce you to another couple who also struggled with this rule. Robert and Stephanie had been childhood sweethearts. Both of their families lived in the area, and they enjoyed a special closeness with their parents. Robert was thrilled when they found a small house to rent right next door to his folks.

While things seemed to go well at first, Robert began to sense some tension after a few months. Both Robert and Stephanie were working full time and going to college. Robert's mom wanted to help the couple, and she had developed the habit of stopping by unannounced and cleaning up around their house. Sometimes she would do the laundry or fix their evening meal. Of course, Robert's mom had the best of intentions, but Stephanie grew more annoyed every time she came home and saw that her mother-in-law had been there.

Robert defended his mother in an effort to help Stephanie believe that his mom was just being helpful. But this only made matters worse. When the stress became unbearable, Robert came to see me (Tim). I explained the first rule of marriage: "Leave father and mother." I described God's plan to establish a new family. The light went on in Robert's eyes. He had been allowing his mother and not Stephanie to meet his needs. By his actions, Robert had caused his wife to feel as though she was less important to him.

Within the month, Robert located a home to rent in the next town. With more distance from his parents, the stress he and Stephanie felt subsided. Stephanie could manage their home as she wanted. She no longer felt so intimidated by her mother-in-law. But this was not the end of their story.

Every Sunday after church, Robert and Stephanie were expected to join his parents for Sunday lunch. As Stephanie gained confidence as a young homemaker, and as the two of them developed friendships with other couples, she began to resent always having to eat Sunday lunch with her in-laws. Stephanie wanted to invite their friends over on Sundays and to cook for them in her home. She tried to express her feelings to Robert, but he was afraid to hurt his parents' feelings by not keeping up the tradition.

Again, the tension grew. The pressure built as Stephanie sat fuming in the second row of the sanctuary, waiting for the worship service to end. She knew they'd be going to her in-laws' for Sunday lunch, and she wasn't happy! This time Robert didn't wait quite so long before he came to see me.

I reminded him again of the first rule for marriage. "But we moved away," he explained. "Isn't that enough?" "That was only the beginning," I answered. "Together, you and your wife must decide what traditions you will make for yourselves. You must form a new family. This is God's plan for you. Together with your wife, you need to create something new." Robert gave a deep sigh, fearful of having to explain this to his parents.

The next Sunday, Stephanie was glowing. On his way out the door after church, Robert grinned as he whispered, "You were right, Pastor, you were right! I explained to my parents that we were not always going to be having Sunday lunch with them. They took it better than I expected. And today, I'm taking my wife out to lunch!" Smiling, I replied, "Actually, Robert, God is the One who is right!"

The physical leaving of father and mother can be difficult for some couples. We see it sometimes in the husband who prefers his mom's cooking to his wife's—and foolishly expresses his preference. "I wish you could make that dessert my mom always makes. My mom is the best cook!" Or, "Why don't you call my mom and get her recipe for apple pie?" We see it sometimes in the young wife who spends more time talking on the phone to her mother than she does to her husband. When she has a problem, her first impulse is to pick up the phone and call her mom or dad for advice.

God said, "Leave!" God wants to create something new and wonderful in your marriage. There must be a physical leaving. The physical aspect of leaving involves two basic things: *responsibility* and *authority*. First, who is responsible for this new couple? Who is paying the rent? Who is buying the food? Who is establishing the family values? Who is responsible when things go wrong? If you have truly left father and mother, then you will take full responsibility for your new family: financially, physically, mentally, emotionally, and spiritually.

The second area is that of authority. Who is in charge? Who makes the decisions for this new family? Who has the last word? It is good to seek your parents' counsel and wisdom (and we do encourage this), but ultimately, the final authority to make a decision is yours, not theirs.

Leaving father and mother does not mean that you should cut off all relationship and contact with your parents. This is not what God means when He says "leave." He Himself exhorts us to "honor your father and mother." Respect, honor, and care for parents are biblical concepts. It is not acceptable to treat your parents with indifference or disrespect under the guise of "leaving father and mother."

Maybe you are in a situation where you must temporarily live in your parents' home. Perhaps your parents need your help and support because of illness. There are times when an arrangement like this is inevitable. If you are in such a situation, there are steps you can take to remain faithful to the command to "leave": First, as a couple, respectfully establish firm boundaries that define you as a couple. Second, do not rely any longer on your parents to care for you, to make decisions for you, or to determine your family values. Finally, become your own family.

LEAVING – EMOTIONALLY

There is much more to this principle than physically leaving your parents' home. The emotional and psychological leaving are far more difficult—and more damaging when they don't happen.

When we were first married, we really left home. Shortly after we were married, Tim joined the Army. After he completed training, he was stationed in Germany. As a result, our first real home together was thousands of miles from our parents. We discovered this was extremely good for us as it allowed us to learn to form our own family. We really had left father and mother. Or had we?

One Sunday morning we had a harsh realization: We hadn't completely left our parents! As we walked out the front doors of the chapel, I (Mary Lou) turned to Tim and said, "Honey, how about if we go out for lunch today?" "No. I think we can fix lunch at home," Tim replied. I was already hungry, and I knew I'd only be more so by the time we'd walked home (we didn't have a car). The mere thought of a long, hungry walk made me cranky.

The walk home that Sunday morning was not a pretty sight. The conversation grew heated as our tempers flared. I wanted to know why we couldn't go out to eat occasionally, and Tim kept insisting it was a waste of money. We reached our small apartment, hot in more ways than one, and slammed our belongings down on the kitchen table. By then, neither of us was very hungry. I couldn't understand how Tim could be so stubborn and stingy. He was frustrated with me for being so extravagant.

Then it happened.

"You sound just like your mother!" I blurted out. "Well, you are acting just like your father!" Tim retorted. It was like being doused with ice-cold water. We suddenly realized what we had been doing: We were living our parents' lives. At that moment we realized we hadn't completely left our parents.

My family had been accustomed to going out to eat. My father had been an officer in the military, and eating out was routine for us. Although Tim's family was on a similar economic level as mine, they seldom went out to eat, and then only on special occasions. Whereas my father was somewhat extravagant, Tim's was more prudent.

Leaving father and mother meant that Tim and I would need to discover together what *our* lifestyle would be. After dishing up generous portions of apologies and forgiveness and scrambling a few eggs for a late lunch, we began discussing what our standard should be. Could we go out to eat as often as my family had? No, we decided we didn't have that much disposable income. But we did enjoy going out together and decided we could do so more than Tim's family had.

On that warm Sunday afternoon we began learning what it meant to leave father and mother. We realized that we were products of two very different families. Our challenge was to create a new family based on who we were and how God had made us. I wish I could say that from that time on we never had a disagreement that stemmed from our different family backgrounds. But that wouldn't be true. Many other instances—relating to everything from finances to child rearing to cleaning the house—revealed that we had not completely "left" father and mother. But as we committed to work through each of these areas of "leaving," we found that these differences became glue that cemented us together. Leaving is a process; it is not something that happens magically as soon as the wedding is over. Many deep-rooted values, beliefs, traditions, and habits may fail to come to light in the first few years of a marriage. (Once children join the family, you will discover differences of which you had been blissfully unaware!) "Leaving" requires that we examine these differences and make decisions based on what is right for our new family. (Questions and exercises at the end of this chapter may help you to apply this first rule.)

Our goal is to blend together the best from both our backgrounds in order to create something new.

God does not ask us to throw away our pasts. Our individual family values, experiences, and traditions are wellsprings. We are thankful for all our families have given us. Our goal is to blend together the best from both our backgrounds in order to create something wonderful and new. A good friend of ours, Pastor Steve D. Felker, expressed it this way:

"Leaving requires becoming aware of the ways and values of my family of origin, evaluating them in the light of Scripture, and making clear and plain decisions to follow Christ when they conflict. Every family has ways they communicate, discipline, and socialize. They also have values they attach to power, wealth, gender, and time. Finally, they have their definitions of success, of status, of meaning and identity. All of these must be evaluated in the light of the Scriptures to see if they are in agreement and to see if they are in proportion to the priorities of God's Word. When a man and woman come together, each will have assets from his or her family and cultural traditions, and each will have worldly perspectives and expectations that he or she must leave behind in order to come together as husband and wife in Christ."

In closing this chapter on "leaving," we want to share a final picture: When you leave your father and mother, you don't just walk away from something; rather, you move toward something new. The Lord didn't give us this first rule so we would simply throw out the old "roots." In His goodness, the Lord wants us to see that in marriage He is making something NEW! Jesus reminds us in Mark 2:22 that "new wine must be put into new wineskins." We should be excited about this first rule! God is going to do something new! *We leave the old behind and move toward something new.*

This brings us to the second rule: CLEAVE.

> *"When you leave father and mother,*
> *you don't just walk away from something;*
> *rather, you move toward something new."*

STUDY GUIDE

Read Genesis 2:24; Matthew 19:5;
Mark 10:2–7; Ephesians 5:31

In this chapter, we introduced God's three rules for marriage: LEAVE, CLEAVE, BECOME ONE. Because these three rules are foundational to marriage, we have considered each of them individually. This chapter is focused on the first rule: LEAVE.

We compared the leaving process to a seed that leaves its parent plant in order to germinate and become something new. Parents should be like the "roots," providing stability and nourishment to the plant. But the new plant cannot grow and be healthy until it *"leaves."* The goal of the root must be to complete its task of providing for the plant until such time as the seed is ready to leave and to become something new.

"Leaving father and mother" is not just the physical action of moving to a new home; it also involves the mental, emotional, and spiritual aspect of leaving. Let's dig a little deeper.

DIGGING DEEPER

1. Do you believe that the three rules stated in Genesis 2:24 are valid today? Why or why not?

2. Name two individuals in the Bible who confirmed the validity of these three rules given in Genesis.

3. Why are rules important for life generally?

4. Can you think of another analogy (other than the car instruction manual) that illustrates how rules can be for our good?

5. Why is it important and logical to obey God's three rules for marriage?

6. Explain in your own words what it means to "leave father and mother."

7. Explain how the analogy of the root and the seed applies to marriage.

8. What can happen when seeds are planted too close together? How does this apply to marriage?

9. The physical aspect of leaving involves two basic things. What are they?

   a.

   b.

10. What is even more difficult to do than to leave physically? Why is this more difficult?

Husbands and wives: Complete statements 11–16 alone and then share your answers with your spouse. Fill in the blanks:

11. "My partner acts just like his/her mom or dad when…"

12. "We always _____ _____ because my spouse's family always did this. This is not what I would like to do. I believe this should change."

13. "We should always do _____
_____because my family always did it this way. I believe
this is the correct way to do it."

14. "When my partner does this _____
_____ I feel like he/she is choosing his/her family over
me."

15. Name three "old roots" that you believe have crept into your marriage
that you would like to see pulled out.

16. What new things should be planted in place of the three "old roots"
you identified in statement 15? Make some practical, specific suggestions of new things you would like to see "planted" into your marriage.

CHAPTER THREE

GRAFTED TOGETHER

Cleave

Join me (Tim) again in my office for another counseling appointment. The couple sitting across from me this time was older. Both partners had experienced failed marriages. They had found each other, and they didn't show any trace of their previous tragedies. They seemed to be very logical about their decision to remarry. Both appeared to have everything under control as they asked me to perform their upcoming marriage ceremony.

As is my habit, I mentioned my requirement for extensive pre-marriage counseling before I would agree to officiate at their wedding. The couple seemed slightly annoyed at this prerequisite, believing themselves to be "experienced." They didn't think they needed any help. They thought they knew what it meant to be married.

They soon realized I would not retract my requirement. They shifted in their chairs, trying to find a comfortable position in which to endure their first session. I opened my Bible and read this passage: "Therefore a man shall leave his father and mother and shall cleave unto his wife..." I paused and asked a question: "How long do you expect your marriage to last?" Their answer shocked me.

"Well, both of our previous marriages lasted around five years. We hope this one will last at least that long, maybe even ten years." With sadness, I closed my Bible. Fixing my eyes on them, I said, "I am sorry. But if this is what you really think, then there is no way I will perform your wedding ceremony. You have already opened the door for this second marriage to fail. There appears to be a lack of commitment to your proposed marriage. It seems that yours will be a marriage of convenience: As long as it is convenient for you to be married, you will stay together. But you are both allowing for an escape should the marriage become inconvenient. You are doomed to fail before you even begin." That was the last time I saw the couple.

What does it mean to "cleave?" This Old English word has lost its original meaning. In your kitchen, you may have a cleaver, a large knife with a square blade that cuts or chops things. But the meaning in the Old English—as well as in Hebrew—is quite the opposite: It means that two things are being permanently joined. (Some Bible translations use the word "join," but this word can be a bit ambiguous, especially in light of contemporary understanding. For example, you join a club, or you join in the fun, or you might join someone for dinner, but none of these usages gives an accurate meaning for this verse. Marriage is not a club that you join and from which you later withdraw your membership.

Marriage is not a club you join and from which you later withdraw your membership!

The Hebrew word translated "cleave" as we read it in Genesis 2:24 is *dabhaq* (daw-bak'), which means 'to adhere to.' In Matthew 19:5, the Greek word translated "cleave" is *proskollao* (pros-kol-lah'-o), which means 'to glue to.' "Cleave" means to glue together! This is a strong image.

The word "cleave" also indicates action and process. Because of the tense that is used, we could say it like this: "Be *being* continually glued together." To cleave is not a one-time action. Rather, it indicates that a union is taking place. It indicates an ongoing process.

It is important to point out the Greek preposition that is part of the word *proskollao. Pros* (**pros**kollao) means 'to move toward something.' Again, this suggests process and action; we are moving toward being glued together.

Unfortunately, in many marriages today, this action is absent. Many couples are unwilling to make the effort—and yes, we do mean effort—to actively move toward becoming 'glued together.' This is hard work!

Many couples today make conditional comments such as "I might be willing to make some changes, but only if she changes first." Is that an attitude of 'moving toward being glued together?' No! Too often we hear couples say things such as "We have a fifty-fifty relationship. I am willing to meet her halfway." Even more common is the statement, "I have my own checking account. After all, this is my money…my savings…*mine, mine, mine!*" There is no movement toward becoming glued together. These couples are focused on their individual rights, not on moving toward being glued together.

In the next chapter, we will look in detail at the third rule for marriage but we need to bring out a critical point here that will help us understand how these three rules fit together. We mentioned in the last chapter the command to "leave father and mother." It is important to reiterate that we don't simply throw away the old; rather, we must *leave the old behind and move toward something new.* This is the image we see in the word "cleave" and in the Greek preposition "pros": We are moving toward becoming glued together.

As we come to the third rule—*"become one"*—we see the completion of God's amazing plan. Here we encounter another preposition: *eis.* Listen carefully: The word means to "go into.' Becoming one involves 'going into' the other. All three rules fit together! It is not enough to *leave* (to throw away the old) or to *cleave* (to move toward becoming glued together); we also must incorporate the third rule: *Become one.*

GRAFTING

An example from agriculture beautifully illustrates the principle of cleaving; it is called "grafting." Grafting involves taking two parts from two different trees and permanently joining them. My cousin, who has a large orchard, explained the process to me. He takes the "rootstock" from a tree with strong roots and the "bud wood" from a tree that produces good fruit. He looks for a rootstock tree that has vigorous roots and that is disease resistant. The rootstock tree is strong, hardy, and can withstand adverse weather and soil conditions. The bud wood is chosen from a tree that produces sweet, delicious fruit.

The process of grafting the two parts must be carefully managed. It must be done at the right time of year. My cousin makes precision cuts into the two trees using a sharp, thin-bladed knife. He then "inserts" or grafts one part into the other. Then he binds them with a special binding tape and allows them to grow together.

Time passes, and the fragile branch grows together with the sturdy tree. The day comes when my cousin removes the binding from the tree. It is difficult to tell where the two were joined. The two have become one. They are permanently joined. To separate them, one would have to cut them apart. They have grown *into* each other.

A tree that is grown from a seed probably will not be as strong as a tree that has been produced through grafting. It takes many years for a tree that has been planted by a seed to produce fruit; when it finally does bear fruit, it often is not very good. By combining (grafting) parts of two trees together, both are enhanced: you gain great fruit from the branches as well as firm support from the roots of a strong, hardy, and long-living tree.

My cousin chose to permanently join the two trees in order to produce something new and better than what the trees could have produced had they remained separate. The sap of the sturdy tree now flowed through the grafted on branch. These two had been *grafted* or *cleaved* together, and this process caused them to become one.

We can learn at least six lessons from grafting that apply to marriage and to this second rule of "cleaving":

- First, both trees have value, worth, and strength separately in the same way that husbands and wives each have individual value, worth, and strength. But when husbands and wives allow themselves to be joined, their individual strengths are enhanced. Together, they can be far more fruitful. This is God's design.
- Second, even as two trees that are not grafted can become subject to disease, unfruitfulness, and death, so the weaknesses of two partners who remain independent of each other also can lead to disease, unfruitfulness, and death (of the relationship).
- Third, both trees had to give up something in order to become one. But what they gained was worth far more than what it "cost" each tree. It was necessary for the trees' greater productivity for the gardener to make cuts in both so as to insert them together. Ouch! Being grafted can hurt, but the end result is worth the pain.

- Fourth, the gardener doesn't use a chain saw to make the cuts. Instead, he uses a special, fine knife. In the same way, we need to be careful with each other as we cleave: Don't chop each other to pieces in your desire to become one! Allow the Gardener to use the sharp, two-edged sword of His Word: The incisions He makes will not destroy your relationship but will bring about new growth.

- Fifth, the process takes time. It is unrealistic to expect that two individuals who hitherto have lived only for themselves will instantly become joined in perfect harmony. The grafting process takes time.

- Sixth, grafting is permanent. Being grafted is not for a day, a month, or a year but for the lifetime of the tree. The gardener will not come back in a few years to cut the branch out and graft it elsewhere. In the same way, we must view our marriage relationships as permanent. If we commit ourselves to God's perfect design, a beautiful, strong, and fruitful "tree" will be produced for His glory!

ATTITUDE

"Cleaving" involves two things: *your attitude* and *your actions*. The couple who were in my office had an attitude that predisposed them to failure. Commitment begins with an attitude—a choice. This couple had already made a choice that their marriage wouldn't last long. Their attitude was not one of commitment. They had no intention of "moving toward becoming glued or *grafted* together."

In the book of Proverbs, we read about the importance of our attitudes and how our attitudes can affect our actions: "Keep your heart with all diligence, for out of it spring the issues of life" (Proverbs 4:23). "As in water face reflects face, so a man's heart reveals the man" (Proverbs 27:19). Jesus also spoke about how important it is to have the right attitude: "A good man out of the good treasure of his heart brings forth good things, and an evil man out of the evil treasure brings forth evil things" (Matthew 12:35).

If we entertain thoughts of giving up, escaping, quitting, or failing, there is a good possibility that we will experience these things. But, if we are going to obey this second rule, we must have the attitude from the beginning that divorce is not an option. It should never even be considered, and it certainly should never be used as a threat.

Divorce was never an option for Mary Lou and me. It did not enter our vocabulary and never was a threat that we used against each other. That does not mean that we never had rough times in our marriage. In fact, we went through some extremely dark valleys in our relationship. There was a point when Mary Lou could not honestly say that she loved me. There seemed to be an insurmountable mountain of ice between us. I felt betrayed, alone and crushed by her indifference. I am convinced that had it not been for our mutual attitude of commitment, we would have divorced many years ago.

When things got rough between us, this attitude became the motivator to spur us to action. When you know that you are not going to divorce each other, then you have only one of two choices: either continue to feel stuck in a miserable, broken relationship or do whatever it takes to fix it.

Do not allow emotions to dictate choices.

It is important to underscore that having an *attitude* is not the same as having an *emotion.* Attitude indicates choice. Often, our emotion does not match our attitude. In fact, we must take great care not to allow our emotions to dictate the choices we make. I may not *feel* like I want to stay in the marriage. I may not *feel* like I love my spouse. But feelings can be deceptive.

Jeremiah 17:9 makes this point quite clear: "The heart is deceitful above all things, and desperately wicked; who can know it?" In the Bible, 'the heart' usually refers to the seat of emotions. Our emotions can easily become tainted and even corrupt.

Recently, we were counseling a couple with significant problems in their marriage. The couple had made many poor choices, and the memory of these sinful actions continued to cause much bitterness and distrust. As we sat with them, we heard the wife express her sorrow and repentance over her past choices. She had asked for forgiveness. But her husband's emotions could not let go. No matter how often she expressed her remorse, it was not enough. The husband continued to operate under the influence of his emotions: He was unable and unwilling to make the choice to forgive. His emotions controlled him, and his emotions were deceived.

Proverbs 28:26 reminds us, "He who trusts in his own heart is a fool, but whoever walks wisely will be delivered." How do we walk wisely? There is only one source of true wisdom—wisdom that will not be tainted or corrupted—and that is God's Wisdom, as found in His Word.

This brings us back to our life verse: "Trust in the Lord with all your heart, and lean not on your own understanding. In all your ways acknowledge Him, and He shall direct your path" (Proverbs 3:5-6). We have discovered again and again that our human "understanding" is completely untrustworthy; it is often deceived. Relying on our own hearts is just plain foolish!

The Lord's way is clear: **cleave!** Make the choice of "moving toward becoming glued together." God has promised that when we choose His ways over our ways, He will direct our paths. As we allow our attitudes to conform to His Word, His Word will change our hearts (that is, our emotions)!

ACTIONS

Cleaving involves not only a correct attitude but also correct actions. We believe that there are many important action steps that couples can take, which will facilitate "moving toward becoming glued or grafted together." Allow us to share a few tips we have learned from our own marriage. This list is by no means exhaustive; rather, it is a starting point of actions you can take as you learn to cleave.

1. **Be a team**. Discover something you can do together. Find something you both enjoy that allows you to work, play, minister, learn, grow, and/or laugh together. Music has been an important part of Tim's and my relationship. We have performed concerts, made recordings, led music at church, and shared our passion for music with our children. We also love co-teaching, leading seminars, counseling, and even writing this book together. A shared passion and goal are important in a relationship. They help provide a direction toward which you can move together and a common interest that can help keep your relationship alive. We have discovered new depth in our married relationship that was gained as a result of becoming partners in other areas of our life.

2. **Be supportive**. There will be areas of your lives that you can't easily participate in together, but you can still be supportive of your spouse. For example, your husband may have his career and you may be a stay-

at-home mom, but you can still be supportive of what he does. Do you understand his job? Take time to learn about it, and become his biggest fan. You may not go to work with him each day, but your husband should know that you are interested in and supportive of what he does.

Husbands, remember that even if your wife has chosen to remain home with the children, it doesn't mean that her chosen career is less important than yours. Show support and respect for your wife. Take time to ask her about her day, and praise her for the great job she is doing raising your children. I have been so thankful for the many ways Tim has been supportive of me in our marriage. He is a huge encouragement to me in the area of my writing. When our children were young, Tim would volunteer to take care of them so I could spend some uninterrupted time writing.

3. **Be purposeful**. Plan time to spend together. Don't offer each other your "leftovers." When Tim was a young pastor, he always had time for everyone in the church—except his family. I felt guilty asking him for any time because he was serving God; who was I to take him away from *that* job? I soon discovered that we were not cleaving, and our marriage was suffering. Tim's ability to minister as a pastor could only be as effective as the strength of our marriage. Tim discovered this truth and made our marriage and family his first priority, and his ministry never suffered. In fact, it became even more fruitful! Be sure to schedule regular date nights, weekends away, or just long walks together. Parents of young children often feel overwhelmed at the prospect of fitting one more thing into an overfull schedule. But this must be a priority! Many marriages suffer and begin to crumble during the early child-rearing years because the couple simply fails to make time for each other. Add to that the fatigue that comes with chasing toddlers and you have a recipe for disaster. Be purposeful! Plan to devote time to each other.

4. **Be prayerful**. We believe this is the most important action you can take. We have discovered that as we move closer to our Lord, we grow closer to each other. Pray together! It is hard to be distant from your spouse when you are seeking the Lord together in prayer. Jesus reminds us in John 15:4, "Abide in Me and I in you. As the branch cannot bear fruit of itself, unless it abides in the vine, neither can you, unless you abide in Me." Our marriages often resemble a withered branch because

we have detached ourselves from the vine. In James 4:1–3, we read a description of many modern marriages: "Where do wars and fights come from among you? Do they not come from your desires for pleasure that war in your members? You lust and do not have. You murder and covet and cannot obtain. You fight and war. Yet you do not have because you do not ask. You ask and do not receive, because you ask amiss, that you may spend it on your pleasures." James provides the key in James 4:8: "Draw near to God, and He will draw near to you. Cleanse your hands, you sinners; and purify your hearts, you double-minded." Consider the following simple illustrations. In the first, we see a man and his wife moving closer to God; as they do, they grow closer to each other. The second illustration shows a man and his wife who have left God out of their marriage and who have gone their separate ways.

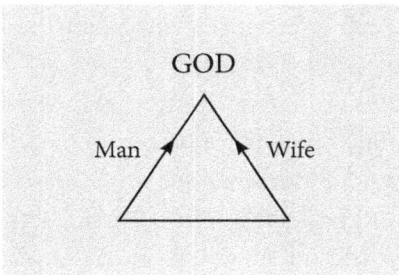

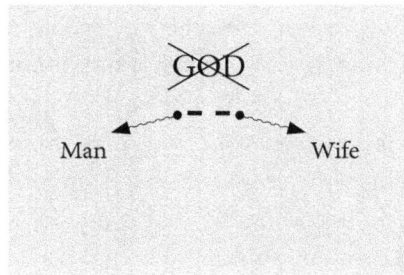

PROBLEMS?

It may be difficult for some of you to even consider implementing the tips we've suggested above. You may feel as though you are facing so many problems that you don't know where to begin. We want to suggest a few more steps that may help if this is your situation. Here are some of the things Tim and I have learned as we have encountered difficulties in the process of learning to cleave.

1. We didn't threaten divorce.

2. We would tell each other, "I am committed to you...*although I may not like you very much at the moment!*"

3. We made it a top priority to work through our problems. This involved a commitment of time, energy, and resources.

4. We communicated our determination and commitment to resolve conflicts. We would tell each other, "I know you are upset right now, and

I understand that neither one of us knows how to resolve this problem. But I want you to know I am not going to give up. Together we will find an answer." Often, just knowing we are not facing a problem alone can help ease the emotional stress and fears that cloud the real issue at hand. Resolving a problem as a team is far easier than trying to deal with an issue that you believe your spouse could care less about. Communication is so important in this area—even when you don't have the solution.

5. We made it our goal to resolve problems as they occurred. We tried not to let problems pile up, unresolved, for days or weeks at a time. Unresolved problems can quickly grow into mountains, which can become seemingly insurmountable. One little misunderstanding gets tangled up with another, and before long, it is impossible to sort out how it all started. We determined not to sweep grievances under the carpet or to ignore conflicts. Solving a problem right away is not always easy, but working through one problem at a time is far more manageable than trying to sort through a mountain of unresolved conflicts.

6. Ephesians 4:26 says "Be angry, and do not sin: do not let the sun go down on your wrath." We tried to be sure that we didn't go to bed angry with each other. It is important to point out what this verse doesn't say: It doesn't say that every problem will be solved before the sun sets! The main point here is that we don't let the sun go down on our anger. Unresolved anger leads to bitterness, hatred, division, and alienation. There were times when we were unable to resolve a conflict before going to bed. When the clock struck 2 a.m., it became obvious that we were not going to solve the problem that night. Whenever this happened, we would agree on four things: first, we loved each other; second, we were totally committed to each other; third, we were committed to finding the answer to the problem, and fourth, we usually set a time to discuss the problem the next day. We then could go to sleep without anger, acknowledging that problems, which seem insurmountable at 2 a.m., can often be solved more easily after a good night's sleep.

7. We learned to view our conflicts as a catalyst for change in the cleaving process. In all our years of marriage, we have accumulated quite a long list of conflicts, problems, struggles, and trials that we have gone through together *and* to which we have found solutions. All these situations have allowed us the opportunity to grow closer together as we

learned to cleave to each other. Our lives are filled with abundant evidence that God's rules for marriage work!

8. We learned to forgive. This is one of the most difficult concepts in any relationship. We often say that we forgive each other, but the truth is that we often hold on to past offenses, ready to throw them back in the face of our spouse like a weapon. Because this is such an important issue, we explore it in greater detail in chapter 9.

Violating Rule Number One—*Leave father and mother*—can result in the collapse of a marriage. Embracing Rule Number Two—*Cleave to each other*—can keep a marriage from collapsing. Now, consider Rule Number Three: the lifelong journey to *become one.*

STUDY GUIDE

Read Genesis 2:24; Proverbs 4:23; Proverbs 27:19;
Matthew 12:35; Jeremiah 17:9; Proverbs 28:26; Proverbs 3:5–6;
Matthew 6:14–15; Matthew 18:32–35

As we explore God's second rule for marriage, we are confronted with an Old English word that has lost meaning in our vocabulary today. "Cleave" does not refer to that huge cleaver or butcher knife in your kitchen *(although many people do a great job of hacking their marriage into tiny pieces!)*. The meaning in the Old English, as well as in the Hebrew and Greek, is quite the opposite. "Cleave" means that two things are being permanently joined. We compared cleaving to *"grafting."* Using this garden analogy, we saw a beautiful image of joining a branch onto another tree, making them one.

We also considered some of the practical things we can do that will help us obey this second rule. This rule has profound implications for our marriages, so let's dig a little deeper.

DIGGING DEEPER

1. Write your own definition of "cleave":

2. What is the importance of the Greek preposition "pros" as it relates to "cleaving?"

3. How do all three rules fit together?

4. What are the six lessons that we learned through the analogy of "grafting"?

5. What two aspects of cleaving did we discuss in detail?

6. Summarize Proverbs 4:23, Proverbs 27:19, and Matthew 12:35, and explain what these verses teach us about our attitudes.

7. What is your attitude about your marriage? (Check any that apply. Be honest! Share your answers with your spouse.)

   ☐ I am 100% committed to my marriage.
   ☐ I have never considered divorce.
   ☐ I have told my spouse that I am committed to her/him.
   ☐ Things are tough, but I won't give up.
   ☐ I have occasionally considered divorce.
   ☐ I think this marriage will last for _____ years.
   ☐ I am tired of trying to make things work.
   ☐ I wish I had an excuse to walk away.
   ☐ I think divorce would be better than what we have now.
   ☐ I have threatened my spouse with divorce.
   ☐ I don't think this marriage can succeed.

8. What do Jeremiah 17:9 and Proverbs 28:26 teach us about the heart?

9. According to Proverbs 3:5–6, how can we bring our emotions under control?

10. We suggested four action steps you can take in regard to "cleaving." They are:
    - Be _____
    - Be _____
    - Be _____
    - Be _____

11. Circle one of the three action steps above that you want to work on this next week in your marriage. Write some practical steps for accomplishing this.

12. We also suggested eight action steps for working through problems. Do you need to put any of these into practice in your marriage? Share with your spouse which of the eight you would like to work on.

CHAPTER FOUR

GROWING TOGETHER

Become(ing)One

The candlelight was reflecting in his eager eyes as he watched his beautiful bride walking down the aisle toward him. It seemed that everyone in the entire room held their breath as the bride reached out and took the groom's hand. With music playing softly, the young couple stood facing each other, engulfed in a sea of happiness. Locked in each other's gaze, it was as if no one else was present as they repeated their vows to each other. Her golden ring glistened as he slipped it gently onto her finger and the pastor repeated those famous words: "I now pronounce you man and wife." As if by magic, they now are *one*, right?

After the fanfare of the wedding ceremony has faded, many couples think, "OK. The wedding is over. We now are man and wife. We are 'one.' Now it's time to get back to normal life." Typically, within a few weeks, this naïve couple hits a brick wall and wonders what happened: Why don't they *feel* like they are one?

The first disagreements start innocently enough: "Where is the proper place for dirty socks to go?" "Who gets to control the TV remote?" "What's all this hair doing in the sink?" "Why can't you help with the dishes?" "Who forgot to refill the water pitcher?" "Why can't you put the toilet seat down when you're done?" And of course, "Why do you squeeze the toothpaste tube from the top/middle/bottom?"

Those of you who have been married for some time may be smiling as you recall those early adjustments. But five or ten years later, it's not so funny if you still are arguing about where to put dirty socks or who does what chores.

These initial adjustments only scratch the surface of the real issue—one often overlooked by couples. Too many couples fail to understand the third rule of marriage: *"...and they shall become one flesh"* (Genesis 2:24).

Many couples have the idea that merely putting on wedding attire, walking down the aisle, repeating vows, and exchanging rings would instantly make them one. Oh, we *say* they are man and wife, and legally, they are. God certainly sees this married couple as one. But the process of *"becoming one"* is only beginning. Consider this story and analogy from our good friend, George Bradley, who had gone with his wife to the beach to celebrate their anniversary.

"We decided to rent an ocean kayak for two hours. We wanted to paddle out about a mile to some sea caves and look for (harmless) leopard sharks. We had never rented a kayak before. So we listened intently to the hasty verbal instructions we were given back at the rental shop, and then we marched down to the beach to go for it.

Our first focus was on getting the kayak through the surf, so we immediately started to feverishly paddle out. We made it! It was tremendous to soak in the beauty of being out there on the ocean. Everything went OK, but we seemed to be having real difficulty paddling the kayak properly. We got to where we needed to go but we went in half circles half of the time. It was frustrating. We didn't know why we were having difficulty paddling the kayak in a straight line. Was it Mary's fault? Was it mine? Or were we just a poor kayaking couple? We didn't know. But we kept working at it. We couldn't give up. If we stopped, the tide would pull us into the cliffs. So though thwarted, we paddled on.

When we were three quarters of the way back to the beach from which we had launched, a kayaking instructor noticed us. He said, "Hey, not to intrude there too much, but you might have a better go of it if you turned around in the kayak. You are paddling the kayak backwards!"

We thanked him and turned around. It was humiliating to learn that we had traveled most of our journey doing something so basically wrong, so absolutely backwards and so functionally messed up. But within seconds of adjusting our positions, we were paddling in a straight line and laughing our guts out! What we had done was so bad that it was hilarious.

Immediately I began to realize that our blunder was an amazing metaphor for life: We see the challenge, joy, and danger of life and go for it, but we sometimes struggle for years and do many things simply backwards from God's perspective. Why? Sometimes it is innocence and ignorance. Other times it is pride. We won't listen to God's instructors. We sin willfully, or we learn how to manage doing it our way and refuse to change."

God sees us as being one. We are in the same "kayak" (we are one) with our spouse, but all too often we ignore His guidelines and end up totally backwards! We often paddle in circles or even capsize. We are one in fact but not in practice! We do not experience all the blessings God has for us through this process of becoming one. Instead, we try to manage on our own, ignoring the Creator and His wisdom. In the same way in which we believe we are instantly one after the wedding ceremony, we think that just getting into the kayak is enough. But getting into the kayak doesn't mean we know how to paddle or even how to sit correctly. There is a process that requires not only that we learn the basics of "kayaking" but also—and even more important—that we become experts at navigating the ocean of life.

This third rule: "BECOME ONE" is a process but it is a process that we must allow God to accomplish in our lives. More than an idea—something you might try for a while and quit when it gets tough—it is a command: Let God do His work in your marriage. Your wedding day is just the beginning. God wants to continue the process of making you one—but only if you allow Him to!

MY WAY? YOUR WAY?

Becoming one means no longer doing things "my way" or "your way" or the "world's way." Rather, becoming one means doing things "our way," a *new* way that is right for us and that means doing things God's way! Becoming one is neither a fifty-fifty proposition nor meeting your partner halfway. Becoming one requires that we learn to live in unison—one voice, one heart, one purpose, and one mind.

It is important that we understand the word 'become.' The verse does not say "and they magically *became* one flesh" (indicating a past, completed action). Nor does it say "and they shall **be** one flesh" (indicating a present state of being). No! The verse says "and they shall *become* one flesh." This word is in the active form; it denotes a process. There is no hint of this action being completed at any specific point in time. And that is exciting news!

Exciting? What's so exciting about that? It means that we don't have to be a perfect couple the day after our wedding ceremony. No! We are "under construction." We can relax the expectations we have of each other and of our marriage because we have a lifetime to figure this out! We get to keep on *becoming one* "until death do us part." What a relief! Repeating some vows and putting on the rings was not the end. It was just the beginning of an amazing journey—the process of becoming one.

> RELAX!
> We are all
> "under
> construction."

For most of your single years, before you were married, you did just what you wanted to, how you wanted to, when you wanted to—you were independent. Now you are married, and all those attitudes, preferences, habits, and values of "singleness" must merge with those of another person. You are not merely roommates living in the same house. You have embarked on a process, designed to last your entire lifetime, of becoming one. And what an adventure it will be!

As we mentioned in the section about cleaving, conflicts become catalysts for change. In our marriages, God uses our problems and conflicts to help us see three things:

- **There may be an area of sin in our life that these conflicts will bring to light.** God will use these problems and conflicts to purify us individually and help us grow. Let's face it: we are often quite selfish! The Lord doesn't want to leave us that way.

- **Our conflicts help to illuminate those areas in our relationships that are not unified and are in discord.** Discord weakens and eventually destroys our relationship. Our goal is to become one. Pretending we don't have conflicts won't make them go away. Face them!

- **As we struggle through** *(and resolve)* **these conflicts, we learn** *how* **to become one, and we gain a new level of unity in our marriage.** The more victories we experience like this in our marriage, the more solid our relationship will be.

Does this mean that we can't have differing opinions? Tim and I often have very different points of view. Tim and I like different kinds of foods. We enjoy different types of activities. We often see things from very different perspectives. Does that mean we aren't *one*? No. Tim and I aren't clones. We are two unique and different individuals. God made us this way. Men and women are *not* the same! (We will speak about this in more detail in Chapter 5.) Two people can have very different personalities, characteristics, likes, and dislikes, and still be one.

We are not clones but we can still be ONE.

The best analogy we can use to illustrate this is by looking at our own human body. We are *one* body, but we are made up of many parts. Each part serves a special purpose, and yet each part is very unique. My mouth enjoys a long drink of water, but I don't like getting water in my eyes or up my nose! My lungs enjoy a deep breath of fresh air but too much air in my stomach causes some serious discomfort.

Does it mean that the body is not "one" just because the individual parts serve different functions and have different preferences? Obviously not. The Lord created the human body to fit together beautifully, as one. In the same way, we may be very different people in our marriage—with different abilities, preferences, likes and dislikes, and even different opinions. We need to understand that the Lord has created us to be unique. He has given each of us strengths, insights, and abilities that help to complete the other. As we learn to respect, appreciate and honor these differences, we will discover a marriage that really works together in amazing ways. Becoming one doesn't mean that we abandon our identities and become carbon copies of our spouses. Becoming one does mean blending two separate lives into one new, dynamic creation.

THE PROCESS

The process of becoming one is not an easy one. If you were sitting in one of our marriage seminars, you would watch me use this object lesson. Imagine that in my right hand I am holding a small, bright red ball of Play-Doh. (The soft, pliable clay that children love to create things with.) In my left hand I am holding a small, bright blue ball of Play-Doh. Sometimes in our marriages we are like these two round balls: We bump heads, each choosing to do things his or her own way and avoiding any real conflicts. (Imagine the Play-Doh balls bumping into each other, but nothing happens.) The balls are still separate, one red and one blue.

But when we commit to following God's rules for marriage and allow Him to do the work, something interesting begins to happen. Instead of running away from conflicts, we begin to face them. Conflicts put a lot of pressure on a marriage. Sometimes we feel as though we are being squeezed as we commit to working through areas of conflict and striving to become one. (Now imagine that I am squeezing the two balls of Play-Doh together, blending them into each other.) Look at what happens: the pressure of those problems creates something new. By working through conflicts and finding God's solutions, the two balls of Play-Doh become one! It took time and pressure to blend the balls of clay. For a while, you could still see streaks of blue mixed with red. Ultimately, though, the red and blue Play-Doh balls become one larger purple ball. No trace of red or blue remains. But notice something important: The red ball of Play-Doh didn't become blue. Nor did the blue ball of clay become red. Rather, they became something new together: —Their individual qualities blended to make something beautiful.

This is what we mean by becoming one. This took time. A process was involved. There was pressure and discomfort. But consider the result: The two have become one. It will be impossible now to separate the red ball from the blue! We love to use the colors blue and red because together they create the color purple. In the Bible, purple often points to the King—to royalty. When we do things God's way, our marriage will be pleasing to the King of kings!

We want to reiterate this point: God holds these two balls of clay! When we allow Him to work in our lives and in our marriages, He will apply just the right amount of pressure to blend us into one. God promises to complete this work of making us one *if we allow Him to:* "being confident of this very thing, that He who has begun a good work in you will complete it until the day of Jesus Christ" (Philippians 1:6).

Time + process + pressure = unity

Imagine a scenario from "real life": Chuck bursts through the front door after work, clearly agitated. Janice is sitting at the table, sipping a cup of coffee. Immediately, Chuck says, "I stopped at the bank on my way home from work, and we only have $5.00 left in the account. What in the world happened to all our money? What did you do?"

Consider three possible reactions to this scenario:

1. Janice grabs the cup of coffee sitting in front of her and hurls it across the room at Chuck, highly insulted that he accused her like that.

2. Chuck snatches Janice's purse and takes away her bankcard and checkbook, convinced he cannot trust her ever again.

3. Together they realize they have a problem and determine that together they need to find a solution.

Janice might say something like this to Chuck: "Oh, sweetheart! Isn't this exciting? We have a problem! But really, this is a wonderful opportunity to become one! I am so happy this happened. We will be able to become one in another area of our marriage! Isn't that just terrific?"

Okay...maybe she wouldn't use those exact words! *(And probably not a sweet tone of voice!)* But in essence, if they are willing to obey this third rule, this is what they are going to do. This conflict will become a catalyst for change, helping them to become one in another area of their life.

Let's see how God's three rules for marriage can be applied to Chuck and Janice: First, they have a problem with how they handle money. Clearly, Chuck and Janice are operating under two very different assumptions and lifestyles. The third rule tells them to become one. They start by agreeing that they are not united in this area.

Remember the second rule? *Cleave.* Chuck and Janice reassure each other of their complete commitment to their relationship. They agree that they will work together to resolve their differences in how they manage money.

Chuck and Janice then consider the first rule: *Leave.* What in their family backgrounds may be influencing the way they handle money? As they begin to talk together, several memories surface: Janice's father always handled the family finances. Janice's mother never knew how to balance the bank account or pay a bill.

Janice had never learned to handle finances and had simply assumed "the money would always be there;" after all, she came from an upper-class family. Whenever she had needed anything as a child, she had gotten it. Her father had given her a generous allowance throughout college. She had lived at home until she married and had never had to take responsibility for her own money.

In Chuck's family, it was his mom who handled the money. She was an accountant and enjoyed managing the family budget. Chuck had assumed that Janice understood how bank accounts and ATM cards work. After all, he had watched his mom competently manage his family's finances. Chuck had thought that Janice had been keeping records of their bank account all along.

After some tearful revelations and a lot of apologizing, Chuck realized that his young bride simply didn't know how to balance their account. She had not intentionally emptied it; she just hadn't known any better.

Together, they talked about what would be the best solution for their new family. Janice admitted that she had never had a good head for numbers; Chuck had excelled in math and was happy to take responsibility for the family bookkeeping.

Chuck explained to Janice that he did not make the same income as her father, and they would need to work together to set a reasonable budget for their family. It took some tweaking, and there were still some tense moments, but Chuck and Janice finally settled on a budget they both felt was workable. It was not the way Janice's family had handled money, and it was not the way Chuck's family had handled money. It was a new way: their way. They were *becoming one.*

WHY BECOME ONE?

There is one last word we want to look at in this passage: "one." Let's consider how Jesus used this word: He said, "I and my Father are one" (John 10:30). We know that Jesus was making clear to His followers that He was God. On the night Jesus was betrayed, He prayed for His followers: "I do not pray for these alone but also for those who will believe in Me through their word; that they all may *be one,* as You, Father, are in Me and I in You; that they also may *be one* in Us, that the world may believe that You sent Me" (John 17:20). Jesus focused on His unity with the Father and on His desire for us to be united with Him. This was one of the last prayers He prayed before going to the cross. Clearly, this was important to Jesus.

Why is it important that we are one? Why can't we live separate, independent lives, doing our own thing, living as we please and not worrying about anyone else? Jesus gives a number of reasons for being "one":

In Mark 3:24–25, Jesus says, "If a kingdom is divided against itself, that kingdom cannot stand. And if a house is divided against itself, that house cannot stand." We cannot have a successful, strong marriage if we are not one. History, culture, society, business, and experience all tell us "united we stand, divided we fall."[1]

> *"If a house is divided against itself, that house cannot stand."*

Jesus provides another beautiful picture in John 15: that of the vine and the branches. "Abide in Me, and I in you. As the branch cannot bear fruit of itself, unless it abides in the vine, neither can you, unless you abide in Me" (John 15:4). Jesus teaches that we must remain connected to—*one with*—Him if we are to produce fruit. In the same way, a marriage cannot be fruitful unless there is unity.

To further illustrate this point, consider Malachi 2:13–15. The chapter begins with the Lord revealing the sins of His people. The Lord says in verse 13, "So He [the Lord] does not regard the offering anymore nor receive it with goodwill from your hands. Yet you say, 'For what reason?' Because the LORD has been witness between you and the wife of your youth, with whom you have dealt treacherously; yet she is your companion and your wife by covenant." The problem was that the Lord's people were not living in proper relationships in their marriages. One result was that the Lord refused to accept their offerings. In Malachi 2:15, we read why the Lord calls us to become one: "But did He not make them *one*, having a remnant of the Spirit? *And why one?* He seeks godly offspring. Therefore take heed to your spirit, and let none deal treacherously with the wife of his youth."

Why does the Lord call us to be "one?" God wants us to produce godly offspring. Can He be any clearer? It is difficult to raise godly offspring in an ungodly home filled with disunity and strife. Today, more than ever, children need to witness unity in their parents' marriages. Sadly, this is not the experience of many children. Worse, many couples have come to the conclusion that if disunity and strife are bad for their children, then divorce must be the only solution. Rather than working to resolve problems and doing whatever is necessary to heal their marriages, these parents believe they are doing their children a favor by divorcing. Certainly it is true that strife is not good, but running away from problems in a marriage does not make things better for the children. Statistics point to serious repercussions in the lives of children whose parents divorce. Consider just a few that are specific to those children who are raised in single-mother homes:

Problem	Single-Mother Family	Two-Parent Family
Hyperactivity	15.6 %	9.6%
Conduct disorder	17.2 %	8.1%
Emotional disorder	15.0 %	7.5%
One or more behavior problems	31.7%	18.7%
Repeats a grade	11.2%	4.7%
Current school problem	5.8%	2.7%
Social impairment	6.1%	2.5%
One or more total problems	40.6%	23.6%

These statistics are from *Growing Up in Canada: National Longitudinal Survey of Children and Youth*[2], which contrasts children being raised in two-parent families with those from single-mother families.

Consider as well the following statistics[3]:

- 63 percent of youths who commit suicide are from fatherless homes. *[U. S. Department of Health and Human Services, Bureau of the Census]*
- 90 percent of all homeless and runaway children are from fatherless homes.
- 85 percent of all children who exhibit behavioral disorders come from fatherless homes. *[Centers for Disease Control]*
- 80 percent of rapists motivated by displaced anger come from fatherless homes. *[Criminal Justice and Behavior,* Vol. 14, pp. 403-426
- 71 percent of all high school dropouts are from fatherless homes. *[National Principals Association Report on the State of High Schools]*
- 70 percent of juveniles in state-operated institutions come from fatherless homes. *[U.S. Department of Justice, Special Report, Sept. 1988.]*
- 85 percent of all youths in prison grew up in a fatherless home. *[Fulton County Georgia Jail Populations and Texas Department of Corrections, 1992]*

How can we expect to have godly offspring when we do not live as God intended? The Lord gave us this rule: "Become one flesh." His purpose is that we produce godly offspring. Contemporary society is replete with the tragic results of couples who choose to ignore God's rules. They have run from their conflicts, having believed the lie that it would be "better for their children" if they divorced. IT IS NOT BETTER! The BEST thing you can do for your children is to learn to become one and allow the Lord to heal your broken marriage.

We believe there is still more in this verse to consider. "Offspring" can refer to spiritual children as well as to natural children. Perhaps you don't have children of your own, or your children are grown. Your marriage should still be producing godly "offspring." It can and should have a positive influence on people around you—neighbors, co-workers, relatives, friends. How many people do you know who have broken lives, shattered relationships, ruined marriages? These people are crying out for answers—not some quick fix or self-help book but rather living examples of what works. What is being produced by your marriage? What kind of "fruit"—sweet or bitter—is your marriage producing? What kind of impact does your marriage have on the lives of those around you?

The Lord has called us to be one so we can bring light and healing to a broken, dark world. In John 17:23, Jesus prays, *"I in them, and You in Me; that they may be made perfect in one, and that the world may know that You have sent Me and have loved them as You have loved Me."* Jesus wants us, His followers, to share His love with a hurting world. How can we do that? By being one! One of the greatest testimonies we have to the world is a marriage that reflects unity and God's love.

> *We are called to bring light and healing to a broken, dark world.*

ONE IN PURPOSE

Throughout the Gospels, Jesus speaks of His oneness with the Father. He says, "For I have come down from heaven not to do My will but the will of Him who sent Me. This is the will of the Father who sent Me, that of all He has given Me, I should lose nothing, but should raise it up at the last day. And this is the will of Him who sent Me, that everyone who sees the Son and believes in Him may have everlasting life; and I will raise him up at the last day" (John 6:38–40).

When we study Jesus' life, we know that He and the Father shared one purpose: to provide salvation for all mankind. Throughout Jesus' life, He had a clear purpose that He was determined to fulfill. In John 12:27, Jesus says, "Now My soul is troubled, and what shall I say: Father, save Me from this hour? But for this purpose I came to this hour."

In our marriages, we too must be one in purpose. What is the purpose of your marriage? Note that the purpose of your marriage may *not* be the reason you married in the first place! Ask engaged couples why they are getting married and you'll get a multitude of answers, many of them having to do with emotions and physical attraction. But what is the purpose of your marriage today? What are your goals for your marriage? What motivates you as a couple? In what direction is your marriage headed? Do you simply live day to day, without a goal or purpose?

Take some time to consider what purpose your marriage serves. We believe that God has a purpose and plan for every marriage: "'For I know the thoughts that I think toward you,' says the Lord, 'thoughts of peace and not of evil, to give you a future and a hope'" (Jeremiah 29:11).

For Tim and me, glorifying God through our marriage and allowing others to see Jesus in us is our purpose. This purpose defines who we are and directs our actions and attitudes. It also brings us together as one.

A football team cannot succeed if the players don't have a common purpose: to win. A business will not thrive if the employees and management are not united in a common purpose. In like manner, having a common purpose in your marriage will draw you closer together on the road of becoming one.

There are no quick fixes for a troubled marriage. We can't wave a magic wand and erase years of pain and sorrow. But there is one thing of which we are convinced: God's Word is powerful! His rules work! By choosing to adopt these three rules: *LEAVE, CLEAVE, and BECOME ONE,* you can lay a solid foundation for your marriage that will help you avoid problems in the future. We are convinced as well that these three rules can help rekindle the flame in a lukewarm relationship or bring healing to a broken one.

In the next chapter, we focus on practical ways to plot a course along the road of becoming one. We consider one of the biggest roadblocks couples face: misunderstandings!

STUDY GUIDE

Read Genesis 2:24; Romans 12:3–5; 1 Corinthians 12:12–25;
John 17:20–23; Mark 3:24–25; Malachi 2:13–16; Jeremiah 29:11

In chapter four, we considered the third rule for marriage: "Become one." We learned that we need to change our mindset: It is not "my way" or "your way" but rather "our new way" as we follow "God's way" together.

This is a process. We do not instantly "become one" the day the minister declares us husband and wife. But on that day we began our journey—a journey designed to last our entire life, a journey in "becoming one." By changing our perspective, we can understand conflicts as opportunities to confront areas in our relationships that are not quite in sync—and to work together toward unity in those areas in which we need to become one.

We also considered the purpose of becoming one as well as the importance of having a common goal for our marriage. Let's dig a little deeper...

DIGGING DEEPER

1. Write your own definition of "becoming one."

2. What were some of the first adjustments you had to make in your marriage?

3. How is "becoming one" a process?

4. Right now, what is the hardest area in which to "become one" with your spouse?

5. What is one area of "oneness" that you and your partner have recently gained?

6. How do you deal with conflict in your marriage?
   (Check whichever answers apply to you. Then place an "X" beside the answers that describe how your partner deals with conflict.) Share your answers with your partner.

   ☐ Head on.
   ☐ Avoid at all cost.
   ☐ Run away from it.
   ☐ Persistently work on it until it gets resolved.
   ☐ Just give in.
   ☐ Become angry.
   ☐ Get very quiet; stop talking
   ☐ Pray about it.
   ☐ We don't have conflicts.
   ☐ Get pushy and forceful.
   ☐ Focus on just one conflict at a time.
   ☐ Bring up every past conflict that might relate.
   ☐ I hate dealing with conflicts.

7. Read Romans 12:3–5. How can you apply this passage to marriage?

8. Read 1 Corinthians 12:12–25.
   The analogy in this passage is of the _____
   The key points are:

   a. We are all _____ (vs. 12).
   b. Each part of the body is _____ and _____
      _____ (vv. 14–17).
   c. _____ has ordained how the body is to fit together, as
      it pleases _____, not as it pleases _____ (vs. 18).
   d. We _____ each other (vv. 22–24)!
   e. God desires that there be no _____ in the body (or
      in our marriages!) (vs. 25).

9. According to Mark 3:24–25, why is unity important in marriage?

10. Describe an example from your marriage that illustrates the truth of
    Mark 3:24–25.

11. Read Malachi 2:13–15. What does this passage say is the reason for
    being one?

12. If you have children, write a prayer in which you ask the Lord to help you and your partner have the kind of marriage that will produce godly offspring.

13. If you don't have children, how can you apply Malachi 2:13–15 to your marriage? How else can you produce godly offspring with your partner?

14. What were your original reasons for marrying your partner?

15. TODAY: What is the purpose or goal of your marriage?

16. If you could choose to work this week on one area in which you know you need to become one with your partner, what would it be? *(Share your answer with your partner.)*

CHAPTER FIVE

DIFFERENCES IN THE GARDEN

A <u>very</u> imaginative narrative....

*A*dam and Eve were wandering around the garden one day when Adam realized he was lost. Eve softly suggested that Adam ask the elephant for directions, but Adam was sure he could find the right path by himself. Besides, Adam loved a challenge! Adam gave his wife a condescending smile and reassured her that he knew exactly where he was going. He took Eve by the hand and proceeded to lead her in circles for the next three hours.

"I think we passed that palm tree before," Eve finally remarked. Adam's jaw tightened as he headed down another path. Eve tried to make conversation, but Adam became more and more tense. Several more hours went by.

"Adam, that monkey looks as if he knows his way around. Why not ask him for directions?" Eve questioned, growing increasingly annoyed at Adam's stubbornness. Adam only huffed. "What is wrong with him?" Eve thought to herself. "We are supposed to meet God for our evening walk together, and we'll never be there on time. Why can't he just ask for directions?"

Adam scowled. He started walking faster, dragging Eve behind him, trampling a few blackberry bushes underfoot in the process. Finally, Eve had had enough. "I am going over there to ask that serpent if he knows

103

anything. You can keep walking in circles if you want to!" And off Eve stomped, leaving Adam alone, grumbling to himself.

We all know that the serpent was more than willing to offer his advice. "Look here! I have just what you need!" suggested the sly serpent. "It's called a 'GPS': that stands for 'Godlike Positioning System.' This GPS (manufactured by "Apple," of course!) will open your eyes, and you'll be as smart as God—and smarter than Adam! You'll be able to navigate anywhere you want to because you'll know the difference between the right and the wrong way!"

This sounded exactly like what Eve needed—especially since Adam had no sense of direction! She willingly accepted the GPS and quickly figured out how to use it, without even reading the directions! Eve programmed the GPS to find Adam, who was still wandering in circles. She generously handed the GPS to her husband and promised to show him how it worked.

Adam took the GPS. He didn't want his wife showing him up—after all, he was the man!

Okay... so that is not *exactly* how it happened! Please forgive our taking a *little* creative license here—but you get the point! From the beginning of time, the differences between men and women have been profound—and have caused many perplexing problems.

In the last chapter, we talked about becoming one flesh. Many of us long to experience this oneness with our partner, but how in the world can we become one with someone we just don't understand? "Why doesn't he/she just behave like a normal person?" In other words, "Why doesn't he/she act like I do?"

We have to start by learning some valuable truths about the differences between men and women. As we gain understanding of these differences, we will learn to respect—and, yes, even *appreciate*—our uniqueness! Our marriages can be either enriched or destroyed by how we view these differences. Men and women think, process emotions, make decisions, learn, and communicate differently. As we explore some of these differences, allow us to state that these are generalizations. Rules often have exceptions. Many men and women will *not* exactly fit the descriptions we provide. The key point really is that men and women *are* different.

In this chapter, we focus on:

- The differences between men and women as seen through God's eyes.
- The differences in the ways we think.
- What do we do with these differences?

THE DIFFERENCES THROUGH GOD'S EYES

"...male and female He created them."

The differences between men and women have been debated for many years and have often provoked explosive reactions. The source of these eruptions is often the false assumption that the differences between men and women imply the superiority of one gender over the other. Let us make one thing very clear: Gender difference does *NOT* mean gender inequality. Simply stated, men and women are different, but this does *NOT* mean that one gender is better or more valuable than the other.

> *Gender difference does NOT mean gender inequality.*

The Bible makes it clear that God created two distinct creatures: male and female. "So God created man in His own image; in the image of God He created him; male and female He created them" (Genesis 1:27). We see the same distinction a few chapters later, in Genesis 5:2: "He created them male and female and blessed them and called them Mankind in the day they were created." In these passages, as well as others, we see the intentional plan of God, reflected in His design, of two very unique creatures: male and female.

We also believe that God loves men and women exactly the same. There is no ranking system with God. He does not place a higher worth or value on one gender over the other. God made men and women unique and different from each other, but God never intended for these differences to denote the greater value of one gender over the other.

The Apostle Paul put it into perspective for us in Galatians 3:28: "There is neither Jew nor Greek, there is neither slave nor free, there is neither male nor female; for you are all one in Christ Jesus." To underscore the importance of what he was trying to communicate, Paul cited three contrasts: Jew and Greek; slave and free; male and female. The culture to which Paul was speaking held to a strong caste system that rated an individual's worth on the basis of race, economics, and/or gender. But that is not God's culture! God's value system is clear: No people group is superior to any other; a person of any given economic status is not of greater value than another; and neither gender is more important than the other.

When we look at the life of Jesus, we see how He valued men and women alike. Misinformed individuals often hold the erroneous belief that the Bible teaches that women are second-class citizens. Nothing could be further from the truth! It is clear from a reading of God's Word that Jesus included many women in His closest circle of friends and followers. Jesus healed men and women alike. Some amazing stories in the New Testament testify of Jesus' love and care of women in particular. (See Luke 7:36–50 and Luke 10:38–42).

We want to make this point crystal clear: *Men and women are different, but God values both equally.* In too many countries, women are treated like dogs—sometimes worse! In some cultures, women are considered the possessions of their husbands, for men to do with as they choose. One pastor in such a culture told us that if he didn't beat his wife, his church would not respect him! But if this pastor truly understood the value God places on his wife, he would not treat her in such a way. Allow us to share an excerpt from a sermon[1] in which Doug Clark shares a beautiful example of how Jesus treated women:

> "...But probably the greatest and most beautiful example is found in Luke 13, where on the Sabbath, in the synagogue at Capernaum, Jesus healed a woman.
>
> The synagogue in Capernaum was about 20 meters wide and 40 meters long, and like the mosque, it was a man's place. On the Sabbath it would be filled with men because Jesus the Teacher was there (Luke 13:10–17). He was going to expound the Word of God. Everyone expected to hear great and revolutionary things from this brilliant new authority on the Law. But as Jesus took the scroll of the Law and began to teach from it, all of a sudden, in the

106

back of the room, He saw a woman who was bent over. For many years she had been a prisoner of an evil spirit that had bound her and kept her a cripple.

Jesus then did five things that are astonishing because what He did broke through the cultural mold of that day: First, He called this woman forward from the place of the women (the back of the room) to the place of the men (the front of the room). He interrupted the teaching of the Word of God—the most sacred time in Jewish life—to minister to a woman.

Second, Jesus broke culture by speaking to her. The Jewish writer Alfred Eidersheim wrote that there were rabbis who prayed every day: 'I thank Thee, God, that I was not born a Gentile, a dog, or a woman.' Isn't that a great prayer? (Do you notice the word order?) No wonder everyone was shocked as Jesus spoke to this woman.

Jesus broke culture a third way: He laid hands on her. Eidersheim explains that in Jesus' day some Pharisees were called 'the black-and-blue Pharisees.' Why? Because they were so strict in their observance of the Law they would not even look at a woman. If they sensed that a woman was going to cross their path, they would close their eyes tightly and walk straight ahead. Sometimes they would smack into a wall or fall over an ox cart and receive their bruises. Here, in contrast to the example of the 'black-and-blue Pharisees,' Jesus laid His hands on a woman.

Fourth, Jesus affirmed her worth in society. These men in the synagogue were probably thinking, 'What is she doing in here? What is He doing? He's touching her. Look at what He's doing in God's holy place.'

Jesus knew their hearts and said to them, 'Don't you loose your ox or donkey and take it to be watered on the Sabbath?' (Luke 13:15). They all knew they broke the Sabbath by watering their animals.

Jesus continued, 'This woman is worth far more than any animal you have. This woman is not an animal; she is a "daughter of Abraham"' (Luke 13:16). By saying this, He restored her rightful position.

This episode is especially important because Jesus willingly risked His life for the sake of a woman. He humiliated His opponents in their own synagogue by ministering sensitivity, kindness, and mercy to a woman. It is for this act of kindness and divine love, and many others like them, that these men sent Him to the Cross."

Jesus never degraded, belittled, or disrespected any woman. He valued men and women alike, and He still does today.

DIFFERENCES IN THE WAYS WE THINK
Taking it from the top!

Men and women's brains are different—literally! Experts have shown that men's and women's brains are structured differently, and these physiological differences affect the way they each react and communicate. Certain parts of the man's brain are larger than the comparable parts of a woman's. For example, an area called the "IPL" is larger on the left side of a man's brain. This is the area that controls mental mathematical ability. Some research has shown that men typically perform better on mathematical tasks than women. But the "IPL" is larger on the right side of a woman's brain, which is the area used for sensory perception. This helps explain why a woman can be tuned in to a special sound, like the cry of her baby, while her husband "doesn't hear a thing."[2]

In women, the two sections of the brain that are responsible for language are larger than the comparable sections in men's brains. Typically, women tend to excel in subjects related to language. We observe this in young children: Girls typically are far more verbal and fluent than boys, and girls often learn to read and write at younger ages.[3]

Tim has never understood why I (Mary Lou) have such difficulty visualizing how a piece of furniture will (or will not) fit in a room. I usually say something like, "Honey, can you just move that chair over there, so I can see how it will fit?" Tim answers, "I can tell you right now, it won't fit there!" Tim can see it in his mind's eye, but I can't visualize it at all. I have to shove the chair into the corner before I will believe he is right! Why is that? It is because a woman has a thicker "parietal region" of her brain, which impedes the spatial visualization ability (this is the ability to mentally manipulate two and three dimensional objects.) In other words, I really can't *"see"* it in my mind. Research has shown that this ability is not gained through environmental or social influences. (That is, it cannot be taught.) Spatial ability has been observed in babies as young as 5 months old. [4]

Men's brains typically are 10 percent larger than women's. But women's smaller, more compact brains are better connected.[5] What do we mean by that? The brain is divided into two hemispheres, with each responsible for various tasks. Nerves connect the hemispheres, enabling the brain to communicate and function as a whole. Women have 40 percent more nerve connectors linking the left and right hemispheres of their brain than men do.[6] As a result, a woman not only can process information between both sides of her brain much more quickly, but she also can use both sides of her brain simultaneously. Men have fewer crossover connectors, with the result that a man typically uses only one side of his brain at a time.

Amazing research has been conducted using brain-scanning techniques (such as magnetic resonance imaging, or MRI), which test the differences in how men's and women's brains react to various situations. The brain scans reveal that whereas a man's brain tended to "light up" (indicating brain activity) on only one side at a time, a woman's brain "lit up" on both sides simultaneously. This has powerful implications for the way men and women communicate as well as for how they respond in various situations.[7]

At this point, I (Mary Lou) often get in trouble with the men who attend our marriage seminars. When I have explained how a man's brain lights up on only one side at a time, I have seen some of the men start to stiffen and look at me crossly. Some have spoken to me afterwards, clearly offended. They have mistakenly thought I was arguing that a man's brain does not function as well as a woman's and that a man thus is not as intelligent or as capable. Let me be clear: That is *NOT* what I am saying!

Rather, I have simply stated scientific facts about how men's and women's brains differ. The quantity of nerves and how well nerve connectors function are not determinants of either intellect or capability. Men, despite having fewer nerve connectors, are not less intelligent.

Nevertheless, the connectors do play an important role in how we communicate with each other—and in how well we understand each other.

So how does this affect our relationships? Consider a few of the job descriptions for the left and right sides of the brain.

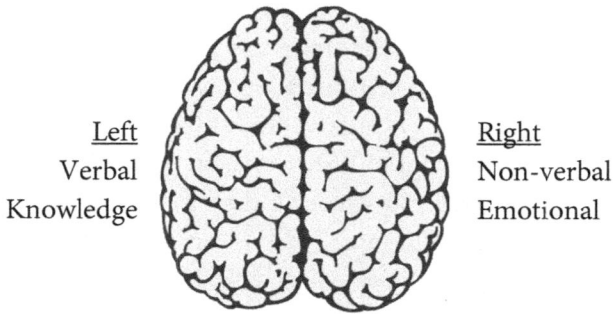

Left
Verbal
Knowledge

Right
Non-verbal
Emotional

The left hemisphere of the brain has the job of verbalizing. It is also the logical side. The right hemisphere picks up on non-verbal cues and is responsible for emotions. A bit of information that is received by the left side of your brain is processed logically, factually. How you *feel* about this information is processed by the right side of your brain. If you want to verbalize your feelings, then this information will need to travel back to the left side.

Now, think about how this bit of information is processed differently by a man and a woman, starting first with the man's brain. Think of the man's brain as a multi-story office building *"connected"* by an elevator.

The man starts with a bit of information. He steps into his *"elevator"* and scans the building directory to determine which floor he needs to travel to in order to process the information. Each floor has offices that serve different purposes: Some store information while others conduct research. He pushes the button for the 7th floor, the "Office of Emotions." He steps out of the elevator and visits the office where emotions are processed. Once he has finished processing the information, he gets back into the elevator, pushes the button for the floor where the "verbalizing" office is, and listens for the elevator bell to signal his arrival on that floor. He steps out of the elevator, ready to communicate what he learned on the 7th floor. His brain works like that: Information is carried from floor to floor, one direction at a time.

Because a man has fewer nerve connectors between his left and right brain, he needs more time to process and verbalize his feelings. He receives the input into the left side of his brain, *"travels"* to the right side of his brain to consider how he feels about the information, and finally returns to the left side to verbalize what he feels. He travels in a straight line, one direction at a time.

In contrast, a woman's brain is more like a wireless Internet hub connecting a variety of devices. Her brain can receive and send multiple signals simultaneously. She can process information and instantly redirect it to various places. How she gathers and transmits this information can seem mysterious: She isn't connected to any cables; rather, her brain appears to work in the "wireless" mode. She has a great antenna that can pick up and transmit signals in a large area. Sometimes the wireless system is protected by passwords and other security that a man can't decipher. No matter how hard he tries, he can't seem to *"log in"* to her network!

A woman can think, feel, and talk all at the same time. She is far more attuned to non-verbal cues. Both sides of her brain "light up" simultaneously. Often, a woman will process information aloud, using both sides of her brain to think through a situation by talking about it. She gets impatient when her husband is in his "elevator," seemingly stuck between floors. (Yet it is possible for a woman to overload and "crash" the system, as when too much information is received and sent out at the same time.)

Is one brain better or smarter than the other? *NO!* They simply function differently. While there are always exceptions to these findings, it is important to acknowledge that differences in brain function do exist. In our marriages, these differences can offer huge benefits if both husband and wife will embrace them and incorporate the strengths the other offers. What follows is a practical example of these differences.

MEET GREG & ANNA

This scene takes place during one of Greg and Anna's pre-marriage counseling sessions. Greg and Anna were obviously in love. It was fun to watch them together. Their love for each other usually bubbled all over the room! As they settled into their chairs to begin the session, we asked a simple question: "How do you feel your relationship is going?"

Immediately Anna replied, "I think we are doing pretty well. We never fight, and we love being together. There is just one little thing. I wish Greg would tell me more often how he feels. I want our relationship to be real and honest. But when I ask Greg to share his feelings with me, he seems cold and distant. I wish he would tell me more often that he loves me. I know he does love me, but I need to hear the words."

Anna continued to talk as Greg sat with a blank expression on his face. When Anna finally finished, there was a long, awkward pause as she waited for Greg to respond. But he didn't. Anna's eyes began to cloud as she looked desperately at Greg, anxiously hoping he'd say something. Finally, sensing the growing tension, we repeated the question for Greg: "How do you feel the relationship is going?" Greg looked sheepish and shrugged his shoulders as he muttered, "Okay."

The atmosphere in the room changed drastically. Anna was filled with doubts. Her thoughts started to run wild: *Did Greg really love her? Why didn't he say he loved her, especially after she had said she wanted to hear the words more often? Did he even care about how the relationship was going?* Anna was ready to burst into tears.

This was a classic case of two very different brains connecting in two very different ways—and *NOT* connecting with each other. Anna's feelings at that moment were not based in reality. The fact was that Greg had heard the first question using the left side of his brain. He then had taken a "journey" to the right side of his brain (the feeling side) to discover how he felt. By the time he had gotten back to the left side of his brain and was ready to give an answer, he took one look at Anna and realized he must have missed something. Just when he thought he knew the answer, he discovered the question had changed!

Greg really did love Anna. He just needed a bit more time to process his feelings. He was not being cold and distant; he just couldn't think about his feelings and express them at the same time, as Anna could.

Remember the brain scan? A man's brain only "lights up" on one side at a time. Greg's left hemisphere received the question *(blink, blink, blink)* and then he "traveled" to the right side to access his feelings *(blink, blink, blink)*. After determining his feelings, he "traveled" back to the left side of his brain to express them. This took time, and Anna couldn't understand the time lapse. Because Greg took longer to respond, Anna assumed he didn't care. But Greg's brain was wired differently from Anna's.

Greg was desperately trying to figure this all out. He could not understand how Anna could be on such a rollercoaster of emotions. It seemed to him that everything was going well. When they had walked into the office for counseling, Greg had thought that Anna was happy. He had felt confident that their relationship was great. How in the world had they gotten to this other point? When Anna blurted out her emotions, it was hard for Greg to understand them—let alone to respond to them.

What Greg didn't understand was that Anna often processed her feelings very differently than he did. Many women process their feelings and emotions by talking out loud —sometimes very loud! Because both sides of Anna's brain "lit up" at the same time, Anna often verbalized her feelings, which helped her sort them out. This was too much confusion for Greg! Sometimes the only thing he knew to do was to keep his mouth shut.

Greg and Anna needed to learn some basic communication skills, beginning with gaining an understanding of the differences between how men and women are wired. Once they began to do so, they were able to appreciate their differences rather than fight against them.

Men and women are wired differently!

We don't pretend to be scientists or experts on brain function, but we think you will agree that men and women are wired very differently!

Sometimes, following our session on brain function, a woman will say, "Actually, my husband has an easier time expressing his feelings than I do. He is usually the first to blurt out his emotions. It often takes me longer." It is true: Some men are far more expressive than some women; some women are very private. Beyond "wiring," many other factors (culture, family, personality, and past experiences, among others) also influence how a person communicates. And while we do want to avoid stereotypes, most couples will agree that differences between men and women do exist—and that they often are the cause of significant problems in relationships.

WHAT DO WE DO WITH THESE DIFFERENCES?
Understand and Honor

The key to dwelling together in unity is to accept that these differences do exist and that they are not wrong. God made us different from each other. God can use these differences to bless our marriages and our lives...if we allow Him to.

During one of our ministry trips to the Middle East, we met a young man who was actively serving the Lord. Gifted and talented, he had a passion for Christ. But he was a terrible husband. We spoke with him about his need to grow in understanding his wife, but he didn't want to listen.

"Why do I have to understand her? She should just respect me and do what I say." The truth was that she didn't respect him but was often forced into submission. This man's marriage was a failure, but sadly, he refused to take any responsibility for the problem.

The truth is clear: This man was being disobedient to Christ. 1 Peter 3:7 teaches, "Husbands, likewise, dwell with them [your wives] with understanding, giving honor to the wife, as to the weaker vessel, and as being heirs together of the grace of life, that your prayers may not be hindered."

> *God created your wife. He will help you understand her if you ask for His help.*

In Chapter 12 of this book, we examine this verse (especially the meaning of "weaker vessel"). But for now, consider two important words: *understand* and *honor*. Even though this passage is directed especially to men, these words are equally important to women.

First, Peter tells husbands to "dwell with them [your wives] with understanding." It is hard work to gain understanding of someone who is "wired" very differently from you. It is far easier to dismiss her as being wrong, inferior, or just plain foolish. But God, speaking through Peter, commands you to dwell with understanding.

You may complain that your partner is beyond comprehending. You may argue that she (or he) is the one with the problem. You may say that your partner is the one who is wired *"wrong!"* You may throw up your hands in defeat and say, "It's just too hard!" But God doesn't want to hear your excuses! It may be hard work to gain understanding of your partner, and it may take a lifetime, but it is an act of obedience; it is what the Lord has called you to do...whether you like it or not! God created your wife (or husband); He will grant you understanding if you ask for His help.

TWO STEPS TOWARD UNDERSTANDING

The first and most important step in obeying this passage from 1 Peter is to ask the Lord to give you understanding. In the Old Testament (1 Kings 3:9–13), we read about King Solomon, who asked God to give him an understanding heart. We learn that God was pleased with King Solomon's request and gave him not only understanding but also riches and honor. Psalm 119:130 says, "The entrance of Your words gives light; it gives understanding to the simple." God's Word will cast light on the sometimes foggy subject of understanding your partner! Even the simplest man can come to understand his wife—if he allows God's Word into the situation!

The next step in understanding comes from the basics of communication: How can you understand someone you don't talk to or whom you don't listen to? Learn to "dwell with understanding" by becoming a "student" of your spouse. Study her (or him). Become an expert on her. Gain knowledge of her moods and attitudes. Learn how to listen to her heart. This does not mean that you will agree with everything your spouse says or feels; but it increases the likelihood that she (or he) will know that you understand.

Consider the following illustration: Imagine that you have just purchased a new, expensive laptop computer. After carefully opening the box and removing all the packing material, you set it on your desk. Would you leave the laptop closed, just sitting there, like some kind of decoration? Of course not! You might take time to read the instruction manual, being careful to follow the directions as you turn it on for the first time. Alternatively, you might invest significant time in exploring the capabilities of the computer, trying this feature and that application. Little by little, as you learn the features of your new computer, you gain understanding and appreciation of all your laptop can do. The more

It is hard work to understand someone who is wired differently from you.

understanding you gain, the better your laptop will function and the fewer "crashes" you will experience. Although it may take some time and hard work, it is well worth the effort to gain understanding.

In the same way, gaining understanding of your spouse is worth the hard work. Everything functions so much better when you take time to

learn everything you can about your spouse. (This includes learning how he or she communicates, which we will cover in the next chapter.)

GIVING HONOR

As you gain understanding, you will be able to follow the next command: to "give honor." To extend the analogy of the laptop, you gain appreciation and respect for it as you gain understanding of what it can do. You value it. You treat it with special care. You likely would not give the laptop to a baby to play with. It isn't a toy. You "give honor" to the computer because you see its value.

In Exodus 20:12, we read "Honor your father and mother that your days may be long upon the land which the LORD your God is giving you." The word "honor" in the original Hebrew means, "to be heavy,"[8] not in the sense of burden but rather in the sense of great importance or impact. Today we may refer to a "weighty decision"—one of great significance. Similarly, we may say, "His opinion carries a lot of weight." Again, the concept is of magnitude or great substance. So, we are to treat our parents with great importance; they should carry "weight" in our lives.

In Matthew 15:4a, Jesus quotes this same passage: "For God commanded, saying, 'Honor your father and your mother';" In Greek, the word "honor" means "to value."[9] It includes the idea of something being precious or a prize. We see the same meaning for honor is used in 1 Peter 3:7. Thus, drawing on the meaning of the word honor in Hebrew and Greek, we find that it means to *"place great weight (importance) on what I value."*

Does this mean that I honor only the person who deserves honor? Do I value only the person who has worth? Is honor to be conditional— that is, should I honor my spouse only when he or she has earned it and retract it when he or she fails? No! If this were the case, none of us would ever receive honor. The fact is that we all are imperfect, flawed beings. Honor is a choice: I choose to value the person to whom I am married.

Have you ever noticed some of the things people collect? A quick online search will amaze you: People collect everything from oil cans to dice, from banana stickers (one woman has more than 7,000!) to bottle caps. At a British restaurant, you can pay 300 pounds for the crumbs left by a member of the royal family who ate there. "One man's trash is another man's treasure." But why do people search, buy, store, and display such things? Because they value—or *honor* them!

You have been given a gift far more valuable than leftover crumbs: The Creator gave you your spouse. That is reason enough to value your partner. He or she is God's creation and His gift to you. If you find it difficult to honor your spouse, then chances are you are using the wrong value system. You are measuring him or her according to the world's standards. Honor cannot be based on what the world values. Instead, ask God to help you see your husband or wife through His eyes. And remember: Apart from Christ, you would have no value either.

Romans 12:10 instructs us, "Be kindly affectionate to one another with brotherly love, in honor giving preference to one another." Does it say, "*IF* the other person deserves it?" No! Here we learn of a second aspect of honor in the phrase "in honor giving preference to one another." Honor also can be defined as 'holding the interest of another person as more important than my own'—not because he deserves it but rather because God commands us to.

The oft-repeated traditional wedding vows include the phrase "*to love, honor, and cherish.*" Never underestimate the power of these three little verbs. How many marriages today would be healed and renewed by simply doing what we promised at the altar to do! The three verbs go hand in hand: You cannot love something you don't honor or value. Although the emotion of love may exist at the beginning of the marriage, true love is not based on feeling alone. It is based on a choice to honor—

to place great value on—someone else. When you value someone, you will cherish, protect, care for, and treasure him (or her).

The man we mentioned earlier showed no honor for his wife. He refused to try to understand the way in which God had made her. Although the man had a public ministry as a servant of Christ, he failed miserably at being obedient to the Lord's command to understand and honor his wife. If you call yourself a servant of Christ, then you need to obey your Master and honor your husband or wife.

AN OCEAN APART

Sometimes it seems that a vast ocean separates men and women: You stand on one shore trying desperately to reach your partner who is thousands of miles away on another. In an effort to navigate this immense ocean, you climb into an inflatable raft. Suddenly, a storm blows in out of nowhere. It takes all your strength just to stay afloat. The waves crash around you, and you fear you will drown! Just when you think there is no hope, you hear the blast of a cruise ship's horn signaling that the ship is coming to help. The captain of the "MS Understanding" throws you a rope. As you hoist yourself up onto the deck, you realize your raft never would have made it across the ocean. But on this ship, you can sail safely to the other shore. Understanding is vital to your survival: The more you understand the differences between yourself and your spouse, the less likely you will be washed overboard. In the next chapter, we describe two other areas of difference: *motivation* and *methods* of communication.

STUDY GUIDE

Read Genesis 1:27 and 5:2; Galatians 3:28;
Luke 13:10–17; 1 Peter 3:7

We began this chapter with an imaginative retelling of the story of Adam and Eve in the Garden of Eden. We hope you'll forgive our creative license as it was intended to help you see an important truth: Men and women are wired differently. And sometimes that's not so funny!

Society abounds with jokes about the differences between men and women. Sometimes it's better to laugh at these differences than to cry about them! In any case, it is important for us to understand that God created man and woman as two unique and distinct beings. The differences between us can be sources of frustration or wellsprings of blessings, depending on what we choose to do with them.

We concluded this chapter by asking, "What do we do with these differences?" *Understanding* and *honor* are the keys to building a strong marriage—and to staying afloat when the storms of life crash upon us.

Let's dig a little deeper.

DIGGING DEEPER

1. Which two verses point out God's design of two unique and distinct beings?

2. What is the truth of Galatians 3:28?

3. Paul contrasts three groups of people in Galatians 3:28. What are these three groups, and what point is he making by describing them?

4. In his sermon, Doug Clark shared five things that Jesus did that were counter to the culture of His day; they revealed how Jesus regarded women. List those five things:

5. What is the difference in the way a man's versus a woman's brain is wired? (Think especially of the 'connectors' between the left and right hemispheres of the brain.)

6. How is a man's brain like a multi-story office building and elevator?

7. How is a woman's brain like a wireless Internet hub?

8. 1 Peter 3:7 is a _____, not a suggestion. The two key words from this passage are:

9. What two steps can you take to understand your partner?

10. What analogy did we give about gaining understanding?

11. How can you become a "student" of your spouse?

12. Choose one area you struggle to understand about your spouse. *Share your answer with him or her.* Take some time to sit together and ask questions about this area. Do not criticize. Do not judge. Do not correct. Simply ask questions and listen. Do not try to "fix" each other; rather try to gain understanding.

13. What does it mean to "honor"?

CHAPTER SIX

TALKING IN THE GARDEN

Communication

We often travel to different countries for ministry. In some of the countries we visit—as, for example, Egypt—our fair skin and light-colored hair make it immediately apparent that we are foreigners. We can forget about trying to blend in! People who meet us on the streets usually guess that we are Americans or at least Westerners.

But in other countries, it is not so obvious that we don't belong. In Russia, France, and Holland, we blend right in. There, it is not uncommon for someone to try to communicate with us in his native language. The reactions can be humorous: Sometimes we are not even aware that we are being addressed; other times, the person speaks more loudly—but still in his native tongue! (as if speaking louder will magically help us understand a language we've never learned!) We have seen people become annoyed or even disgusted at our lack of understanding. And some have just kept on talking, ignoring the fact that we have no idea what they are saying.

This reminds us of what can happen in our marriages. We take for granted that our spouse understands us. After all, we speak the same language! Or do we? The fact is, we often don't! Men and women often speak different languages—and they don't even realize it.

The results in our marriages can be similar to those we have experienced in our travels: some people speak more loudly when they think you don't understand them; others become annoyed, disgusted, and even angry at your lack of comprehension; and still others just keep talking, oblivious to the fact that no real communication is taking place.

In the last chapter, we described a few of the basic differences between men and women. In this chapter, we continue to explore them, focusing on two communication distinctions—

- The differences in motivation for communication
- The differences in methods of communication

We conclude the chapter by providing some practical tips for bridging these differences. We hope you will come to understand that even though these differences exist, it is possible to learn a "new" language.

Proverbs 24:3 says, "Through wisdom a house is built, and by understanding it is established." We read more about the benefits of understanding in Proverbs 3:13–14: "Happy is the man who finds wisdom, and the man who gains understanding; For her proceeds are better than the profits of silver, and her gain than fine gold." Isaiah 50:4 declares what we should seek: "The Lord GOD has given me the tongue of the learned, that I should know how to speak a word in season to him who is weary. He awakens me morning by morning, He awakens my ear to hear as the learned." Our desire should be to speak words in the right way, in the right season, to any who are weary; to have ears open to hear and learn more.

DIFFERENCES IN HOW WE COMMUNICATE
Motivation for communication

What four words can strike fear in a man's heart? *"We need to talk!"* What usually goes through a man's mind when he hears his wife say those words? He thinks, "What did I do? What is she upset about? I need the facts! How can I fix it?" He'll ask himself how to fix *"it"* before he even knows what *"it"* is! However, the woman who speaks those four words may just be thinking, "I miss you. I want to spend time with you. I want to share my feelings with you."

It is important to understand the motivation and purpose that underlie a man's versus a woman's communication.

- A man's motivation for communication is primarily to discover and express facts.
- A woman's motivation is to build relationships.

When a man's wife says, "Let's talk," she is saying, "I want to build a better relationship with you." But her husband is apt to think "There is a problem, and I have to figure out how to fix it. I need the facts!"

Let's revisit the elevator analogy from chapter five: The man's brain is task-oriented. He wants to get into his "elevator," push the appropriate button *(and only one button)*, go to that floor *(and only that floor)*, get off, accomplish what he needs to, and then get back into his elevator and travel back to where he started. He has a goal—to discover and communicate facts—*but not whatever facts may be on every floor!* The man's wife can stand outside his closed elevator doors, pressing the elevator call button all she wants, making it repeatedly go *"ding, ding, ding,"* but if his elevator is in motion, she won't be able to stop it. She has to learn to wait until her husband "comes back down" and the "doors" reopen.

Remember that we described a woman as being like a wireless Internet hub: She constantly receives and sends out information. She is tuned in to everything around her and processes all of this data simultaneously. In so doing, she builds new "connections" with those around her. She loves being in sync with others and is equally adept at sending and receiving information. The more information she sends out, the more connections she makes, and the happier she is.

Because a woman's motivation for communication is to build relationships, she is usually a good listener. She is not focused on the goal of exchanging facts but instead wants to build relationships. She understands this as being a two-way action.

There is a fun way to observe this difference. Ask a man and a woman to describe a meeting they both attended. Typically, the man will focus on a few main points—"headlines" - such as you might read in a newspaper. But the woman typically will share more in-depth and personal insights—the "fine print." Men tend to be about the headlines, women about the fine print.

In a relationship, this can cause problems—when a wife seeks communication that is personal and detailed and interwoven with emotion but her husband seeks to communicate "just the facts" or, when the husband grows impatient with his wife for providing "too much detail" when all he wants is a quick overview ("just the facts"). The husband is in his metaphoric elevator, discovering and delivering the facts. His wife

A woman wants communication that is personal and interwoven with emotions; a man is content with just the facts.

has her antenna up, sending and receiving information at high speed in order to build relationships.

Consider this example from our marriage: Tim comes home after a busy day of ministry. He has been counseling people all day, and he is tired. But I want to talk! Tim wants to turn on the TV, but I ask, "Can we just talk?" Tim reluctantly agrees and responds with a logical question: "What do you want to talk about?" Tim needs a goal, a purpose. But my only purpose is to be near him and *talk!* I begin to rattle on about some rather unimportant trivia, and Tim begins to get impatient. "What's the point?" he finally asks. Because my goal was not to exchange information but rather to build our relationship, I am offended by his abruptness and wonder "Why is he being so rude? Doesn't he want to spend time with me?"

Do you see what is happening? We had two very different motivations for (and methods of) communication: Tim was in his elevator, trying to figure out which button to push, becoming annoyed that the elevator door kept opening and closing while he waited for me to get to the point. And I was sending out signals like crazy, trying to get in sync with him, in order to feel more connected.

As Tim began to understand that building our relationship was my underlying need, he became more willing to accept what he viewed as trivial conversation. He finally had a goal: to strengthen our relationship.

As for me, I could have avoided having my feelings hurt had I stated my "goal" more clearly from the outset. I needed to understand that Tim's impatience was based on the fact that he didn't understand the purpose of my chattering. Of course he seeks a closer relationship with me; he just needed to understand the bottom line. Once I expressed my desire, Tim was happy to snuggle up next to me and just sit and talk.

WORDS, WORDS, WORDS!

There is a lot of discussion about how many words a man speaks in a day versus how many a woman speaks. Low figures range from 2,000 for a man to 7,000 for a woman; highs range from 25,000 for a man to 50,000 for a woman! But no matter which expert you believe, all are consistent in their finding that on average, a woman speaks at least twice as much as a man. (Our personal experience aligns with these findings.) *Women talk more than men!*

As we begin to understand the motivation behind communication, we begin to also understand why this is often the case. A man doesn't need many words to deliver the facts. He doesn't use communication to build relationships, which would require more talking and more words. Remember a woman's motivation for communication? Building a relationship can't be accomplished with a few monosyllabic words! Because she has simultaneous access to both sides of her brain, a woman has an unending supply of words!

Consider this scenario:

A husband goes to work in the morning and spends his day in a stressful office. By the end of the day, he has used up his allotment of 25,000 words (assuming the high estimate is correct). He is done talking; all he wants to do is go home and enjoy some peace and quiet.

But his wife has had a very different kind of day. A young mother with two small children under the age of 3, she has been home all day, chasing after little ones. The extent of her word usage has been perhaps seven words: *"No!" "Come here!" "What are you doing?"* (She may have repeated those words numerous times, but she has not engaged in what she likely would consider "meaningful conversation.")

She hears her husband walk through the door and she thinks, "Finally! An adult with whom I can communicate! Someone who will understand me and actually listen to me!" She hasn't come close to using her 50,000 words reservoir! But at the same time, her husband is thinking, "Finally! I don't have to answer the phone or deal with any angry customers. I can just turn on the TV and turn off my mind."

As soon as her husband walks into the living room, his wife corners him. She needs to talk! She needs to reconnect! You can imagine the growing tension because he is too tired to listen, and she won't be quiet! It gets even worse when his wife expects a two-way conversation. Remember, he is done talking. He's used up his words for the day!

This tension can be avoided if both the husband and wife come to understand this difference and learn ways to meet both of their needs.

One solution may be for the wife to give her husband a specific period of time to "recharge his battery" after work—a period of time during which she doesn't "require" anything of him. (Note that this should be a reasonable amount of time—not 12 hours!) Ask your husband how he can best "recharge." Does he need to be alone? Would he prefer a short rest? Once his battery is recharged, the husband should seek to give his wife the attention she needs, especially by listening to her as she seeks to communicate with him and to use her reserves of words.

Give your husband time after work to "recharge his battery."

Consider the following scenario:

A man walks in the door, where he is greeted by his wife, who hands him a glass of iced tea. She says, "Hi! I know you've had a long day, and there is a lot I would like to tell you, but I want to give you some time to rest. So take this drink, and I'll keep the kids busy for the next half hour so you can unwind." A half-hour later, the man approaches his wife, who now is busy in the kitchen. "Thanks. I really needed a bit of quiet. Now, let me help with the kids, and then you can tell me about your day."

This sounds simple, and our lives are not always easy to control. But even if you can't give your husband or your wife time or space to rest or to talk, a great place to start is by showing that you understand the need.

THINKING OUT LOUD

Another motivation for communication that is particularly important to women is the discovering and processing of feelings by thinking out loud. When we considered the physiology of the brain, we learned that a woman's brain processes information in both hemispheres simultaneously. As a result, a woman can think, feel, and talk at the same time. And frequently, she will process her feelings and emotions out loud.

This has been a point of contention for my husband and me. Consider this classic example: It was one of those days. I (Mary Lou) had been struggling with how to balance my schedule. Like many women, I have numerous responsibilities as a mother and wife as well as many relating to ministry and our church. Sensing my frustration, Tim asked, "What's wrong?" I replied, "I feel so overwhelmed today! I have three projects that are overdue; I need to help Josef with his schoolwork; the house is a mess; and I haven't even thought about what I should fix for dinner. Plus, we have Bible study tonight. There are several ladies I really need to call and talk to, but I don't have time for that either. I just don't know how to handle this workload!"

Tim actually heard only the first sentence, when I said: "I feel so overwhelmed." Hearing my distress and wanting to fix the problem, Tim immediately switched into *"solution hunter"* mode: He missed everything else I said because he had started to search for solutions as to how he could fix my problem. He had stopped listening!

And here is where the problem started: He interrupted me and began to offer solutions. That should have made me feel better, but it didn't. I felt even more frustrated because I started to feel alone with my problem. My emotions told me Tim didn't understand. I felt he was trying to offer a quick fix, but he was not willing to listen to my heart.

So I did what many women do: I got louder—and I repeated myself, hoping I could make my husband understand how I was feeling. Of course, Tim was still trying to fix the problem—which was not what I really wanted. Tim had focused on the problem; I was focused on how to resolve the emotions underlying the problem.

As our discussion continued, Tim began to feel frustrated because he thought he had found the solution to my problem. He didn't understand why I kept reiterating the problem. Why didn't I just accept the solution, do what he said, and be done with it?

Our communication broke down because I did not clearly state my expectations from the outset of the conversation. I did not want a solution; I wanted a sounding board. Tim eventually realized he was missing something and said, "Tell me again what it is you are really trying to say."

Having thought out loud about the problem, I was able at that point to rephrase the real issue. I replied, "Tim, I don't need a solution. I know I need to be more realistic during this busy time. First, I need to think through my problem out loud. I only need you to listen. Second, I need to hear from you that I am not a failure as a wife and mother. I need some comfort from you during this time of stress. Finally, I need to know that you understand how I am feeling and that I am not alone."

Now that I had Tim's attention, I could process the rest of my feelings out loud. I went on to explain, "I know this is just a particularly stressful and busy time for us. I know the stress will not go away right now. I just need to know that you are my partner through all of this and that together we'll make it." (Here you see the two aspects of my motivation for communication: *build relationship* and *discover and express feelings.*)

Finally, Tim understood. He switched out of "solution hunter mode" and simply listened to my heart. He could offer me the encouragement and empathy—not the "quick fix"—I needed and he could relax, knowing I didn't expect him to fix the problem. Together, we agreed to pray about the situation and place it into the hands of the One who could handle it. (We talk about this in more practical terms later in this chapter.)

METHODS OF COMMUNICATION
Pockets and Purses

Have you noticed that many women are amazing multi-taskers? Consider, for example, the young mother with a toddler. She is a juggler! This super-mom can repair the broken toy, wipe her child's runny nose, stir the potatoes, sort the mail, start another load of laundry, set the table, and never miss a second of the conversation she is having on the phone with her girlfriend!

And men? They are very focused—usually on one thing. It always amazed me that when Tim was reading, he was completely unaware of the chaos around him, especially when our children were very little. One child was crying, another was throwing a toy across the room, and the third was screaming to get the toy back. Tim is a wonderful father, but he was focused on one thing; he was reading his book and had an incredible ability to tune out everything else!

Earlier, we compared a man's brain to an elevator and a woman's to a wireless Internet hub. Here is another image to think about as we consider the differences in men's and women's methods of communicating: Men have pockets; women have purses. Usually, a man will have just one thing in his pocket—perhaps his wallet or his keys. He puts his hand into his pocket and finds just one thing there. Pockets are not connected; one pocket typically contains only one item. That is how most men are wired: Their lives are separated into "pockets." If a man has his hand in his "work pocket," then that is all he is thinking about or dealing with. Nothing else is in the work pocket. Of course, a man is aware that he has other pockets, but typically he deals only with what is in any given pocket. He focuses on one thing at a time.

Women, in contrast, have purses—often, rather large ones! Everything is in there! Everything touches everything else; it's all jumbled together. When a woman reaches into her purse in search of her wallet, she likely will have to move her comb, lipstick, old receipts, loose change, pens, tissues, gum, keys, a letter from a friend and a granola bar! Most women are wired that way: Everything is connected, and everything touches everything else. If a woman is talking to her husband about the kids, she may also mention his work, the house, the car, and the vacation, because for her, everything is connected!

If we want to grow in our understanding of each other, we need to remember that a man's method of communication is focused, usually on one thing at a time. A woman's method of communication is more panoramic: she views the big picture and sees everything as connected.

Women, when you communicate with your husbands, focus on one "pocket" at a time. If you want to talk about the children, be careful to focus only on the "child pocket." If in your conversation you require your husband to reach into other "pockets," he will become frustrated—

or he may stop listening. His method of communication is to focus on one thing at a time. If you seek to communicate effectively, you must address one topic at a time.

Men, learn to be patient with your wives when they start emptying their "purses" over your heads! Don't be surprised when you talk to her about the car and she suddenly starts talking about your next vacation or her friend's new job or a funny movie she just saw. Remember, in her "purse," all these topics are connected. You may want to talk about the car, but for her, the car is related to your next vacation (she is thinking about whether the car will be big enough) and her friend's job (her friend just got a company car) and the funny movie she saw (it included a scene with a car like yours.) Yes, this can be exhausting! But gently remind her that you need to talk only about the car at this particular point in time. Be patient!

"Pocket" versus "purse" often becomes an issue when I talk about something with Tim. One day, I needed to talk with him about my schedule. I made the mistake of mentioning first that I might have to miss one of our son's basketball games. Tim immediately focused on his "basketball game pocket" and stayed there. I continued to talk about my schedule, not about the game. But Tim kept talking about attending our son's game; he never heard anything about my real concern, which was scheduling.

Finally, I said, "Tim, it's not about basketball. It's about my schedule." He finally understood as he was directed to a different "pocket!" My mistake was to have mentioned the basketball game at the outset. (But remember, I have a "purse" in which everything touches everything else. So when I was thinking about my schedule, I was also thinking about everything else that was connected to it in any way.

Our different methods of communicating can be assets. My panoramic method, in which everything is connected, offers perspective. Case in point: Tim is a great Bible teacher. I love listening to him teach. But there have been times—particularly during small group Bible studies—when he has been overly focused on teaching the material and has missed the emotions of those listening to him. He was excited about sharing what he found in his "Bible study pocket." But with my "purse," I saw how "everything was touching." I was focused not only on the lesson but also on the confused look on the face of the teenager sitting across from me. I noticed when an older man started to fidget because it was getting late. I was able to offer this information to Tim and so to help him become a more sensitive teacher.

On the other hand, a purse that is crammed full of objects can also lead to a lot of frustration, especially when you are in a hurry and look-ing for your keys! It is so much more efficient to put keys into a pocket so you can easily reach into it and find them. In the same way, having a brain that processes information all the time and in both hemispheres simultaneously can be exhausting—and sometimes confusing! Tim's brain typically is far more focused. Often, he has helped me sort through my "purse" to find the one thing I was looking for! My husband brings clarity and focus to me when life seems blurred. As we learn to under-stand and respect our differences, we will be less impatient and demand-ing of each other.

Paul taught the church at Corinth that each member needs every other member. His teaching applies as well to our marriages. "If the whole body were an eye, where would be the hearing? If the whole were hearing, where would be the smelling? (v. 17) But now indeed there are many members, yet one body. And the eye cannot say to the hand, 'I have no need of you'; nor again the head to the feet, 'I have no need of you.' (vv. 20–21) But God composed the body, having given greater honor to that part which lacks it, that there should be no schism [disunity] in the body, but that the members should have the same care for one another." (vv.24b–25) (1 Corinthians 12:17, 20–21, 24b–25)

We may communicate differently, but these differences can bless us as we learn to accept, trust, and rely on the strengths of our partner.

DIRECT AND INDIRECT

A man's method of communication typically is more direct. How many times has your wife said something like "The backyard is such a mess!" A man hears a fact and thinks, "Hmm. She's right; the backyard is a mess." But that is not at all what she is trying to say. She might have uttered the words: "The backyard is a mess." But, her meaning *behind* those words is: "Please clean up the backyard!" A woman's method of communication is often indirect.

This difference in how men and women communicate gets men in trouble all the time: Their wives *assume* their husbands understand what they mean, but quite honestly, they don't! A man doesn't intentionally ignore his wife's request to clean the backyard; he just didn't hear it!

A woman uses a less direct method of communicating for a variety of reasons. One is that she believes an indirect request is more polite and shows respect. Unfortunately, most men don't perceive it that way. In fact, most men prefer a direct approach (of course, women still should use a respectful tone of voice and manner).

Another reason why a woman may communicate indirectly stems from the misconception that if she has to ask her husband specifically to do something, then his action won't be based on his love for her. A woman tends to equate actions that are solely her husband's idea with proof of his love. This misconception results in many hurt feelings. Remember: men have pockets. If they are "in" their work pockets, they may forget to do something for their wives. It is not that men don't love their wives; rather, it is that they are preoccupied with a different "pocket."

For example, I don't want to tell Tim, "Tomorrow is my birthday. Please remember to do something special." If I were to do so, then he might do something special only because I reminded him. If I have to tell him to remember my birthday, then it doesn't mean much to me when he does. I want it to be his idea! So I choose not to say anything—at least, nothing direct! (I might, however, offer plenty of hints!) I cling to the hope that he won't forget and that he will fulfill my unspoken expectation.

But this is hardly fair or realistic. I may drop a truckload of hints, but Tim doesn't communicate that way. He needs to hear things directly. This is an area in which many women need to grow. We need to learn how to be more direct in our communication.

Men, you also need to learn some new skills. If you ask your wife to do something directly, she may interpret your request as demanding and pushy. It is likely that she doesn't understand that your communication style is to be direct. It can be challenging for men to learn to be a bit more indirect in their conversations. Understand that your wife often will perceive your directness as harsh. Strive to speak in quieter tones, and mix in plenty of patience and gentleness. Usually, your wife will respond in a more receptive manner. Proverbs 15:1 reminds us "A soft answer turns away wrath, but a harsh word stirs up anger." The NIV uses the term 'gentle' rather than 'soft. Most men's voices are deeper and coarser than most women's. Men, learn to soften your voices; speak gently, and your wives will hear you. Proverbs 16:24 says "Pleasant words are like a honeycomb, sweetness to the soul and health to the bones." (This is likely where the proverb "You can catch more flies with honey than with vinegar" originated.)

By way of review, allow us to remind you of a few of the differences in how men and women communicate:

- Men = focused and direct
- Men have "pockets."
- Women = panoramic and indirect
- Women have "purses."

Practical Communication Tips

Many excellent books have been written on how to improve communication. In just one chapter, we have barely scratched the surface of this vast topic. Nevertheless, we conclude this chapter with eight practical tips for improving communication. We have found them to be invaluable!

Communication Tips for Women from Mary Lou:

1. **Focus on one topic at a time**. Don't "overload" your husband by enumerating a long list of problems. Men tend to communicate in a very focused way, so learn to communicate one thing at a time. Don't grow impatient if he needs time to get out of one pocket and go into another one! If you need to talk to your husband about your children, be sure you allow him time to shift his focus to his "children pocket," and then be careful to discuss *only* those issues that have to do with your children. *(See Proverbs 10:19.)*

2. **State facts**. For example, if you tell your husband that you don't feel that he respects you, he really won't know how to respond. Men need facts. Help your husband by giving him specific examples *(facts)* of when you felt he didn't respect you. Again, list only enough to help him understand. *(See Proverbs 15:2.)*

3. **Make direct requests**. Often, women try to be "sweet" and don't clearly say what we mean. For example, if I say, "The trash can is overflowing" *(indirect statement),* my husband will think, "Yes, it is." But it may not occur to him that what I really mean is "Would you please empty the trash can?" *(direct statement).*

Most men need to hear direct requests. They cannot read women's minds! Don't become angry if you make an indirect request and your husband doesn't do what you hope he will. He isn't ignoring you; he likely just didn't realize that you actually wanted him to take out the trash. He thought you were stating a fact, and he agreed with you. State your requests clearly and respectfully. *(See Proverbs 15:23.)*

4. **Rating system**. A rating system is a helpful tool for improving communication. When you have something really important to communicate, help your husband focus on the issue by rating its importance before you start talking. For example, you might say, "I would like to talk with you about a problem that is a #10 for me" (10 being the highest in importance). Giving the problem or topic a point value will provide your husband with a "fact" to which he can respond.

However, every issue or topic of conversation cannot be a "#10!" Using a rating system has the added benefit of helping you to evaluate the problem and speak in more factual terms. As you determine the relative importance of any given problem, you will be better equipped to communicate and to find an appropriate solution. Often, when I ask myself what point value I would give a problem, I am surprised to discover that the problem in fact was not such a big deal. Assigning a point value to a problem has helped me see through clouds of emotion and understand the real facts of the matter. *(See Psalm 37:30.)*

5. **State expectations clearly at the beginning of the conversation**. Do you need your husband just to listen? Then ask him to just listen! Sometimes I get crazy, new ideas. I like to think about them out loud because it helps me determine whether they really are good ideas. Whenever I would say to Tim "I have an idea," he would be filled with dread. "What does Mary Lou want to do now? What changes does she want to make? How much time, effort, and resources will this cost me?"

But more often than not, I was only brainstorming. There was nothing for Tim to be worried about because I wasn't yet to the point of knowing whether any given idea was good. I have learned to state my expectations clearly at the outset: "Tim, I am just thinking out loud. I am not making any plans to change or to do anything crazy. I just want to bounce this idea around with you and see what you think." You can almost hear Tim breathe a sigh of relief! When I make my expectations clear, Tim can switch off his "solution hunter mode" and brainstorm with me. *(See Proverbs 15:14, 28.)*

6. **Allow time for your husband to process information on both sides of his brain!** Ladies, be patient! Allow your husband time to get into his "elevator," determine the correct "floor," push the button, travel to that floor, and process the information. If he doesn't give you an answer right away, don't assume the worst—and. don't accuse him of being cold or insensitive. Give him time to think and to process information on both sides of his brain. *(See Proverbs 31:26.)*

7. **Choose the right time, place, and manner in which to discuss issues with your husband.** We cannot overemphasize this point. There will always be problems and situations to discuss and resolve, but *how* you deal with them can make all the difference. *(See Proverbs 21:23; Colossians 4:6; Psalm 141:3; and 2 Timothy 2:14.)*

Choose the right time. If you have to leave for church in 5 minutes, then that probably is not the best time to start talking about a problem that is a #10 for you. It may be painfully obvious that a situation has arisen that must be resolved. However, if you know you don't have enough time to discuss it, then say that you know you need to talk and suggest that you make an "appointment"—that is, set a time—to work through the issue. That said, do *not* ignore a problem (or postpone discussion of it) for weeks at a time. Doing so will undermine your relationship.

Often, women attempt to talk to their husbands when they are in the middle of doing something. Perhaps your husband has a big project he has to finish for work. He may feel a great deal of stress because he has a tight deadline, and he may feel overwhelmed. If you interrupt his work in an effort to settle an unrelated issue, it is quite likely that the stress he is feeling will inhibit his ability to focus on your problem; the result may be even more conflict. Ask your husband when would be a good time to talk. Accept his answer if right then is a bad time, but ask him to suggest an alternative.

Tim and I have learned that trying to solve a disagreement at 2 AM is a bad idea. When we are tired, our emotions can become raw and we are more likely to be unreasonable. Some women should avoid difficult conversations during certain times of the month. Similarly, it is unwise to try to resolve a conflict when you are sick. Choosing the right time is critical to good communication. Choosing the right time involves:

- allowing adequate time to resolve an issue.
- making an "appointment" to resolve any unresolved problems.
- asking your husband if now is a good time (or when a good time would be).
- avoiding times when you are tired or sick.

Choose the right place. Tim and I agreed to avoid having heated discussions in front of our children. Some people say that it is important for children to see their parents argue and disagree, the rationale being that children need to understand that differing opinions are normal. We respectfully disagree with this philosophy. Arguing in front of your children can result in their feeling insecure, particularly because the argument involves the two people they love most. Many children may become fearful and uncertain. Some will blame themselves for any disagreements. Note as well that a child cannot remain "neutral" and that too many parents involve their children in their arguments. *NEVER USE YOUR CHILDREN AS A WEAPON AGAINST YOUR SPOUSE.* Personal issues between you and your spouse should be discussed by the two of you. *(See Matthew 18:15–17.)*

Certainly, children should have the opportunity to witness a godly role model for conflict resolution. However, we believe this can better be achieved by modeling this process in your relationship with him or her (i.e., parent to child) as well as by teaching them how to resolve conflicts with their siblings. Conflicts between mom and dad are sure to arise when children are present. This is unavoidable. But when this happens, it is crucial for both parents to apologize that the children became party to what was a private disagreement. Explain the principle articulated in Matthew 18:15. Then be sure you communicate to your children how and why your actions were wrong. If either of you spoke disrespectfully to your spouse, then confess that before your children and ask their forgiveness for treating their father or mother in such a way. Finally, reassure your children of your love for and forgiveness of each other.

We know that when you have a matter to discuss with your spouse, it can be difficult to find a private place—especially when you have young children. But it is critical that you and your spouse do so. Take a long walk together. Go and sit together in your parked car. Lock yourselves in the bathroom. Wait until your children are in bed. Ask the Lord to give you wisdom. But protect your children (as well as other family members and guests) from getting caught in your problems.

We also believe that heated discussions should NOT take place in the bedroom. Rather, the bedroom should be the place where spouses' love for each other is expressed. The bedroom should be a sanctuary for both husband and wife. That said, we do understand that the bedroom may be the only place where some couples have any privacy—and thus the place they can go to talk. But to the greatest extent possible, try to keep your bedroom a place where you show love, not where you have disputes. Every couple is unique, but do your best to find a private place to discuss your problems. Choosing the right place means:

- seeking a place to discuss problems that is apart from your children, other family members, or guests; and
- safeguarding your bedroom from becoming a battle zone.

Choose the right manner. The final and the most important choice we all must make is the manner in which we discuss a problem. Our words can become weapons. It is easy to become disrespectful and belittling when we talk to our spouse. When we let our anger get out of control and lash out with our tongues, we are not focusing on the problem but instead are attacking the person.

The Bible has much to say about our tongues: James 1:26 reminds us to control them; in chapter 3 of the same book, we read about their dangers (vv. 2–10). Why do we use our tongues to attack each other rather than to work together to attack the problem? How often does a small misunderstanding grow into a mountain of anger, all because of a misspoken word or hurtful retort? James 3:10 is so important for us to remember: "Out of the same mouth proceed blessing and cursing. My brethren, these things ought not to be so."

Avoid using trigger phrases such as "You always do this!" "How could you?" "What were you thinking?" and "What's wrong with you?" Remember Proverbs 15:1: "A soft answer turns away wrath, but a harsh word stirs up anger." Choosing the right manner includes:

- attacking the problem not the person;
- answering with gentleness, softness, and respect; and
- not using trigger phrases.

8. **Remember, he is not wrong…just different!** Celebrate your differences! The Lord created you to be the completion of each other. His differences bring strengths into your life that you need! I have learned to see Tim's differences as blessings.

Remember that women have "purses." Sometimes my purse is so packed with stuff that I can't find anything! I start to feel overwhelmed, and I don't know where to begin. Both sides of my brain are processing information at a furious pace, and I feel that I am overloading. It is at times like these that I have come to appreciate Tim's strengths and differences. Tim is able to focus on just one thing at a time. He can reach into just one pocket, find the one thing that is important, and help me deal with my confusion and stress. It is a good thing he has to make that "journey" from the left side of his brain to the right and back; the process helps him think more deeply and identify far more effective solutions to the problems than all my frantic activity ever would. Tim is my calm. He is my rock. He may be very different from me, but he is not wrong. He is wonderful! *(See Ephesians 5:33; Titus 2:4; Proverbs 12:4; 1 Timothy 2:1)*

Communication Tips for Men from Tim:

1. **Allow your wife to talk. She may not need you to solve her problem. She might just be thinking out loud. Just listen!** Remember

that your wife's motivation for communication is different from yours: She will communicate as part of her process to understand and express her feelings. She may not be talking in order to communicate facts; rather, she may just be "processing out loud." As she verbalizes her feelings, questions, and thoughts, she becomes better able to "process" the situation. Learn to listen. *(See James 1:19 and Proverbs 29:20.)*

2. **Ask clarifying questions before you try to solve the problem.** For example:

a. *"Do you want an answer, or do you just need to talk?"*

b. *"How can I help you?"*

Learn to keep the "solution hunter" mode in your brain turned off until you ask some questions. Don't get stuck in the wrong "pocket." Wait until your wife asks for your help. *(See Proverbs 18:13.)*

3. **Take some time to learn how to express your feelings.** It is wrong to think that men don't have feelings. Reading through the Book of Psalms will give you great insight into the depth and range of emotions King David experienced. He was a "man's man": outdoorsman, soldier, leader. He was no "mama's boy." God created both men and women as emotional beings. But because men process emotions differently, it is harder for us to readily express them. But we can learn! Sometimes it is helpful to put our feelings into writing. Ask your wife to help. Admit to her that this isn't easy for you but that you want to learn. Learning to be honest and open about your emotions will bring greater unity to your relationship with your wife. And it is good for your health as well! *(Read through the Psalms.)*

4. **State your expectations clearly but gently.** When you need to discuss a topic with your wife, be sure to explain it to her gently. If she seems to stray off topic, patiently redirect the conversation to the topic at hand. Understand that your wife gets "sidetracked" because she sees everything as being connected. When your wife begins to talk about issues you perceive as peripheral, reassure her that you understand her concerns and that you are willing to discuss them later; emphasize that for now, you would like to address just the one topic. Be patient! *(See Proverbs 17:27 and Ecclesiastes 9:17.)*

5. **Show respect for your wife's uniqueness. Learn to ask for her opinions and listen to her observations.** God has given you your wife as a gift. She sees things that you may not. She has abilities, talents, knowledge, and strengths that you do not have. She is to be your completion. Accept this gift the Lord has given you. Allow her to speak into your life. She can offer a panoramic perspective, which may be just what you need to keep from becoming short-sighted. God made her different from you for a purpose. You are not meant to be self-sufficient. It is a strong man who recognizes that he needs help!

I praise God for the gift of my wife. Mary Lou has amazing insights and ideas. More than anyone else, she has helped me grow in my walk with Christ. In the early years of our marriage, I didn't realize how valuable she was. I had the idea that I was the man and I didn't need anyone. How wrong I was! My ministry has become more effective and productive because of the talents, skills, sensitivity, and discernment of my wife. I am the man I am today because of her influence in my life. *(See Proverbs 5:18; Proverbs 18:22; and Proverbs 31:10–12, 28.)*

6. **When your wife is offended, do not become defensive or try to justify your actions**. Accept that your wife's feelings are valid, and respond respectfully. You may not always agree with the details of what she is saying, but she needs to know that you understand and accept her feelings. Remember: her motivation for communication is to build your relationship. Her underlying reason for sharing her feelings with you is her desire for a deeper relationship. Don't fixate on the mere facts of what she is saying. Instead, focus on understanding her feelings. Our feelings are not necessarily right or wrong. Our feelings are *our* feelings! When your wife is offended, try to hear what she is feeling. And even though she may not express her feelings clearly, your job is to dig deeper: discover the source of the hurt and don't just try to treat the "symptoms."

One of the worst things you can do when your wife is offended is to tell her she is wrong and to defend yourself. You probably think that if she just heard the facts, then she would understand that there was no reason to be offended. Unfortunately, it usually isn't that easy. When my wife opens her heart to me by sharing a hurt, she closes up like a clam when I respond by telling her she is wrong. My own pride wants to defend my honor, so I respond in turn by making excuses or by trying to justify my actions. I have learned that instead, I must start by listening. I need to ask my wife questions about what she is feeling.

If you want to diffuse a potentially explosive situation, try these two little words: "I'm sorry." Admit that your actions hurt your wife, even if the hurt wasn't intentional. Avoid using the word "but" followed by some justification of your actions. Once your wife feels assured that you really want to understand her and that you are not rejecting her feelings, she will be able to hear your explanations. Perhaps she won't even need to because she already will have forgiven you. *(See Psalm 17:10 (NIV); Proverbs 28:25; Ecclesiastes 7:8; and 2 Corinthians 5:18, 19.)*

7. **Remember that your wife has a "purse."** Everything is packed into your wife's "purse": everything is connected. It is not easy for her to ignore her emotions or to stop feeling concerned about something. Even after you have finished talking about a problem, your wife's emotions may still be churning. You might think the problem is resolved, but your wife may need some time to finish processing. She may no longer feel angry, but she may still feel "raw" or sensitive.

Men, we have an amazing ability to compartmentalize our lives – a separate pocket for everything, even our emotions. Our wives are not wired like that. The best way to help your wife process her emotions is to be patient and allow her time to finish processing. Be gentle with her. Reassure her of your love. Don't expect her to have "pockets." She may not be able to tuck the problem into a "pocket" and act as though it never happened. Don't hurt her further by saying, "Hey, I told you I was sorry. Why can't you just let it go?" Give her time. *(See 2 Timothy 2:24 and Galatians 5:22.)*

8. **Remember: She is not wrong...just different**. Chances are good that all those wonderful differences were the little things that attracted you to your wife in the first place. Unfortunately, what you once found charming can turn into something that annoys and frustrates you. Ask the Lord to change your perspective. Ask Him to help you understand and honor your wife. Remember that He commands you to. The Lord created her for you. Become a student of her. Make it your goal to under-

stand her. Stop thinking and saying that she is wrong. She is different, but that doesn't make her wrong.

Do not be one of those men who belittles, ridicules, demeans, or humiliates his wife. Negative comments about your wife should never come out of your mouth. This is a direct act of disobedience against the command of the Lord to honor your wife. *(See 1 Peter 3:7 and Psalm 19:14.)*

OUR PRAYER FOR YOU

Our prayer is that you will discover the joy of walking hand in hand through the Garden. We pray that you will become a student of each other; that you will seek the Lord daily to give you wisdom and understanding. May your marriage reflect His love in the way you communicate with each other. May your differences become a source of blessing, not a curse!

STUDY GUIDE

Read Proverbs 24:3; 3:13-14;
Isaiah 50:4; Proverbs 15:1

We often have the feeling that our spouse is speaking a different language. Misunderstandings can ensue because of our inability to comprehend the differences in the ways men and women speak. Men and women have different motivations for and methods of communication. As we grow in our understanding and appreciation of these differences, we can begin to accept, trust, and rely on the strengths of our partners. Our personal lives as well as our marriages will be enhanced as we incorporate these unique strengths.

This chapter contains many practical suggestions. We have not written out all of the Bible passages that correspond to the eight communication tips we have provided, but we encourage you nevertheless to read each of these references. The topic of communication is immense: Volumes have been dedicated to resolving communication issues—within the family, marriage, school, the workplace, the political arena—even with dogs! In this chapter, we have barely peeled back the first layer. Our prayer is that you will use this chapter as a starting point from which to learn how to grow together through healthy communication. Let's dig a little deeper.

DIGGING DEEPER

1. According to Proverbs 24:3 and Proverbs 3:13–14, why is *understanding* important (especially as it relates to your marriage)?

2. Isaiah 50:4 states the importance of:

3. What is a man's motivation for communication?

4. What is a woman's motivation for communication?

5. Name two methods of communication on which a man typically relies:

6. Name two methods of communication on which a woman typically relies:

7. How is a man's method of communication like "pockets?"

8. How is a woman's method of communication like a "purse?"

9. How does Proverbs 15:1 relate to making direct or indirect requests?

10. **Women**: Read through the list of communication tips for women and write down two that you know you need to work on.

11. **Men**: Read through the list of communication tips for men and write down two that you know you need to work on.

12. **Women:** Read through the list of communication tips for **men** and choose one that you would like your husband to work on. *Share your answer with your husband.*

13. **Men:** Read through the list of communication tips for **women** and choose one that you would like your wife to work on. *Share your answer with your wife.*

CHAPTER SEVEN

ENEMIES IN THE GARDEN— WEEDS

The Lust of the Eyes

*T*he delicate fragrance of flowers and fruit caressed Eve's senses as she wandered through the garden. The sun glistened on leaves still damp with the morning dew. Birds began singing their opus to the day. The garden's tranquility was interrupted unexpectedly by a silky baritone voice calling to Eve as she passed under the branches of the tree.

It was as though all creation held its breath, straining to hear, knowing instinctively that this moment would change everything. Eve stopped and gazed up with fascination at the magnificent serpent resting in the branches of the tree. The serpent appeared to be clothed in light, and when he spoke, it was almost like singing. He held his head high in regal fashion, and his black eyes glinted like onyx.

"Good morning, Eve. You must be hungry, wandering in the garden so early in the morning. But I heard that God doesn't allow you to eat from the trees of His garden. Is that really true?" the serpent inquired.

Eve smiled at the serpent. "Oh, that's not quite right. We may eat from any of the fruit trees in the garden, just not from this tree. God said we must not eat its fruit or even touch it, lest we die."

The serpent shook his head sympathetically, feigning benevolence and goodwill. His eyes narrowed and he stared at Eve for a moment. "You shall not die," he stated with authority. "God is withholding this fruit from you. God knows that this fruit will give you the power to be like a god. Your eyes *will be opened. You will gain real knowledge. You will be able to discern between good and evil." The serpent's lips curled slightly as he allowed his words to resonate.*

Eve tilted her head back and let her eyes gaze at the fruit-laden branches of the tree. She hadn't paid much attention to this tree before. The fruit was beyond comparison: it was the most colorful she had seen, luxurious and rich, gleaming in the morning light. And such a sweet aroma! She imagined its sweet, succulent flavor. Her mouth began to water.

"Would God really withhold something from us that is good?" Eve mused. "The fruit looks delicious, and I am quite hungry. And to think: this fruit has the power to make us wise and able to know what is good and evil." Eve reached up and plucked the juiciest fruit she could find. She took a bite and offered some to Adam. And he ate it.

As they licked their lips, all of creation moaned, a deep agonizing groan. And their eyes were opened—to sin, shame, and death. (Based on Genesis 3:1–6)

ENEMIES IN THE GARDEN

Yes, it all started in the garden! The first institution given to man—marriage—began in the garden. The foundational rules to bless this union were also given in the garden. And tragically for all of us, sin took root in the garden. God had provided everything Adam and Eve needed. Have you ever wondered, "How could Eve have been so foolish?" Why didn't Adam stop her? How could they have made such a huge mistake? They knew God face to face. They lived in paradise! Why did they disobey God?

In Genesis 3:1–6, we are introduced to the Serpent (Satan) and his classic strategy to deceive, tempt, and ultimately destroy mankind. The Serpent used five weapons to attack Eve—the same five he used when he later tempted Jesus in the wilderness. In fact, they are the same weapons he uses to assault mankind today. What are Satan's five weapons?

1. Lust of the flesh
2. Lust of the eyes
3. Pride of life
4. Doubts
5. Lies

Our goal is to become familiar with these weapons and to learn how they can be defeated. 1 John 2:16 admonishes "For all that is in the world—the lust of the flesh, the lust of the eyes, and the pride of life—is not of the Father but is of the world."

Many people equate the word *lust* with sensual or sexual cravings. But in the Bible, the word is translated from five different Greek words; not all of them refer to sexual passion. In 1 John 2:16, John uses the Greek word *epithumia*, which means "desire, craving, longing, desire for what is forbidden."[1] Lust has two aspects: the first focuses on the "object" that is forbidden: it may be something sinful or something that is forbidden *because it is not yours to have.* The second meaning focuses on the desire: an excessive, inordinate, or uncontrolled craving for anything. Consider your desire for food: It is legitimate and healthy. Food is not forbidden or sinful. But excessive or inordinate desire for food is gluttony.

There are many good things we desire; problems arise when we lust after those things, for then our motivation is selfish and evil. A person can lust after any thing—person, place, object, or activity. The danger of lust is that these "things" we desire (be they good or bad) become idols.

Let's examine Genesis 3:1–6 to see how Satan (the Serpent) used each of these five weapons against Eve in the garden.

1. **Lust of the flesh:** "*...the tree was good for food...*" (v. 6). The Serpent subtly drew attention to the tree in the middle of the garden by indirectly asking Eve about the other trees. As we read this account, we almost get the feeling that Eve was noticing for the first time how delicious this tree's fruit looked. Certainly she had wandered past this tree before! Why at that moment should she crave its fruit? Her thought process is revealed in verse six: "So when the woman saw that the tree was good for food, that it was pleasant to the eyes, and a tree desirable to make one wise, she took of its fruit and ate." The Serpent had told her that the tree would make her wise. It is likely that the other two ideas—that the tree was good for food and pleasant to the eyes—also were planted by him. The Serpent tempted Eve by focusing her attention on physical craving—the lust of the flesh.

2. **Lust of the eyes:** "*...that it was pleasant to the eyes...*" (v. 6). We are not told what kind of fruit was growing on the tree (though many

artists have rendered it an apple). But we do know it looked beautiful. Not only was Eve tempted by her physical desire to taste the fruit, but she also was tempted by its beauty. Eve had unrestricted, unlimited access to every other tree, plant, flower, and fruit in the garden. The garden was filled with perfect samples of all God had created. Yet the Serpent was able to tempt Eve through the lust of the eyes so that she coveted this fruit for herself.

3. **Pride of life**: *"...and a tree desirable to make one wise..."* (v. 6). The Serpent attacked Eve with one of his most heinous weapons: pride. He told Eve, "You will be like God" (v. 5). He offered wisdom and enlightenment: "Your eyes will be open" (v. 5). He appealed to her pride by inferring that she was missing something—that her life was incomplete. The insidious nature of this weapon is that it often seems so noble: Eve wanted wisdom; what was wrong with that? The problem was, Eve was being tempted to act independent of God—and in so doing she sought to claim for herself something that only God can give and acted in disobedience to Him. The Serpent tempted Eve with the pride of life.

4. **Doubt**: *"Now the Serpent was more cunning than any beast of the field which the LORD God had made. And he said to the woman, "Has God indeed said, 'You shall not eat of every tree of the garden?'"* (v. 1) Was the Serpent merely curious about God's rules? No! His question clearly was designed to create doubt: Did God *really* say that? Is that *really* true? Eve's failure was the result of her allowing room in her heart for doubt to grow. Eve should have gone directly to "the Source"—to God—to ask Him to explain the truth. The Serpent tempted Eve by cultivating doubt and this led to his final weapon – lies.

5. **Lies**: *"Then the Serpent said to the woman, 'You will not surely die'"* (v. 4). Eve was susceptible to defeat by this final weapon because she had given in to doubt. The serpent's subtlety was replaced by a blatant lie. He called God a liar and questioned His nature and goodness. The serpent portrayed God as a selfish Being who was only interested in depriving Eve of something good. Did you notice that the Serpent did not begin

with a bold-faced lie? Eve might have seen through that. Instead, the Serpent tempted Eve by turning her heart from the truth.

Satan used these same weapons against Jesus when he tempted Him in the wilderness (see Matthew 4:1–10). Jesus went into the wilderness to fast and pray. After not eating for 40 days and nights, Jesus' body was weak. Satan thus began by tempting Jesus with instant gratification of His flesh: "Turn these stones into bread." Then Satan attacked with the pride of life, daring Jesus to prove who He really was. Next, Satan tempted Jesus by showing Him the glorious kingdoms of the world. Twice he attacked by attempting to sow seeds of doubt. Finally, Satan twisted and perverted God's Word. Let's examine the passage in Matthew to see how Jesus responded to each of Satan's tactics.

1. **Lust of the flesh:** *"Now when the tempter [Satan] came to Him, he said, 'If You are the Son of God, command that these stones become bread'"* (v. 3). Jesus had been fasting for forty days and nights. He was hungry and weak. Jesus had a physical body with physical needs. Satan attacked Jesus by appealing to his flesh. But Jesus answered, "Man shall not live by bread alone but by every word that proceeds from the mouth of God" (v. 4). Jesus answered with God's Word and God's priority.

2. **Pride of life:** *"Then the devil took Him up into the holy city, set Him on the pinnacle of the temple, and said to Him, 'If You are the Son of God, throw Yourself down. For it is written: He shall give His angels charge over you, and in their hands they shall bear you up lest you dash your foot against a stone'"* (vv. 5–6). Satan dared Jesus to prove who He really was (if You *really* are the Son of God…). Satan tempted Jesus to act in pride and presumption to establish Himself and demonstrate His power. This time, Satan even quoted Scripture to validate his suggestion. But Jesus answered, "It is written again, 'You shall not tempt the LORD your God'" (v. 7). Jesus made it clear that He was submitting to the authority of God's Word. He would not exalt Himself above God the Father.

3. **Lust of the eyes:** *"Again, the devil took Him up on an exceedingly high mountain and showed Him all the kingdoms of the world and their glory. And he said to Him, 'All these things I will give You if You will fall*

down and worship me'" (vv. 8–9). Satan showed Jesus the kingdoms of the world and their glory and offered to give everything to Him. But Jesus answered, "Away with you, Satan! For it is written, 'You shall worship the LORD your God, and Him only you shall serve'" (v. 10). Jesus remained focused on the glory of God the Father; He would not worship any other.

4. **Doubt:** *"If You are the Son of God, command that these stones become bread"* (v. 3). *"If You are the Son of God, throw Yourself down"* (v. 5). Coupled with Satan's first two temptations of Jesus was the phrase *"If* you are…." Satan is masterful at sowing seeds of doubt. Deeply rooted within the temptation for Jesus to give in to His physical desire (lust of the flesh) and to validate Himself (pride of life) was doubt. Satan repeated the scheme he debuted in the garden: "Did God *really* say that?" Jesus answered, "It is written…." Jesus was able to resist temptation because He never doubted God's truth.

5. **Lies:** *"And he [Satan] said to Him, 'All these things I will give You if You will fall down and worship me'"* (v. 9). Satan loves to make promises that he never intends to keep. Satan promised Eve "You won't die." But he lied. Satan promised to give Jesus the kingdoms of the world. Again, he lied. Satan also perverted God's Word by taking it out of context and seeking to use it to his own benefit. But Jesus answered, "Away with you, Satan!" (v. 10) Jesus never played around with lies. He exposed them to the light of His Word and cast them out.

Satan seeks to implement these same schemes in our marriages today: He fills our homes and marriages with the lust of the eyes, the lust of the flesh, the pride of life, doubts, and lies. These five weapons can wreak havoc. In this chapter (as well as the three that follow), we consider each weapon individually in order to discover how we can guard against and defeat these enemies in the garden.

Let's begin by thinking of Satan's weapons metaphorically.
- Lust of the eyes: weeds
- Lust of the flesh: fungus
- Pride of Life: rocks
- Doubts: moles
- Lies: mice

LUST OF THE EYES:

Weeds

One afternoon, as I was working in our garden, I noticed some lovely white flowers. Gardening is not my strong suit, so I was pleased to see some flowers growing without my help. But my pleasure was short-lived. The lovely flower turned out to be bindweed, or *convolvulus arvensis,* from the Latin *convolere* meaning "to entwine." I learned that this perennial vine is invasive and has a deep root system. Bindweed entwines itself around "desirable" plants and, like a boa constrictor, chokes the life out of its victims. Suddenly, my pretty white flowers didn't seem so attractive!

This weed reminds me of the first enemy in the garden: the lust of the eyes. Lust is not only sexual cravings; it can refer to any strong desire or excessive craving for anything, good or bad. I was attracted to the beautiful white flower. I hadn't planted it, yet there it was. But weeds are "forbidden" in my garden: they choke out and kill what is desirable; they don't belong there.

The lust of the eyes refers to looking and longing for anything that is not yours to have. It is covetousness. God warned against this enemy when He gave the Ten Commandments: "You shall not covet your neighbor's house; you shall not covet your neighbor's wife, nor his male servant, nor his female servant, nor his ox, nor his donkey, nor anything that is your neighbor's" (Exodus 20:17). Notice that God did not say to not steal these things ("do not steal" is a separate commandment); here He said not to covet. Most dictionaries define 'covet' as 'having an inappropriate desire or longing to have or possess something that belongs to someone else.'

Why does it matter to God if we do a little "window shopping" with our eyes? After all, we are just looking, right? Wrong! The first look leads to the second… which leads to covetous thoughts and, finally, taking action on the basis of those thoughts. James 1:14–15 warns, "But each one is tempted when he is drawn away by his own desires and enticed. Then, when desire has conceived, it gives birth to sin; and sin, when it is full grown, brings forth death."

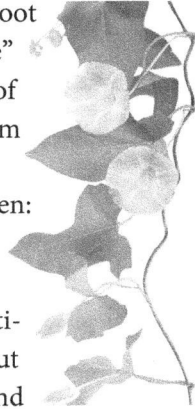

Consider two examples from the Bible of men who got in trouble because of "looking." Abraham and his nephew Lot lived together in an area of Canaan that was not big enough to support both of their expanding flocks and herds. With conflicts between the two families escalating, Abraham suggested that they move apart from each other. Abraham gave Lot first choice of where he would like to move his family. By tradition, the younger man should have relinquished to his elder the right to

It started with a look!

choose first. But not Lot: Genesis 13:10 tells us "And Lot lifted his eyes and saw all the plain of Jordan, that it was well watered everywhere...." Lot saw the rich farmland in the plain of Jordan and lusted after it. He wanted it for himself. Later we read that Lot faced his tent door toward the city of Sodom; eventually, he moved to this wicked and depraved city. He was a righteous man. What was he doing in this evil city? It started with a look. God sent His angels to rescue Lot and his family from the city before He destroyed it with fire and brimstone, but Lot's wife turned around to have one last look...and became a pillar of salt. Righteous Lot lost everything: his wife, his home, his possessions— and it all started with a look. (Genesis 13:1-13; Genesis 19:1-26)

King David also got into trouble because of a look. Sitting on his rooftop one evening, he saw a woman on a nearby rooftop taking a bath. King David, a brave and valiant warrior, was defeated by a look. He committed adultery with the woman, conceived a child with her, arranged to kill her husband, and tried to cover it all up. King David, a man after God's heart, brought heartache and tragic consequences to his family— and it all started with a look. (Read 2 Samuel 11:1-27.)

The lust of the eyes is a dangerous enemy in our marriages. In the sections that follow, we look at two of the ways in which this "weed" entangles itself in marriage: through pornography and through coveting material possessions.

PORNOGRAPHY

Jesus says in Matthew 5:28-30, "But I say to you that whoever looks at a woman to lust for her has already committed adultery with her in his heart. If your right eye causes you to sin, pluck it out and cast it from you; for it is more profitable for you that one of your members perish than for your whole body to be cast into hell." That seems extreme, yet Jesus is making the point that a lustful look is the same as committing adultery. The truth is that most men and women don't simply wake up one morning and decide to commit adultery. Rather, it begins with a look and is quickly followed by the thought, "Wow. I wish my wife looked like that!" Or, "I wish my husband had that man's body." Let us be direct: That longing, lustful look is sin. There is no place in your marriage for pornography.

The noxious weed of pornography doesn't belong in your garden because:

- It is sin.
- It damages marriages.
- It creates a distorted view of sex.
- It is addictive.
- It destroys righteousness.

It is sin. Men and women: It is not okay to look at pornography. If you choose to, you open the door for an enemy to walk right into your home. You may think, "I am not hurting anyone. It is natural that I have these desires. It's not like I am sleeping with a prostitute or having an affair." These rationalizations are lies. You *are* hurting yourself, your spouse, and your family. You are created in God's image: You are not an animal, which can't control its urges. God gave you these natural desires, but He also gave you guidelines for enjoying them in a godly manner—that is, within your marriage. Jesus says, "If you lust after a woman in your heart, you have committed adultery with her." **It is sin**.

> *The noxious weed of pornography doesn't belong in your garden.*

It is important that men and women alike heed this warning. More and more women are addicted to pornography: In 2004, more than 32 million women visited at least one porn site; more than a third (41 percent) of those women downloaded pornographic pictures and videos. One report states that one in six women struggle with pornographic addiction.[2]

Pornography damages marriages in many ways. It is completely self-centered. When a man or woman views porn, he or she is focused only on fulfilling his or her own desires. Such acts of selfishness will never produce anything but sorrow in a marriage. Pornography is like having an affair with yourself. One of the primary goals of marriage is intimacy. Porn causes an increase in desire for sexual activity but not for intimacy. The husband may begin demanding more sex from his wife, but in reality he is just using her to relieve his sexual tension. Eventually, he may choose to masturbate rather than to enjoy his wife as the primary source of sexual relief. This allows him to continue his cycle of self-centered gratification. Studies reveal that 80 percent of the women who involve themselves in pornography act out in real life what they view online: They become involved in casual sex and/or adulterous relationships.[3] Intimacy is destroyed by self-fulfilling lust. Oneness is restored by self-sacrificing love.

> *Intimacy is destroyed by self-centered lust; oneness is restored by self-sacrificing love.*

This enemy creates a distorted view of sex: It presents a perverted picture of sexuality and creates expectations that are not realistic. Discontent is the inevitable result. Husband and wife are equally disillusioned—the one because his (or her) spouse cannot meet his (or her) unrealistic expectations and the other because he (or she) feels like a failure and perhaps is not even aware why she (or he) can't satisfy her (his) partner.

Pornography is addictive. What begins as a quick glance at an inappropriate magazine cover soon unlocks the desire to seek more graphic sexual images. Pictures of women in lingerie are not enough to sustain the thrill. The Internet can bring explicit video right into your home. And much of it is free and allows for complete anonymity. When amateur YouTube sex videos lose their appeal, cyber-sex and hard-core porn sites are readily available. The addictive nature of pornography is well substantiated.

Pornography destroys righteousness and "right thinking." If you still believe pornography is harmless, consider the findings of this study:[4] "When experimental subjects were exposed to as little as six weeks' worth of non-violent pornography, they:

- Began to trivialize rape as a criminal offense or no longer considered it a crime at all.
- Developed distorted perceptions about sexuality.
- Developed an appetite for more deviant, bizarre, or violent types of pornography. ('Normal' sex no longer seemed to satisfy.)
- Devalued the importance of monogamy and lacked confidence in marriage as either a viable or a lasting institution.
- Viewed non-monogamous relationships as normal and natural.

A STORY OF VICTORY

Debbie was troubled. Her husband again had come to her, guilt ridden, to confess that he had been viewing pornography. The familiar fear and pain swept over her like a riptide ready to pull her under. For ten years this had been an ongoing problem. She felt that she bore all the consequences of his addiction. Rob seemed sorry but not really repentant—and certainly not sorry enough to stop. Couldn't he see what it was doing to her and to their relationship? When she learned that during a business trip he had ordered a "massage" (which actually involved sexual activity), she knew she could no longer trust him.

After a painful confrontation, he agreed to seek counseling. He found a center about 1,000 miles away that offered an intensive two-week recovery program. Grandparents would watch the children, and Rob and Debbie would participate in the program together. During counseling, both Rob and Debbie were confronted with their sin. It was an uncomfortable two weeks as they both realized they were trying to satisfy themselves in different ways, apart from God. Rob was using pornography and illicit sex in an attempt to meet his needs for intimacy. Debbie, somewhat self-righteously, had been using her Bible knowledge and supposed "spiritual maturity" to feel good about herself. In arrogance, she had preached to Rob and unknowingly had contributed to the chasm between them.

By the end of the program, both were repentant and were able to forgive each other. With changed actions and attitude, Rob really was different this time. "We both had idols to get rid of," Debbie said. She was challenged to put her hope wholly in God, for there would be no guarantee that Rob wouldn't revert to his former ways. Sometime after they returned home, Rob was baptized and confessed before his church,

"I sinned. But now I know that Jesus died for me, and His Holy Spirit has made me clean." Of course, this did not mean that Rob and Debbie would no longer struggle in their relationship. They continued to benefit from counseling and support from their church. Today, Rob and his wife minister to other couples who struggle with similar issues. They are a living testimony to the healing power of Almighty God.

A NOTE TO WOMEN

Have you considered the message you communicate to men through your manner of dress? We are deeply grieved by the open disregard many Christian women display toward men's struggle with lust. I (Tim) recently spoke at a Christian conference. When some of the women came forward for prayer, I found it almost impossible to speak comfortably with them because of their low-cut necklines and other revealing clothing. My desire was to minister Jesus to them, but their clothing made it difficult for me to focus on their hearts!

Certainly, men must combat the lust of the eyes. But when a man can't even go to church without being exposed to a woman's breasts, the problem is serious. In Chapter 15, "Tools for the Garden," we include the link to a recent survey that reports the types of clothing many men find problematic. You may be surprised—and even convicted. (If you think we are nothing more than two old people with old-fashioned ideas, we challenge you to review the survey. Its findings are significant.)

Scripture is clear about the consequences of causing your brother to stumble. Romans 14:21 reminds us, "It is good neither to eat meat nor drink wine nor do anything by which your brother stumbles or is offended or is made weak." Did you catch the last phrase—"*nor do anything by which your brother stumbles or is offended or is made weak*"? Women, do you know how many men struggle with lustful and sinful thoughts because of the way in which you dress? Do you really want them to think of you as a sex object? Is this the message you really want to communicate? Like it or not, your clothing sends a message that may lead many men to entertain sinful thoughts about you.

1 Corinthians 8:12 teaches, "But when you thus sin against the brethren and wound their weak conscience, you sin against Christ." That seems quite clear. And yet I (Mary Lou) have heard women say, "Well,

I can dress as I like. There is nothing wrong with showing off my body. I can't help it if these guys are so depraved." Women, that is a lie! You are responsible for—and you will answer to God for—your actions. "But beware lest somehow this liberty of yours become a stumbling block to those who are weak" (1 Corinthians 8:9).

At some churches we visit, women who serve on the worship team wear short skirts and low-cut and/or very tight-fitting tops. How can such women be pleasing to God if the majority of the men in the congregation are utterly distracted from thinking of Jesus? Women who dress in this manner invite men to focus on them and their bodies. This is wrong.

Ladies, there is nothing wrong with allowing our husbands to enjoy our bodies. There is nothing "lustful" when a husband delights in his wife's body. But your husband alone should delight in your body. In the privacy of your home, dress in any way you like. Only remember: Your body belongs *exclusively* to your husband—not to every other man who passes by.

While much of the clothing in stores today is low cut, tight fitting, and revealing, it is possible to make wise choices in the clothing you buy—and in how you put your outfits together—and to honor the Lord through your modest dress. A woman does not need to look like a bag: Frumpy clothing doesn't bring glory to God either. There is nothing wrong with looking our best. Women can look fashionable and stylish without wearing clothing that draws the focus of a man to the wrong place. The question to ask is, "Is my manner of dress drawing inappropriate attention to my body, or am I drawing attention to Jesus?"

1 Timothy 2:9 instructs, "In like manner also, that the women adorn themselves in modest apparel, with propriety and moderation, not with braided hair or gold or pearls or costly clothing." Here are three easy checkpoints:

- Is my appearance modest (i.e., not drawing attention to my body in an inappropriate manner)?
- Is my appearance decent (i.e., not exposing to other men what is to be reserved for my husband alone)?
- Is my appearance appropriate (i.e., not inappropriate or unsuitable for the situation)?

As we consider this problem of pornography, we women must ask ourselves—and answer honestly—whether our appearance is contributing to this rampant problem. We must learn to be sensitive and supportive of our Christian brothers.

DEFEATING THIS ENEMY

How can you defeat this enemy of pornography? Some excellent resources are referenced in chapter 15 ("Tools for the Garden"). Pornography is not an addiction from which it is easy to break free. For many, it is absolutely vital to seek help from a pastor, counselor, or other organization. And while it is beyond the scope of this book to address this enemy adequately, we pray that this section will provide the motivation and conviction you need to stage a counter-attack. Here are a few suggestions:

1. **Confess this sin to your spouse.** We know this is a frightening task. However, chances are good that your spouse has felt that something was wrong for some time. You cannot truly be one if you keep secrets from each other. Satan wants you to keep this a secret. He knows that if you keep hiding this problem, you will remain in bondage to it. Remember the bindweed? The only way to get rid of it is to pull it up by its roots. Metaphorically speaking, that is confession. You must get down to the roots of your sin.

James 5:16 encourages us, "Confess your trespasses to one another, and pray for one another, that you may be healed. The effective, fervent prayer of a righteous man avails much." *Note:* This may not necessarily be the first step. It may be important for the man (or woman) to speak first to his (her) pastor. A pastor can provide counsel about how to approach this subject with one's spouse and which words to use. It may be important to get a realistic sense of what to expect as well as to outline the road to healing. The level of addiction and the quality of the couple's relationship are factors to consider. The pastor may need to mediate this time of confession. Pornography addiction can be devastating, but a confession that is handled improperly, without adequate support, can be just as damaging. The injured spouse may require counseling, and it is possible that the guilty spouse will not be the one to help his (her) partner negotiate this difficult time.

2. **Find an accountability partner.** This may or may not be one's spouse. Again, this will depend on the level of addiction and the status of the couple's relationship. It may be preferable to have an account-ability partner who is not personally affected by the problem. One's spouse may find it difficult or even impossible to be objective. The por-nography addict may feel reluctant to confess his (her) struggles to his (her) spouse, if only for fear that he (she) will hurt him (her) again. An accountability partner must be someone with whom one can be honest, without fear of repercussions. For many men and women, it is vital to have a Christian brother or sister who understands the struggle and who will ask the hard questions.

An accountability partner is someone with whom to meet regularly, to pray, and to confess sin. One's spouse should be allowed to contact the accountability partner at any time, whether to express concerns or to ask questions. Many organizations provide excellent accountability as well as recovery programs. The local church should also play a key role in this battle, providing support and encouragement for both partners. This is not a battle to fight alone. Being alone is what caused sin in the first place. If pornography is a problem in your marriage, prayerfully ask God to lead you to the right person to provide help. Ecclesiastes 4:9–10 says, "Two are better than one because they have a good reward for their labor. For if they fall, one will lift up his companion. But woe to him who is alone when he falls, for he has no one to help him up."

3. **Clean house.** Get rid of anything inappropriate. Throw out any DVD that has even a hint of evil. Cancel magazine or newspaper sub-scriptions that contain anything unacceptable. Ask your wife to sort the mail and throw away anything containing indecent advertising. Get rid of cable TV, or establish firm guidelines about never watching TV alone. Install filtering or monitoring software on your computer. Keep the computer in a public area. Psalm 101:3 says, "I will set nothing wicked before my eyes; I hate the work of those who fall away; it shall not cling to me." And Job 31:16 says, "I have made a covenant with my eyes; why then should I look upon a young woman?" Remember, sin too often starts with that first look.

4. **Develop new habits and interests.** Pornography can dig deep channels into your mind. Images will come screaming back at you,

uninvited. While it is good and necessary to "clean house," you also need to fill your mind with new, healthy, enjoyable activities. It is particularly beneficial to identify activities you and your spouse can enjoy together. Perhaps you can find a ministry in which to participate. Or maybe you can learn a new sport together. Take a class or start a new hobby together. Talk about what you both enjoy, and prayerfully ask the Lord how you can fill your home with good things. Luke 11:24–26 says, "When an unclean spirit goes out of a man, he goes through dry places, seeking rest; and finding none, he says, 'I will return to my house from which I came.' And when he comes, he finds it swept and put in order. Then he goes and takes with him seven other spirits more wicked than himself, and they enter and dwell there; and the last state of that man is worse than the first."

5. **Let God become your passion.** "Love the Lord your God with all your heart, with all your soul, with all your mind, and with all your strength" (Mark 12:30). Notice the little word in this verse: *"all."* This reveals true passion for God. Pornography addiction breeds in the rancid soil of self-gratification. Quit living for self. Galatians 2:20 says, "I have been crucified with Christ; it is no longer I who live, but Christ lives in me; and the life which I now live in the flesh I live by faith in the Son of God, who loved me and gave Himself for me." "And do not be drunk with wine, in which is dissipation [squandering or wasteful abuse]; but be filled with the Spirit" (Ephesians 5:18). When a person is drunk, he is under the influence of alcohol. Rather than letting wine (or pornography) control you, allow the Holy Spirit to reign in your life.

Pornography is a merciless dictator, ruling over a person's thoughts, motives, and actions. Romans 6:16–18 instructs, "Do you not know that to whom you present yourselves slaves to obey, you are that one's slaves whom you obey, whether of sin leading to death or of obedience leading to righteousness? But God be thanked that though you were slaves of sin, yet you obeyed from the heart that form of doctrine to which you were delivered. And having been set free from sin, you became slaves of righteousness." James 4:7–8 teaches, "Therefore submit to God. Resist the devil and he will flee from you. Draw near to God, and He will draw near to you. Cleanse your hands, you sinners; and purify your hearts, you double-minded."

6. **Take the offensive.** "For the word of God is living and powerful and sharper than any two-edged sword, piercing even to the division of soul and spirit and of joints and marrow, and is a discerner of the thoughts and intents of the heart" (Hebrews 4:12). This enemy cannot be overcome with good intentions. God's Word is powerful. Learn to use the Bible to counter-attack the enemy. "How can a young man cleanse his way? By taking heed according to Your word. Your word I have hidden in my heart, that I might not sin against You" (Psalm 119:9, 11). Read and study God's Word. Memorize specific verses. Speak Scripture out loud—especially when you find yourself fighting temptation. Invest in audio Bible CDs, and listen to them often. Let God's Word cleanse your heart and your memories.

7. **Fast and pray.** Jesus told his disciples, "Watch and pray, lest you enter into temptation. The spirit indeed is willing, but the flesh is weak" (Matthew 26:41). The key is to watch and pray *before* you fall into temptation. Don't wait until you are in the middle of it! In Mark we read about the inability of the disciples to cast out a demon. Jesus explains, "This kind can come out by nothing but prayer and fasting" (Mark 9:29). Satan has many people in bondage to pornography. We believe that fasting can help break those chains. Fasting also expresses repentance of sin (read 1 Samuel 7:6 and Nehemiah 1:4) and reveals our total dependence on God (Ezra 8:21). Andrew Murray shared these great truths about fasting in his book *With Christ in the School of Prayer:*[6]

"Fasting helps to express, to deepen, and to confirm the resolution that we are ready to sacrifice anything, even ourselves, to attain the Kingdom of God.

The truly consecrated soul, however, is like a soldier who carries only what he needs for battle. Because he frees himself of all unnecessary weight, he is easily capable of combating sin. Afraid of entangling himself with the affairs of a worldly life, he tries to lead a Nazarite life as one specially set apart for the Lord and His service.

Prayer is the one hand with which we grasp the invisible; fasting, the other, with which we let loose and cast away the visible.

Prayer is the reaching out after God and the unseen; fasting, the letting go of all that is of the seen and temporal."

COVETOUSNESS

The lust of the eyes is not just about pornography. You can lust after any number of things: the new home your friend just bought; the sports car parked next door; your colleague's promotion; the dream vacation you could never afford; the latest fashion; or the newest tool. The list is endless. These things may not be evil or bad in and of themselves. But if you covet things that are not yours, you open the door to sin. Jesus spoke about the dangers of covetousness: "Take heed and beware of covetousness, for one's life does not consist in the abundance of the things he possesses" (Luke 12:15).

This reminds me of the bindweed's lovely white flower. At first glance, it seems so desirable. But its insidious vines entangle themselves around other plants in the garden and choke the life out of them. Allow us to share a story about how the lust of the eyes almost destroyed a couple we know.

Dave was a young pastor serving in a small village church. Because the church couldn't afford to pay Dave an adequate salary, he also had to work at a part-time job. Dave and Heidi had two small children and lived in a small apartment. Their family had a very tight budget; whenever anything broke, it often remained broken. Although they had enough money to meet their basic needs, Heidi grew frustrated and discontent with their limited income. Frequently, she complained to her husband about their shabby apartment. She grumbled about their old appliances.

Dave felt the pressure rising. He wanted to please his wife and to give her the nice things she longed for. He felt trapped between his limited salary and his desire to care for his wife. Heidi became more unhappy, and Dave felt like a failure. It seemed that their marriage was on the brink of falling apart.

Out of desperation, Dave left the ministry and sought full-time employment as a salesman. For years, Dave fought feelings of resentment over having to leave his calling. He felt unfulfilled as a salesman. It was a miracle that the marriage survived. Like Lot's wife, Heidi was entrapped by the lust of the eyes. She was so consumed with lust for things she didn't have that she failed to appreciate the ministry she could have shared with her husband. More important, she failed to trust the Lord for what she needed. Her love for the things of this world obscured her love for the Lord. Like bindweed, the lust of the eyes entangled itself around Heidi's life and marriage so that her marriage was almost choked out.

By the grace of God, Dave and Heidi's marriage was restored. Many years later, Dave returned to full-time ministry. But how much ministry was lost because of this one enemy, the lust of the eyes?

I did a quick survey of websites that purport to identify the "top ten problems in marriage today." Problems with finances was cited—often in the number one slot—on every list. Arguing and worrying about money can cause immense stress in a marriage. Often, husband and wife must both work full time to maintain the lifestyle they have chosen. But often this lifestyle is built upon the lust of the eyes—that new car, a bigger house, nicer furnishings, an up-to-date entertainment system. The couple ultimately may possess a lot of "stuff," but often they also find their lives so busy and stressed that they can't enjoy it. Worst of all, they can't enjoy each other.

Consider this statistic: In 2010, the U.S. Census Bureau reported that U.S. citizens had more than $886 billion in credit card debt. The report specified that on average, each cardholder had credit card debt of $5,100.00.[5] Much of this is the direct result of the lust of the eyes: coveting things one cannot afford and yet choosing to buy anyway—on credit. When will we learn to be content with what we have? The lust of the eyes devastates marriages every day.

> *When is enough enough?*

There is one more thing to know about bindweed: One plant can produce as many as 500 seeds, and these can remain viable for as long as 50 years! The danger of this enemy lies not only in entanglement but also in the "fruit" it produces. The lust of the eyes gives rise to rotten "fruit" in our lives: greed, discontentment, bitterness, anger, idolatry, and broken relationships with God and with others. We need to eradicate this weed, right down to the roots.

The root of this weed is actually idolatry: the worship of things, not God. If you truly worshiped God, you would seek Him and His righteousness first (Matthew 6:33). God would have first place in your heart. If you trusted Him, you would be content with what He has given you. When needs arise, you would look to Him for provision. You cannot worship God and the things of this world. "No one can serve two masters; for either he will hate the one and love the other, or else he will be loyal to the one and despise the other. You cannot serve God and mammon [riches]" (Matthew 6:24). Who is your master? Who is master in your marriage?

Paul speaks directly about this enemy in Ephesians 5:3–5: "But fornication and all uncleanness or *covetousness*, let it not even be named among you, as is fitting for saints; neither filthiness, nor foolish talking, nor coarse jesting, which are not fitting, *but rather giving of thanks*. For this you know, that no fornicator, unclean person, nor covetous man, who is an idolater, has any inheritance in the kingdom of Christ and God." Paul doesn't mince words. He clearly warns about the danger of this enemy. Does it seem as if a shroud has settled over your marriage? "The lamp of the body is the eye. If therefore your eye is good, your whole body will be full of light. But if your eye is bad, your whole body will be full of darkness. If therefore the light that is in you is darkness, how great is that darkness." (Matthew 6:22-23) The lust of the eyes clouds judgment and blocks out the light of the Son. How can we guard against this enemy?

The lust of the eyes clouds judgment and blocks out the light of the Son.

DEFENDING AGAINST THIS ENEMY

1. **Give thanks.** Paul admonishes "...but rather giving of thanks" (Ephesians 5:4). Rather than being filled with covetousness, give thanks. In Colossians 3:15, we read "And let the peace of God rule in your hearts, to which also you were called in one body; and be thankful." 1 Thessalonians 5:18 instructs, "In everything give thanks; for this is the will of God in Christ Jesus for you." An attitude of gratitude will change your focus from lusting after things to being filled with worship of the Giver of things. The more I worship God, the more I am able to identify idols and dethrone them in my life.

2. **Be content.** 1 Timothy 6:6–10 says, "Now godliness with contentment is great gain. For we brought nothing into this world, and it is certain we can carry nothing out. And having food and clothing, with these we shall be content. But those who desire to be rich fall into temptation and a snare and into many foolish and harmful lusts, which drown men in destruction and perdition. For the love of money is a root of all kinds of evil, for which some have strayed from the faith in their greediness and pierced themselves through with many sorrows."

3. **Pray together for your needs.** "Be anxious for nothing, but in everything by prayer and supplication, with thanksgiving, let your requests be made known to God" (Philippians 4:6). We see both lines of defense in this verse: thanksgiving and prayer!

4. **Clean house.** You try to be content, but every time you leaf through the latest advertising circular from the electronics store, you find yourself lusting after more stuff—stuff you really don't need. Get rid of the flier! Don't even look at it! Psalm 119:36–37 expresses this beautifully: "Incline my heart to Your testimonies, and not to covetousness. Turn away my eyes from looking at worthless things, and revive me in Your way."

5. **Become a giver.** If you have not yet discovered the joy of giving, now is the time! Look around you: Whom could you bless with an anonymous gift? One of our family's greatest joys is to find creative, anonymous ways to meet someone's needs. Luke 6:38 says, "Give, and it will be given to you: good measure, pressed down, shaken together, and running over will be put into your bosom. For with the same measure that you use, it will be measured back to you." This is a promise! We can never "outgive" God. We may not receive material wealth in return, but I guarantee that we will receive treasure in heaven, "where neither moth nor rust destroys and where thieves do not break in and steal" (Matthew 6:20).

We thought the bindweed was a lovely plant—until we realized how deadly it is! The lust of the eyes is equally deadly to our marriages. Eliminate it! It does not belong in your garden. In the next chapter, we will learn about another enemy—equally dangerous and even more subtle: the lust of the flesh.

STUDY GUIDE

Read Genesis 3:1–6; Matthew 4:1–10; 1 John 2:16;
Genesis 13:1–13; Genesis 19:1–26; 2 Samuel 11:1–27;
and Luke 12:15

I admit it: I am quite challenged by gardening! My neighbors have beautiful yards, and they make it seem effortless. I can spend hours weeding, planting, and watering and still struggle to keep anything alive— anything but weeds, that is! I was thrilled to spot the lovely, white flowers that appeared in my front yard. I soon learned, however, that they were weeds that had no place in my garden. In the same way, enemies that seem lovely may "appear" in our marriages. But they have no rightful place there.

We began this chapter by reviewing the story of Adam and Eve's fall. We learned that the Serpent—Satan—still uses the same tricks to tempt and deceive mankind. This chapter focuses on the first enemy: the lust of the eyes. We considered one of the most noxious weeds— pornography—in detail. We discussed the dangers of this enemy as well as ways to defeat it. The lust of the eyes involves other areas of our lives as well. Covetousness is a serious problem that is destroying many marriages today. It is vital to learn how to defend against this enemy. Let's dig a little deeper.

DIGGING DEEPER

1. What are the five weapons Satan used in the garden—and that he still uses today?

2. How did Satan use these five weapons against Jesus in the wilderness?

3. The Greek word for lust *(epithumia),* as used in 1 John 2:16, can be defined as:

4. Write your own definition of lust:

5. How is bindweed like the lust of the eyes?

6. What two men in the Bible demonstrate the danger of "just looking?" What was the result of their lustful looks?

7. What are the five reasons that pornography should have no place in your marriage?

8. What are some additional dangers of pornography?

9. What are seven ways to defeat the enemy of pornography?

10. If pornography addiction is a problem in your marriage, confess your sin to your spouse and agree on a plan of attack.

11. The lust of the eyes also includes:

12. What does Jesus say in Luke 12:15?

13. What "things" have become idols in your life?

14. What "things" do you believe have become idols in the life of your spouse? *(Share your answers with your spouse.)*

15. What are the five action steps you can take to defend against the enemy of covetousness?

16. Choose to implement at least one of these action steps this week. *(Share your plan with your spouse.)*

17. Paraphrase Matthew 6:22–23.

18. Whom can you bless with an unexpected, anonymous gift? (The gift could take any form—cash, clothing, food, an appliance, etc.) *Plan with your spouse to give this week to someone in need.*

CHAPTER EIGHT

ENEMIES IN THE GARDEN— FUNGUS

The Lust of the Flesh

*T*he sweet taste of the forbidden fruit quickly turned sour as Adam and Eve realized what they had done. Filled with shame—and not knowing how to deal with it—they tried to cover it up. First, they attempted to hide their shame by covering their bodies with fig leaves. Then they tried to hide from God. They realized they were naked. They had been naked all along, but now sin had stripped them of their innocence. Eve had lusted after knowledge...but she got far more than she bargained for. Yes, they had gained knowledge, but because it came from the wrong source, it brought shame. This was a new emotion for man. Adam and Eve knew they couldn't face God, and this knowledge broke their relationship with Him. In the cool of the day, God came into the Garden and lovingly called out to them. "Where are you?" God called. (He knew where they were but wanted them to respond.) Adam answered, "I heard Your voice in the garden, and I was afraid because I was naked; and I hid myself." Adam was afraid—another emotion new to mankind.

"Who told you that you were naked?" God inquired. "Have you eaten from the tree of which I commanded that you should not eat?" Adam pointed his finger at God and said, "The woman You gave to be with me— she gave me of the tree, and I ate." Adam's knowledge supplied him with a *new skill: shifting blame. In essence, Adam said, "God, if you hadn't given me this woman, I wouldn't be in this mess!"*

God turned to the woman and asked, "What is this you have done?" A quick learner, Eve pointed to the Serpent and blamed him: "The Serpent deceived me, and I ate."

God didn't need to hear any more. He pronounced the punishment for their disobedience. Adam and Eve had given in to the lust of their flesh. But rather than find their desires fulfilled, they received curses. Most of these were directly related to the flesh: Eve would have sorrow and pain in childbirth, and Adam would experience drudgery and hard labor as he worked the cursed earth. Thorns and thistles replaced the beauty of the tree after whose fruit they had lusted. They would eat their bread by the sweat of their brow—no longer in the coolness of the garden. And they would die, returning to the dust from which they had been taken (Genesis 3:7–19).

LUST OF THE FLESH

The lust of the flesh is another enemy that can attack our marriages. We learned in the last chapter that Satan uses five weapons to tempt and destroy: the lust of the eyes, the lust of the flesh, the pride of life, doubt, and lies. "Lust" is a craving, longing, or intense desire for anything that is forbidden. The object of our lust is not necessarily good or evil in and of itself. It is possible to lust after good things that we are not meant to have. John Calvin said, "The evil in our desire typically does not lie in what we want, but that we want it too much."[1] The lust of the eyes is covetousness, which is idolatry. In this chapter, we consider in detail the second enemy in the garden: the lust of the flesh.

Many people equate the lust of the flesh with sensual sins: fornication, adultery, gluttony, drunkenness, and immorality. Although these sins are aspects of the lust of the flesh, we believe the definition is far broader. Galatians 5:19–21 reveals a much longer list, "Now the works of the flesh are evident, which are: adultery, fornication, uncleanness, lewdness, idolatry, sorcery, hatred, contentions, jealousies, outbursts of wrath, selfish ambitions, dissensions, heresies, envy, murders, drunkenness, revelries, and the like; of which I tell you beforehand, just as I also told you in time past, that those who practice such things will not inherit the kingdom of God."

The lust of the flesh can be defined as the pursuit of sensory plea-sures—hedonism. Hedonism is "the self-indulgent pursuit of pleasure as a way of life."[2] Hedonism says, "I want it all, and I want it now. Who cares about tomorrow? I am living for today! Gimme, gimme, gimme! Life is short: Eat dessert first! In fact, *only* eat dessert, and take as much as you can, from anyone you can."

The Greek word *hedone* is the root of the word 'hedonism.'[3] In English, *hedone* is translated 'pleasure.' In each of the five times the word is used in the Bible, it is used negatively and refers to sin. In Luke 8:14 we read the parable of the sower. Jesus explained to His disciples what hap-pened to the seed (God's Word) that was sown in people's lives: "Now the ones [seeds] that fell among thorns are those who, when they have heard, go out and are choked with cares, riches, and pleasures *[hedone]* of life and bring no fruit to maturity." Paul says to Titus, "For we our-selves were also once foolish, disobedient, deceived, serving various lusts and pleasures *[hedone],* living in malice and envy, hateful and hating one another" (Titus 3:3).

In James 4:1–3 we read, "Where do wars and fights come from among you? Do they not come from your desires for pleasure *[hedone]* that war in your members? You lust and do not have. You murder and covet and cannot obtain. You fight and war. Yet you do not have because you do not ask. You ask and do not receive because you ask amiss, that you may spend it on your pleasures *[hedone]."* In 2 Peter 2:13, Peter describes people who are hedonistic: "And [they] will receive the wages of unrigh-teousness, as those who count it pleasure *[hedone]* to carouse in the day-time. They are spots and blemishes, carousing in their own deceptions while they feast with you." The Bible is clear that the pursuit of sensory pleasure is sin.

Do we have a right to be happy?

How many times have you heard someone say, "I have a right to be happy"? Do we have a right to be happy? Is this a Biblical teaching? True happiness is the by-product of seeking God first and others next. Nowhere in God's Word do we find the admonition to pursue or seek happiness on the basis of some intrinsic *right* to happiness. That is not to say that we won't experi-ence this emotion. But we are not to assert our right to be happy. To do so is hedonism—living for my pleasure, my desires, me, me, me! Paul reminded the Christians at Corinth: "Or do you not know that your body is the temple of the Holy Spirit who is in you, whom you have from God, and you are not your own? For you were bought at a price; therefore glorify God in your body and in your spirit, which are God's" (1 Corinthians 6:19–20).

Happiness in and of itself is not a bad thing. The Bible does speak about gladness and joy. But we challenge you to consider that joy, gladness, and happiness are by-products of a relationship with God. We serve the Lord with joy. In God's presence is fullness of joy. God fills us with gladness. He restores our joy. He leads us in joy. The fruit of the Spirit—the by-product of a life yielded to the Holy Spirit—is joy. But to pursue joy (or happiness) as the ultimate goal of your life is wrong. We are to pursue God. Joy, gladness, and happiness flow naturally into a heart that seeks God first.

Contemporary culture has brainwashed us to believe the lie that we deserve to be happy. Unfortunately, we see the result of this deceit all too often in our marriages: Whenever something doesn't make us happy, we get rid of it and find something new that will. The lust of the flesh is a deadly enemy not only because it is hedonistic but also because it is cloaked in a philosophy that says, "The world revolves around me!"

Whenever something doesn't make us happy, we get rid of it—including marriage!

This attitude of entitlement has become prevalent among young people. It affects the education system, the workplace, government, church, and marriage. Students who fail to complete an assignment or who turn in shoddy work believe they have the right to be excused. Many employees believe they have a right to excessive benefits. Proper work ethic and taking pride in one's accomplishments has been supplanted by an entitlement mind-set that says, "I'll do my job if my needs are met first. I have the right to be treated better." America's social welfare system is plagued by this entitlement attitude: "The government should pay me a monthly salary because I lost my job. I also have the right to a place to live, and I expect the government to provide decent housing for me. And of course, I need food and other basics. I have the right to receive these compensations. After all, I pay my taxes." Too many churches are filled with people who also demand their rights: "I give my tithe to this church. I will tell the pastor what I think about this new worship music. Why can't we sing my favorite hymns? I also think he needs to preach shorter sermons. After all, we have the right to get out of church on time."

Marriages are being destroyed by attitudes of entitlement: "I have the right to be happy in my marriage." "My partner doesn't satisfy me any more so I am getting a divorce." "I have needs, but they aren't being met. I am going to find someone new who will meet my needs." Asserting one's right to happiness is nothing less than hedonism in the guise of humanism. It is the lust of the flesh, and it is sin. At the core of hedonism is SELF.

SOLOMON

King Solomon exemplifies hedonism in its purist form. If anyone could explain the lust of the flesh, King Solomon would be the man for the job. Solomon was not only a powerful ruler but he possessed wealth beyond measure. He built the magnificent temple in Jerusalem as well as his own palaces. Gold was used for table service, and silver was as common as plastic is today. He had more than a thousand chariots and the finest horses. Exotic food and animals, precious stones, elegant clothing, and the highest quality of wood were abundant in Solomon's court. He also had 700 wives and 300 concubines. This was a man who sought sensory pleasure.

In Ecclesiastes 2:3–10a, King Solomon describes his life and his insatiable pursuit of pleasure:

> "I searched in my heart how to gratify my flesh with wine, while guiding my heart with wisdom, and how to lay hold on folly, till I might see what was good for the sons of men to do under heaven all the days of their lives. I made my works great, I built myself houses and planted myself vineyards. I made myself gardens and orchards, and I planted all kinds of fruit trees in them. I made myself water pools from which to water the growing trees of the grove. I acquired male and female servants, and had servants born in my house. Yes, I had greater possessions of herds and flocks than all who were in Jerusalem before me. I also gathered for myself silver and gold and the special treasures of kings and of the provinces. I acquired male

and female singers, the delights of the sons of men, and musical instruments of all kinds. So I became great and excelled more than all who were before me in Jerusalem. Also, my wisdom remained with me. Whatever my eyes desired I did not keep from them. I did not withhold my heart from any pleasure."

King Solomon had it all. He should have been happy with all this "stuff." Whatever his eyes desired, he obtained. He sought every pleasure: wealth, power, entertainment, food, wine, and sex. But what does Solomon say about his life? "Then I looked on all the works that my hands had done and on the labor in which I had toiled; and indeed all was vanity and grasping for the wind. There was no profit under the sun" (Ecclesiastes 2:11). The Hebrew translation for 'vanity,' as used throughout the book of Ecclesiastes, is 'emptiness.' Solomon continues, "Therefore I hated life because the work that was done under the sun was distressing to me, for all is vanity and grasping for the wind" (Ecclesiastes 2:17). How could a man who had everything hate life? In Ecclesiastes 5:10 Solomon writes, "He who loves silver will not be satisfied with silver; nor he who loves abundance, with increase. This also is vanity." By the end of the book, you get the sense that King Solomon was throwing up his hands in utter despair: He writes, "'Vanity of vanities,'" says the Preacher, 'All is vanity." (Ecclesiastes 12:8).

What a tragic commentary from the man who had it all! Yet the book of Ecclesiastes contains vitally important teaching for our hedonistic world. King Solomon clearly portrays the emptiness—the vanity—of living for the lust of the flesh. But he doesn't stop there. He concludes the book with this statement:

"Let us hear the conclusion of the whole matter: fear God and keep His commandments, for this is man's all. For God will bring every work into judgment, including every secret thing, whether good or evil" (Ecclesiastes 12:13–14).

Solomon discovered the truth of Matthew 10:39, where Jesus says, "He who finds his life will lose it, and he who loses his life for My sake will find it."

A FEW MORE EXAMPLES

Solomon has been dead for hundreds of years, but the lust of the flesh is alive and well. A few examples illustrate the danger of this enemy.

Troy and Heather

Troy and Heather were newly married. Because Troy had relocated to the city where Heather lived, he had to change jobs. The job market in this new city was very competitive, and Troy was thankful to have landed a good job. However, within the first year of their marriage, Troy's company offered him a yearlong interim position with a sister company hundreds of miles away. He would receive a pay increase as well as opportunities for advancement within the firm. The problem was that Heather didn't feel she could quit her job and move away with Troy for a year. Over many years, she had worked her way up in her company; she was afraid that if she took a year's leave, she wouldn't get her job back when she returned. Although we counseled Troy (and Heather) not to take this new position given that it would mean a year of separation, they decided the financial benefits would be too great to pass up; Troy agreed to take the job and make the move—without Heather. But God graciously intervened so that Troy became ineligible for the new position. Not long afterward, Troy found a better job in the same city where he and Heather lived. We shudder to think what might have happened to their marriage had they proceeded with their yearlong separation—and all because of money.

Brad and Nicole

Brad and Nicole live disconnected lives. Nicole longs for intimacy and closeness, but Brad lives for himself. Their home reveals much about this couple: Brad loves technology and has bought all the latest in computer equipment and entertainment systems. He has a high-paying position and sees no need to consult with Nicole about any purchases he makes. Whether he is considering buying a new house or taking a vacation (usually without her), Brad lives to please himself. Nicole has asked numerous times whether she might help choose furnishings for their home, but Brad refuses. The house is his! Nicole also has suggested making charitable donations to worthy organizations, but Brad's constant reply is, "Where is the profit in that?" Brad and Nicole's marriage is in trouble. Nicole feels completely abandoned by her husband; wealth is his god.

Darren and Vicky

Darren and Vicky are getting a divorce. Darren has allowed the lust of the flesh to consume him, especially in regard to sex. His need for sex has become an addiction, and his demands often become aggressive. Vicky has given in to him time and again. She loves him and has been willing to do whatever it takes to save their marriage. But Darren's sexual appetite has caused so much brokenness and hurt in the marriage that it is difficult to see how it can be saved. Darren often buys his wife expensive gifts, always with the ulterior motive of sex. If she is sick or if the children need her attention and she fails to meet his demands, he becomes angry and antagonistic. Darren has been involved in pornography and in other illicit affairs. He often says cruel and mean things to his wife, comparing her to an old piece of meat. He openly ogles other women, praising their bodies while criticizing his wife about her appearance. The lust of the flesh has destroyed this marriage.

All three of these couples allowed the lust of the flesh to creep into their marriages. The lust of the flesh is like a fungus that attacks a plant subtly—almost undetected—but that is insidious and ultimately deadly.

FUNGUS

I have a rose bush in my front yard. I am amazed each year when this thorny bush produces beautiful flowers. But there is an enemy of the rose bush that not only can destroy its beauty but that also can kill it outright. It is a fungus called "black spot," so called because it attacks the leaves and causes black spots. The fungi spores travel by air and water. Black spot germinates when the temperature is mild and the air humid. The fungus thrives when a rose bush is overwatered or watered incorrectly. Rose bushes planted in shade or without adequate drainage are more susceptible to this fungus.

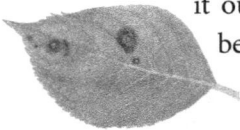

Left untreated, the spots on the leaves increase in size and eventually grow together. This continues until the rose bush is defoliated. When a rose bush loses all its leaves, it is unable to convert and store enough energy to survive the winter (let alone enough for growth in the spring). Eventually, the rose bush dies.

Black spot is like the lust of the flesh: It begins to grow in comfortable surroundings (e.g., mild temperatures, too much water, and shade). The lust of the flesh can undermine our marriages in a similar way: We get comfortable and become spiritually lazy. We avoid anything that requires sacrifice. We seek instant gratification. We prefer not to be in the Light and instead are attracted to the "shade." We deceive ourselves into believing that a little shade isn't so bad. But the Light of God's Word will reveal the junk in our lives that doesn't belong there. We think that if we avoid exposing ourselves to truth, we won't have to feel guilty about our disobedience. But we are deceived.

In the same way that the black spots of the fungus increase in size and grow together, so the lust of the flesh will pervade our marriages. The more stuff we have, the more we want. And the result? Just as infected leaves fall off the rose bush, so, too, our marriages become "sick" and unfruitful. A defoliated rose bush is ugly; a marriage plagued by the lust of the flesh is similarly unattractive. Even more critical is that without leaves, the rose bush cannot benefit from the sun. So it is in our marriages: The lust of the flesh hinders us from receiving, understanding, and benefiting from the light of God's Word. We begin to perceive truth as relative, and we remain powerless to change our lives. Like the rose bush infected with black spot fungus, marriages afflicted by the lust of the flesh will have difficulty surviving the "winters" of life. "Winter" comes into all of our lives; trials and troubles are inevitable. And if we do not have the "energy of the sun" stored in abundance, winter will destroy us. Spring should be a time of new growth, but a rose bush (like a marriage) afflicted by fungus (the lust of the flesh) will produce nothing.

Black spot fungus provides some good analogies for our marriages. So do prevention and treatment methods

1. **Plant your rose bush in full sun. Roses love sunlight!** *(The Light is God's Word.)* Just as fungus cannot thrive in direct sunlight, so the lust of the flesh cannot

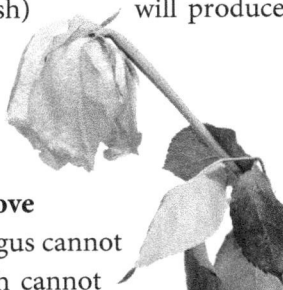

abide the purifying light of God's Word. The more time we spend in God's Word—studying it, memorizing it, meditating on it, and applying it—the less influence the lust of the flesh will have in our marriages. God's Word not only will purify those attitudes and habits that are ungodly, but it also will guide and direct us along safe paths, helping us avoid contact with this fungus.

It is important for married couples to study God's Word together as well as individually. If you do not know how to study the Bible, visit a Christian bookstore and find a Bible study book that you can work through together. Something we have done as a family is to pray through the book of Psalms. We read one psalm together and then pray it back to God. For example, we might read Psalm 5 and then pray, "Lord, in verse four it tells us that You do not take pleasure in wickedness. Show us areas in our lives where we have allowed wickedness to creep in." Or, "Father, lead me in your righteousness. Many enemies surround me. I am not sure what to do. Lord, make my path straight" (verse 8). This is a powerful way to apply God's Word to our lives in practical ways. Praying through Scripture together allows the light of God's Word to permeate even more deeply. We have been amazed at how many times the psalm we read spoke directly to a need or circumstance we were facing. It is exciting and encouraging to experience God's Word coming alive in one's marriage!

What about you? Where is your marriage "planted?" What are the priorities of your life? How do you spend your time and resources? Do you spend more time watching TV than you do together in God's Word? Do you use the excuse that you need some "family time" and so skip going to church? (What better place is there for family time than with the family of Christ?) Have you allowed your love of pleasure and your avoidance of anything uncomfortable to produce shadows—dark places—in your spiritual lives?

"And this is the condemnation, that the light has come into the world, and men loved darkness rather than light, because their deeds were evil. For everyone practicing evil hates the light and does not come to the light, lest his deeds should be exposed. But he who does the truth comes to the light, that his deeds may be clearly seen, that they have been done in God" (John 3:19–21).

2. **Plant your roses in a way that permits good air circulation.** *(This is prayer.)* Roses need adequate air circulation to help them grow properly, resist diseases and pests, and produce beautiful blooms. When a rose bush is planted too close to other plants and the garden is overcrowded, the bush can't get sufficient air. Sometimes it is necessary to prune the bush to promote better air circulation. Similarly, if you overcrowd your life with "stuff," you will find yourself consumed by materialism—in short, "diseased." Just as a rose bush needs to *breathe,* so we need to breathe spiritually.

Prayer is like breathing: If you don't get sufficient air—or if you breathe polluted air—you will become sick. If you want to combat the lust of the flesh, you must have a healthy prayer life. You inhale—that is, you talk to God, listen to His voice, worship Him, and seek His presence; you exhale—that is, you confess sin, allow the Holy Spirit to purify any ungodly attitudes and actions, and remove any hindrances or idols from your life. But take care that your prayers are not mere shopping lists of all the stuff you covet (see James 4, below).

Through prayer, we can defeat the subtlety and trickery of the lust of the flesh. If we pray correctly—that is, not by telling God what we want but by listening to discern what He wants—then we find our hearts realigned with His will. We can pray as Jesus taught us: "Your Kingdom come, Your will be done" (Matthew 6:10). The Holy Spirit will convict us of sin, remind us of truth, and teach us the correct way to go.

Do you pray with your spouse? Do you pray for your spouse? Do you spend more time nagging your spouse about bad habits than you do praying for him or her? The Holy Spirit will do a far better job of convicting your spouse than you can! Get out of the way by getting on your knees! Often, a disobedient husband (or wife) remains disobedient because the only voice he hears screaming in his ear is that of his spouse. Be quiet and pray, and let God speak to your spouse.

Consider keeping a prayer journal. Perhaps you have trouble remaining focused during your times of prayer. A journal is a great tool for directing your thoughts. Writing your prayers will help keep your mind from wandering. Be sure to record the answers to your prayers. I love to reread entries in my prayer journal. I use red and green ink pens—red for prayer needs (the color reminds me to pray again about the situation) and green for answers to prayer (my way of saying "Watch God go!" or "Go, God!"). Isn't this exactly what King David did in the Psalms? "I sought the LORD, and He heard me, and delivered me from all my fears" (Psalm 34:4). The following verses remind us of the importance of prayer:

> "...rejoicing in hope, patient in tribulation, continuing steadfastly in prayer" (Romans 12:12).

> "...praying always with all prayer and supplication in the Spirit, being watchful to this end with all perseverance and supplication for all the saints" (Ephesians 6:18).

> "Pray without ceasing" (1 Thessalonians 5:17).

> "You lust and do not have. You murder and covet and cannot obtain. You fight and war. Yet you do not have because you do not ask. You ask and do not receive because you ask amiss, that you may spend it on your pleasures" (James 4:2–3).

3. Water correctly, and be sure the rose bush has good drainage. (*Acts of service*) Black spot fungus flourishes in overwatered places. Water your rose bush from the base so that water does not accumulate on the leaves. If a rose bush doesn't have proper drainage, fungus will grow with ease. Water is good...but too much water is not. I am reminded of the attitude of many Christians today: They come to church week after week and enjoy good teaching and worship, but then they go home and do absolutely nothing with it. They become like overwatered rose bushes rife with fungus. Often, they change churches because they don't "get" anything out of attending—or the worship isn't what they like. Many Christians are hedonistic, seeking comfortable seats, flashy entertainment shows masquerading as "worship," sermons that tickle their ears...for them, Christianity is really all about pleasure.

So what happened to service? What happened to "presenting your body as a living sacrifice" (Romans 12:2)? If you are not doing anything with what you are receiving from church or God's Word, then you are "overwatered" and have poor "drainage." Stop thinking only about yourself; allow the Living Water to flow outward from you to others.

In our marriages, this tendency toward "overwatering" can cause serious problems. Husband and wife cling to their own possessions; neither is willing to share (let alone sacrifice) anything for the other. Jealousy grows like black spot fungus when one partner makes a purchase. "How could he spend all that money on himself? He knows I need a new coat." Or, "I can't believe she bought another new outfit. She already has more than she can wear. I really wanted to buy that new tool for my workshop. Now I won't have enough money to do that." Ultimately, jealousy gives way to bitterness, deceit, and selfishness. Anger takes root when one partner doesn't show respect for the other's "idol."

Husband: "I'm not letting her drive *my* car. She is so careless, and she always leaves it dirty." Wife: "I can't believe he left his coffee cup on *my* new table. It will be ruined!" Notice that it is *my* car...*my* piece of furniture. The best way to prevent this fungus is to learn first to serve each other.

Before you make that next purchase, ask yourself, "Should I really spend this money on myself? Am I willing to sacrifice my pleasure in order to bless my partner?" Even more important, look around your home: Is it filled with too much stuff—stuff you really don't need or use? Have you "overwatered" your marriage? Serving others is an effective weapon to use to defeat this enemy. When you serve others, your focus changes, and selfishness is replaced with generosity. Become a channel of blessing in your marriage, and as you reach out to others you will quickly discover this fungus is defeated.

"I beseech you therefore, brethren, by the mercies of God, that you present your bodies a living sacrifice, holy, acceptable to God, which is your reasonable service" (Romans 12:1).

"For you, brethren, have been called to liberty; only do not use liberty as an opportunity for the flesh, but through love serve one another" (Galatians 5:13).

"Be kindly affectionate to one another with brotherly love, in honor giving preference to one another" (Romans 12:10).

"Therefore lay aside all filthiness and overflow of wickedness, and receive with meekness the implanted word, which is able to save your souls. But be doers of the word, and not hearers only, deceiving yourselves. For if anyone is a hearer of the word and not a doer, he is like a man observing his natural face in a mirror; for he observes himself, goes away, and immediately forgets what kind of man he was. But he who looks into the perfect law of liberty and continues in it, and is not a forgetful hearer but a doer of the word, this one will be blessed in what he does." (James 1:21–25).

4. **Remove leaves that show signs of infection** *(Confession and repentance)* Once the black spot fungus appears on a leaf, it must be removed immediately. Any leaf that shows even a small spot should be thrown away. It is vital to discard all infected leaves—even those that may have fallen to the ground. No infected leaves should be left near the bush or other plants lest the fungus spread. This is not a fungus you can ignore: Left untreated, it soon will infect and kill the entire bush. In the same way, any evidence of the lust of the flesh must be dealt with in our marriages or it will destroy marriages.

Confession and repentance are critical in routing this enemy. Confession means 'to tell the whole truth,' without making excuses or shifting blame. It means I take full responsibility for my poor choices. If you really want to get rid of this fungus, you must confess sinful actions. A number of years ago, a man in my church approached me (Tim) about a terrible sin he had committed when he had been stationed overseas, away from his family. He had committed adultery and still lived with the devastating guilt of his past action. He had confessed and repented of his sin before God, but he was afraid to confess it to his wife, for fear she would leave him. He asked me what he could do to be free from this bondage of guilt. I told him he needed to confess his sin to his wife. I explained that he would never experience real freedom and oneness in his marriage until he was willing to do this.

It took some time before the man found the courage to confess to his wife. Of course she was hurt, but she was also relieved. For some time she had felt that something was terribly wrong, and she didn't know how to deal with the invisible wall that seemed to have grown up between them. Many tears were shed, but healing came. The Sunday after he had confessed to her, I saw them sitting together in church, holding hands, and with looks of renewed love and joy on their faces. Confession had broken the bondage sin had wrought in this man's life. He had repented before the Lord, but it was the act of confessing to his wife that helped bring restoration. The lust of the flesh brings unspeakable sorrow and pain, but confession opens the door for healing and renewal.

However, confession alone would not have been enough. Both confession *and* repentance were vital for this couple to experience restoration. We often hear individuals confess their sins, but within a short time they return to wallow in the mud of that sin again. Repentance is not the same as confession. The Greek word that we translate 'repentance' is *metanoia,* which means 'to change your mind, or a reversal.'[5] In Greek, the word 'confess' means to 'acknowledge or fully agree with.'[6] Confession must be accompanied by repentance. Repentance says, "I am not only sorry for what I have done, but I am convinced it was wrong. I have changed my thinking, and I want to go in a completely different direction."

Often, we are saddened only by the results of what the lust of the flesh has brought into our marriages. We grieve because of the results of the sin without truly being sorry for the sin itself. This type of grief is often based on self-pity: We feel sorry for ourselves because of the mess we are in but not truly repentant of the sin which caused the mess. We know the sin was wrong, but we are unwilling or unable to take the next step—that is, to turn away from it and eliminate it completely.

Confession is like identifying the infected leaf: I openly point out the "infection" (sin) to anyone else who has been affected by it, and I communicate my sorrow about what I have allowed to grow. Repentance is like cutting off the leaf and throwing it away: I don't want to leave even a small portion of the "infection" in my life. It may be necessary to ask for help, but I am willing to do whatever it takes to make a permanent change.

How about you? Are you hiding things from your spouse, hoping you won't get caught? Are you in bondage to guilt over past sins? Have you been upset by the mess you got yourself into (because of the lust of the flesh), but you don't really hate the sin itself? Are you willing to turn away completely from this enemy? You can't ignore this fungus. It will destroy your marriage.

"For I will declare my iniquity; I will be in anguish over my sin"
(Psalm 38:18).

"He who covers his sins will not prosper, but whoever confesses and forsakes them will have mercy" (Proverbs 28:13).

"I acknowledged my sin to You, and my iniquity I have not hidden. I said, 'I will confess my transgressions to the LORD,' and You forgave the iniquity of my sin. Selah" (Psalm 32:5).

"Therefore say to the house of Israel, 'Thus says the Lord GOD: "Repent, turn away from your idols, and turn your faces away from all your abominations" (Ezekiel 14:6).

"Let him turn away from evil and do good; let him seek peace and pursue it" (1 Peter 3:11).

"Remember therefore from where you have fallen; repent and do the first works, or else I will come to you quickly and remove your lampstand from its place—unless you repent" (Revelation 2:5).

5. **Keep your garden clean.** *(Be separate from the world.)* Black spot fungus loves to breed in dark, damp places—as, for example, under piles of dead leaves. You may have taken all of the steps listed above: You planted your bush in full sunlight; you were careful to ensure adequate air circulation; you avoided overwatering and removed any diseased leaves. But if you fail to keep your garden clean, you invite disease to attack. In the same way, we must protect our marriages from the destructive enemies of this world.

Contemporary society bombards us with sensual images; advertising urging instant gratification; a thousand voices screaming that we need more, more, more. How do we combat the myriad temptations and opportunities? How can we protect our marriages from succumbing to this fungus? Our marriage is like a tiny rose bush planted in the middle of a junkyard!

We cannot run and hide in a monastery (though at times this may appeal). We live and work in the real world. We have neighbors, family members, work colleagues, and friends who not only are comfortable living in a "junkyard" but who have no idea there is anything better! You strive to keep your marriage—your "rose bush"—healthy and blooming, but the air around you—not to mention the ground—is polluted.

What can we do? First, we can choose what we allow in our homes. Keeping our "gardens" clean involves intentional choices about our entertainment—music, books, magazines, games, movies, and TV shows. Would you watch that TV show if Jesus were sitting beside you on the couch? The fact is that He is always in your living room! A friend of mine complained that her daughter was becoming quite worldly in her dress; she was wearing immodest clothing in an effort to look sexy. My friend didn't know what to do. But when I visited her home, I noticed a number of glamour magazines around the house, and especially in her daughter's room. The magazines featured sexual themes and promoted an immoral lifestyle. My friend had allowed ungodly influences into her home, and the results were evident.

Second, we must choose our friends wisely. If your colleagues enjoy telling dirty jokes, flirting with co-workers, and going out to bars, they are likely to bring you down to their level. We are called to be light to the world, but we need to take care that "bad company" does not extinguish our light. Make it a priority to have godly friends—friends who will challenge you to grow in your faith, who exemplify a godly marriage, and who will help you keep your garden clean.

"Do not be unequally yoked together with unbelievers. For what fellowship has righteousness with lawlessness? And what communion has light with darkness? And what accord has Christ with Belial? Or what part has a believer with an unbeliever? And what agreement has the temple of God with idols? For you are the temple of the living God. As God has said: "I will dwell in them and walk among them. I will be their God, and they shall be My people." Therefore "Come out from among them and be separate," says the Lord. "Do

not touch what is unclean, and I will receive you" (2 Corinthians 6:14–17).

"And do not be conformed to this world, but be transformed by the renewing of your mind, that you may prove what is that good and acceptable and perfect will of God" (Romans 12:2).

"For you were once darkness, but now you are light in the Lord. Walk as children of light (for the fruit of the Spirit is in all goodness, righteousness, and truth), finding out what is acceptable to the Lord. And have no fellowship with the unfruitful works of darkness, but rather expose them" (Ephesians 5:8–11).

OUR STORY

More than 21 years ago, we were invited to consider taking a ministry position in Austria. We had felt the pull on our hearts to serve in Europe, but when we saw this open door, we were apprehensive. We had four children. We were serving a good church in Kansas. Our salary was adequate, and we lived in a lovely home. Taking the position in Austria would mean a huge decrease in salary (basically, we would be living by faith); we would have to sell almost everything we owned and start over in a new country. (You often don't realize how attached you are to things until you have to get rid of them!) The Lord continued to tug on our hearts and made it clear that we were to take this step of faith.

We decided an auction would be the easiest way to get rid of our belongings, and we hoped it would provide us with enough money to furnish a home overseas. Were we ever wrong! Naively, we didn't set price minimums for our household goods. Many people got great deals that day—but we made very little money. We felt sick when our new washing machine was auctioned off at a fraction of the price we had paid for it. Other appliances were snatched up for next to nothing. We felt frustrated as our antique furniture was sold for mere dollars as we knew it was worth ten times as much. Piece by piece, all of our possessions disappeared. At the end of the day, we felt a bit lost as we stood in our empty house.

But then, an amazing thing happened: It was as if a huge weight had been removed from our lives! Suddenly, we felt such freedom! We hadn't realized how much our "stuff" controlled us. The lust of the flesh had crept into our marriage, and we had almost missed the greatest adventure of our married life because of fear of giving it all up. For the next year, prior to moving to Europe, we lived in a rusty, old van as we traveled throughout the United States and shared in churches about the work we would be doing in Austria. That was one of the best years of our life as a family. We learned to live simply, and it was so liberating. We discovered the joy of trusting the Lord to be our sole Provider. We experienced so many miracles during that year. When we finally arrived in Austria, we continued this walk of faith. We have been amazed time and again to see how the Lord provides for our every need. It was a battle for us to defeat the lust of the flesh, but the victory has been truly amazing! Despite our limited income, we have traveled all over the world and have enjoyed more blessings than we can name. God is good!

Jim Elliot was a missionary who was killed in Ecuador by the Waodani Indians, the very people group he had gone to serve. A man who understood what was truly important in life, he said, "He is no fool who gives what he cannot keep to gain what he cannot lose."[7] Similarly, Martin Luther said, "I have held many things in my hands and I have lost them all. But the things I have placed in God's hands I still possess."[8] Luke 12:16–21 records one of Jesus' parables:

> "'The ground of a certain rich man yielded plentifully. And he thought within himself, saying, "What shall I do, since I have no room to store my crops?" So he said, "I will do this: I will pull down my barns and build greater, and there I will store all my crops and my goods. And I will say to my soul, 'Soul, you have many goods laid up for many years; take your ease; eat, drink, and be merry.'" But God said to him, "Fool! This night your soul will be required of you; then whose will those things be which you have provided?" So is he who lays up treasure for himself, and is not rich toward God."

We have explored two of the enemies in the garden: The lust of the eyes is a lovely weed that will choke the life out of your marriage; the lust of the flesh is a fungus that subtly spreads and attacks the health of your marriage, leaving it diseased and, eventually, dead. In the next chapter, we will examine the third enemy: the pride of life.

STUDY GUIDE

Read Genesis 3:7–19; Galatians 5:19–21;
Luke 8:14; Titus 3:3; James 4:14;
2 Peter 2:13; 1 Corinthians 6:19–20;
Ecclesiastes 2:3–17, 12:13–14; John 3:19–20

In this chapter, we explored the second enemy in the garden: the lust of the flesh. The lust of the flesh refers not only to sensual sins, such as fornication, adultery, gluttony, drunkenness, and immorality, but also to sins such as greed, selfishness, and the love of pleasure. We explained that the lust of the flesh is hedonism and that hedonistic attitudes can destroy marriage.

Many people live for instant gratification, pursuing their wants and unwilling to do anything that might require sacrifice. These individuals will throw away their marriages, claiming they have a "right" to be happy; some may justify their actions by claiming that: "my partner doesn't satisfy me any more." Me! Me! Me! The lust of the flesh is all about me! This attitude is a fungus that creeps into our marriages, causing us to become diseased, unfruitful, and, eventually, dead. How can we combat this fungus? Let's dig a little deeper.

DIGGING DEEPER
1. Some of the curses Adam and Eve received in the garden for their disobedience were directly related to their flesh. What were these curses?

2. Galatians 5:19–21 provides a good definition of the lust of the flesh. What sins are listed in this passage?

3. Write your own definition of the lust of the flesh.

4. What is hedonism? What is the relationship of hedonism to the lust of the flesh?

5. The Greek word *hedone* is translated 'pleasure' in English. Explain how this word is used in the following passages:

   - Luke 8:14
   - Titus 3:3
   - James 4:1–3
   - 2 Peter 2:13

6. Do you think people have a "right" to be happy? Explain your answer.

7. What does 1 Corinthians 6:19–20 reveal about God's attitude toward our "rights"?

8. How has the attitude of entitlement caused serious problems in society today? How have attitudes of entitlement caused problems in marriages?

9. King Solomon was a man who had it all. List a few of the things from which he tried to gain satisfaction (Read Ecclesiastes 2:3–17):

10. What is the important lesson King Solomon shares in Ecclesiastes 12:13–14?

11. Name some of the ways in which the lust of the flesh is like black spot fungus.

12. We identified five ways to help prevent and/or cure black spot fungus. Each of these tips has an analogy to our marriages. What is the first tip for preventing black spot fungus?

   a. What is the analogy to our marriages?

   b. Paraphrase John 3:19–21.

13. What is the second tip for fighting black spot fungus?

   a. What is the analogy to our marriages?

   b. Paraphrase one of the verses cited in Section two.

14. What is the third tip for preventing black spot fungus?

    a. What is the analogy to our marriages?

    b. Paraphrase one of the verses cited in Section three.

15. What is the fourth tip for fighting black spot fungus?

    a. What is the analogy to our marriages?

    b. Paraphrase one of the verses cited in Section four.

16. What was the fifth tip for protecting against black spot fungus?

    a. What is the analogy to our marriages?

    b. Paraphrase one of the verses cited in Section five.

17. Which areas of your marriage have been affected by the "fungus" of the lust of the flesh? *(Share your answers with your spouse.)*

18. If there is anything you should confess to your spouse, commit now to do so.

19. Choose one of the five tips to work on this week in your marriage. *Make a practical plan with your spouse to implement this in your marriage.*

CHAPTER NINE

ENEMIES IN THE GARDEN— ROCKS

The Pride of Life

L et's wander back into the garden and revisit the fall of man. Adam and Eve stumbled on a huge "rock" that the Serpent cleverly left in their path: This was the pride of life.

The Serpent said, "For God knows that in the day you eat of it [the fruit] your eyes will be opened, and you will be like God, knowing good and evil" (Genesis 3:5). The Serpent presented two reasons that Eve should take the fruit: It will make you like God, and you will have knowledge of good and evil. The appeal was to self-exaltation and self-aspiration; two traits God never intended man to have. In essence, the Serpent was tempting mankind to aspire to a position above God.

This was exactly what the Serpent himself had aspired to—and the reason he found himself in the garden. The Serpent, Satan, was a created being, an angel of much importance. He is often called 'Lucifer,' which means "Morning Star." Ezekiel 28:13–17 says,

"You were the seal of perfection, full of wisdom and perfect in beauty. You were in Eden, the garden of God; every precious stone was your covering: the sardius, topaz, and diamond, beryl, onyx, and jasper, sapphire, turquoise, and emerald with gold. The work-

manship of your timbrels and pipes was prepared for you on the day you were created. You were the anointed cherub who covers; I established you; you were on the holy mountain of God; you walked back and forth in the midst of fiery stones. You were perfect in your ways from the day you were created, till iniquity was found in you."

We often envision Satan as some hideous creature, but clearly this was not the case. He was beautiful. So what happened to him? How did he become the enemy of God and of His people? He had walked with God, just as Adam and Eve had. He had been given a high position. How did he end up in the garden?

Isaiah 28:12-14 provides the answer:

"How you are fallen from heaven, O Lucifer, son of the morning! How you are cut down to the ground, you who weakened the nations! For you have said in your heart: "I will ascend into heaven, I will exalt my throne above the stars of God; I will also sit on the mount of the congregation on the farthest sides of the north; I will ascend above the heights of the clouds, I will be like the Most High."

Do you notice how many times the word "I" occurs in this text? Satan fell because of pride. And he uses this same tactic on Eve in the garden. Satan had said, "I will be like the Most High." This was exactly what he offered Eve: "You will be like God." Satan still throws the rocks of pride into the garden of marriages today.

FIVE KINDS OF ROCKS

Come walk with us through the garden of marriage. In the last two chapters, we described the weeds and fungus that often grow there. Now we want to consider the rocks of pride. As we enter the garden, we see a pile of rocks stacked six feet high and forming a kind of statue. The rocks are packed together with mud, and flowers are strewn at the foot of the statue. The rocks form an idol. The first type of "rock" we find in the garden is **self-exaltation.**

We walk a little further and come to a rock wall. It has been built in a strange place and doesn't provide protection; it only divides the garden into two awkward parts. This second kind of "rock" is **self-sufficiency.**

Walking around the wall, we find the third rock structure. Built in the corner of the garden, it is larger than the rock wall and is a completely secure enclosure. These are the rocks of **self-centeredness.**

Turning away from this small prison, we wander to another part of the garden where we see some rocks stowed in a treasure chest and others prominently displayed. Although they don't seem particularly valuable, someone has deemed them to be of great worth and has been collecting them. These are the rocks of **self-gratification.**

Finally, we pass through the last section of the garden. Some rocks lie buried in the soil; others are in small piles but have been filed so their tips are pointed. They look like weapons. These are the rocks of **self-righteousness.**

None of these rocks adds anything to the garden. They don't provide beauty, protection, or value. They hinder the ability of things to grow, and they waste space. At their core, they all are pride, at the heart of which is "I." Consider the English word 'PRIDE'; "I" is in middle. Now consider the word 'SIN'; again, "I" is right in the middle! "I"—"SELF"—is at the center of pride and sin. Now let's examine each of these rocks individually—and learn how we can remove them from our garden.

- self-exaltation
- self-sufficiency
- self-centeredness
- self-gratification
- self-righteousness

ROCK OF SELF-EXALTATION

A monument to me! "I am above all!"

This first rock best describes the fall of Satan as well as the fall of Adam and Eve. It says, "I will be like God." It is building an idol of self. In the Greek Bible, the word we translate 'pride' means "being full of smoke" or "a puff of smoke, rising up." It also means "being high-minded or lifted up."[1] Yet another meaning is "a haughty attitude, appearing to be above others or looking down on others contemptuously."[2] All of these describe putting oneself above others.

What does this look like in marriage? It reveals itself in the husband who says, "I can do what I want with my time and money. I expect my wife to cater to my every wish. I demand complete submission and obedience" or "I am the king of my castle. My wife is not very bright. I certainly would never trust her opinion." It is evident as well in the wife who says, "I deserve better than this bum. I want to be treated like a queen. I have my own interests and future to think about. I have no intention of sacrificing my career for my husband. My husband makes so many foolish choices. I always tell him he is wrong, but he never listens to me."

This "rock" also demands respect. Many couples describe this as one of the biggest problems in their marriage: "My wife doesn't respect me. She treats me like dirt. I deserve a little respect." To which the wife retorts, "If he would do the right thing, then I would respect him! He hasn't earned my respect!" God does command wives to respect their husbands, but God never tells husbands to demand respect from their wives. Whenever we start demanding our "rights," we are presumptuously proclaiming that we deserve to be treated in a certain fashion. (We discuss respect in greater detail in chapter 11.) The point is that we do not have the *right* to *demand* respect. That is arrogance and pride.

As we described in the previous chapters of this book, we are called to be one! How can you be one with someone who believes he or she is better than you? How can there be unity with your partner when he or she looks down at you or sees no value in you? The Apostle Paul reminds us, "There is neither Jew nor Greek, there is neither slave nor free, there is neither male nor female; for you are all one in Christ Jesus" (Galatians 3:28).

> *The rocks of self-exaltation corrupt your mind because they present a counterfeit system of value.*

In Romans 12:3, Paul admonishes, "For I say, through the grace given to me, to everyone who is among you, not to think of himself more highly than he ought to think, but to think soberly, as God has dealt to each one a measure of faith." The rocks of self-exaltation corrupt your mind because they present a counterfeit system of value. The truth is that you are no better nor more valuable than your spouse. Before the Lord, you stand on even ground. It is time to adjust your "standards."

Not only does this rock of pride come between husband and wife, but it also raises itself up against God. When couples say, "We know the Bible says divorce is wrong, but God doesn't want us to be unhappy," what they really are saying is "We know better than God. We don't believe God really meant it when He said this was sin. God is a God of love. We will create God in our own image. We will be like God."

But God replies, "'For My thoughts are not your thoughts, nor are your ways My ways,' says the LORD. 'For as the heavens are higher than the earth, so are My ways higher than your ways, and My thoughts than your thoughts'" (Isaiah 55:8–9). "The wicked in his proud countenance does not seek God; God is in none of his thoughts" (Psalm 10:4). It is unfathomable pride that presumes to know more than God! God is the Creator of marriage. He made the rules. He created you! How can you be so foolish as to reject His ways?

Consider this passage from Proverbs 6:16–19: "These six things the LORD hates, yes, seven are an abomination to Him: a proud look, a lying tongue, hands that shed innocent blood, a heart that devises wicked plans, feet that are swift in running to evil, a false witness who speaks lies, and one who sows discord among brethren." Did you notice that pride is listed first? The rocks of self-exaltation will destroy your marriage and your relationship with God. God is a jealous God. Isaiah 42:8 is clear: "I am the LORD, that is My name; and My glory I will not give to another, nor My praise to carved images." God has no intention of sharing His glory with you! You can have no other gods before Him—and that includes the god of your pride.

How can we remove the rocks of self-exaltation? The antithesis of pride is humility, and herein lies the key. To understand what humility is, let us first say what it is NOT: Humility is not being a doormat; it is not putting yourself down; and it is not a lack of confidence. Humility says, "I am inadequate, but I can do all things through Christ." Humility is being honest about weaknesses but not groveling in the dirt of self-pity. Humility stands in the strength of the Lord. Humility doesn't fight for "my rights." Humility means I am secure and satisfied with who I am in Christ and therefore am neither threatened by nor afraid of putting others first.

Someone once said, "Humility is a strange thing: The moment you think you have it, you have lost it." Indeed, pride often sneaks in the back door of our attempts to be humble. We must start by realizing that humility is a choice. 1 Peter 5:6 says, "Therefore humble yourselves under the mighty hand of God, that He may exalt you in due time." Humility is a choice we make—a choice to obey. But how can we choose to show humility in our marriages?

We can start with two areas: *our actions and our words.* Do you remember when you were in elementary school? You probably had a bully at your school who loved to push his way to the front of the line. He would take the best seat and always wanted to be first. He did not model humility. But now that we have grown up, some of us still behave like bullies in our marriages. We don't consider our spouse's needs. We "get in line" first, whether it is deciding what to watch on TV, how to spend some extra income, or even who gets to use the bathroom first. An act of humility would be marked by the questions "How can I serve you first? What do you need?" You may have worked hard to earn that "first place" in line, but humility willingly gives it up, with no strings attached—even if the other person doesn't deserve it.

Humility should also be evident in our words. I can choose to keep my mouth shut even when I know I am right. I can choose to stop making fun of my spouse. We often fail to see that innocent teasing can be quite hurtful and can be another reflection of pride. Even ostensibly "constructive" criticism can be mixed with pride; you can almost hear Pride saying, "You shouldn't do that. I would never do that! I know more than you do." Humilty speaks words of encouragement, praise, and thanks. It focuses on the positive things your spouse has done, and does not demand recognition of one's own accomplishments.

Philippians 2:3 exhorts, "Let nothing be done through selfish ambition or conceit, but in lowliness of mind let each esteem others better than himself." When I see myself through God's eyes—that is, as a sinner saved by grace—it is not difficult for me to put others first. Jesus is the supreme example:

"Let this mind be in you which was also in Christ Jesus, who, being in the form of God, did not consider it robbery to be equal with

God, but made Himself of no reputation, taking the form of a bond-servant, and coming in the likeness of men. And being found in appearance as a man, He humbled Himself and became obedient to the point of death, even the death of the cross" (Philippians 2:5–8).

Humility is a byproduct of drawing close to God. Throughout the Bible, we read the stories of people who had an encounter with God. Although they usually found themselves flat on their faces before Him, He never left them groveling in the mud. That is grace. James 4:6–8 says, "But He gives more grace. Therefore He says: 'God resists the proud, but gives grace to the humble.' Therefore submit to God. Resist the devil and he will flee from you.

> *Humility comes as a natural by-product of drawing close to God.*

Draw near to God and He will draw near to you. Cleanse your hands, you sinners; and purify your hearts, you double-minded."

We love the word picture James provides a few verses later: "Humble yourselves in the sight of the Lord, and He will lift you up" (James 4:10). This does not mean He will "lift you up" to be above Him or above others. Rather, it means He will lift you up out of the horrible mud pit—pride—in which you are stuck and bring you into relationship with Him. That is grace.

ROCKS OF SELF-SUFFICIENCY
Walls that divide. "I don't need anyone!"

The rocks of self-sufficiency are used to build walls in the garden. These rocks shout, "I can do it myself. I don't need any help. No one else can do this as well as I can, so I don't trust anyone else to get this job done."

Consider the life of King Nebuchadnezzar, a Babylonian king who learned a harsh lesson when he foolishly believed he had built his kingdom by his own power. King Nebuchadnezzar struggled with the rocks of pride. A powerful military leader who conquered Israel, he is credited with having built the Hanging Gardens of Babylon, one of the "seven wonders of the world."

You might remember the story of the 90-foot golden statue that Nebuchadnezzar commanded to be erected and before which his subjects were ordered to bow. But three Jewish captives, Shadrach, Meshach, and Abed-Nego, refused to do so. These men were brought before the king and testified of their faith in God. They resolutely refused to worship this statue. Enraged, Nebuchadnezzar had them thrown into a fiery furnace. But God miraculously delivered Shadrach, Meshach, and Abednego: Not only were they unharmed by the flames, but they didn't even smell of smoke! When Nebuchadnezzar saw that the mighty power of God had saved these three men, he decreed that no one in his kingdom could speak against God; he acknowledged, "There is no other God who can deliver like this" (Daniel 3:29b). As we read this story in Daniel Chapter 3, we get the sense that Nebuchadnezzar had learned a lesson about who really has the power.

But this was not the end of Nebuchadnezzar's story. In Daniel Chapter 4, we read that pride continued to be a problem for the king. God gave Nebuchadnezzar a dream to warn him about the danger of his pride. Not understanding what the dream meant, Nebuchadnezzar sent for Daniel to interpret it for him. (Daniel, another captive from Israel, had proven himself a valuable advisor to the King. He was also a prophet who had the gift of interpreting dreams.) Daniel explained the dream to Nebuchadnezzar and instructed him to repent, but to no avail.

Daniel 4:29 says, "At the end of the twelve months, he [King Nebuchadnezzar] was walking about the royal palace of Babylon. The king spoke, saying, 'Is not this great Babylon, that I have built for a royal dwelling by my mighty power and for the honor of my majesty?'" This boastful statement aroused God's judgment. Nebuchadnezzar was driven from his palace. He lost his mind and his kingdom and lived like a wild beast in the fields. Some time passed before King Nebuchadnezzar finally came to his senses and acknowledged God and His supreme power. In Daniel 4:34–35 we read Nebuchadnezzar's own testimony:

"And at the end of the time I, Nebuchadnezzar, lifted my eyes to heaven, and my understanding returned to me; and I blessed the Most High and praised and honored Him who lives forever: for His dominion is an everlasting dominion, and His kingdom is from generation to generation. All the inhabitants of the earth are reputed as nothing; He does according to His will in the army of heaven and

among the inhabitants of the earth. No one can restrain His hand or say to Him, "What have You done?""

Mighty King Nebuchadnezzar humbled himself before almighty God and recognized that all power, majesty, and glory came from God's hand. King Nebuchadnezzar continues his story:

King Nebuchadnezzar discovered a vital truth: "And those who walk in pride He [God] is able to put down" (Daniel 4:37). We prefer to portray God as all-compassionate, long-suffering, gentle, and kind; these traits are accurate, but let us never forget that God is also the God of discipline and correction. If you continue to build walls of self-sufficiency, God will take steps to correct you—and to smash your walls to pieces. Many times, the punishment for your pride will be the natural consequences of your sin. Proverbs 16:18 is clear: "Pride goes before destruction, and a haughty spirit before a fall." The pride of self-sufficiency has led individuals to bankruptcy, unemployment, broken relationships, and utter loneliness. Proverbs 29:23 says, "A man's pride will bring him low, but the humble in spirit will retain honor."

Paul admonishes Christians to evaluate their motives and behavior lest they fall into God's hands. If we humble ourselves (as we read earlier in James 4:10), then God will not need to intervene. But do not be deceived: God will step in and discipline His children because He loves them. "For if we would judge ourselves, we would not be judged. But when we are judged, we are chastened by the Lord, that we may not be condemned with the world" (1 Corinthians 11:31–32). These rocks cause us to forget what Adam learned in the garden: "I am alone, and it is not good."

The rocks of self-sufficiency form walls that divide us.

The rocks of self-sufficiency form walls that divide us; we think we really don't need each other. This enemy creeps into our marriages in many subtle ways. It says, "I know I have an addiction (to pornography, alcohol, drugs, overspending, etc.), but I can deal with it myself. I don't need my spouse's help or anyone else's." Or it may say, "I don't see any reason we need to get help for our marriage. We can solve our problems alone." This enemy—the rocks of self-sufficiency—is echoed in the words of husbands who say, "I am the man of the house. My wife has no idea how to handle anything. I need to do it all myself. Her opinion doesn't matter." They also are echoed in the words of the wife who claims, "I am more spiritual than my husband. I need to take charge of the spiritual training of our children because my husband can't do it."

How do we break down this wall of self-sufficiency (before God does)? *First, confess your self-sufficiency as sin to God,* and repent—turn away from your prideful attitude and acknowledge your utter dependence on God. King Nebuchadnezzar was healed and restored when he confessed, repented, and acknowledged God's absolute authority. These three steps—*confess, repent, and acknowledge*—are important in destroying this wall. Begin by confessing the sin of prideful self-sufficiency. *Next, repent: turn away from this sin,* determined not to continue living behind walls of pride. *Finally, acknowledge your complete dependence on God*—on His power, authority, provision, and redemption. "Not that we are sufficient of ourselves to think of anything as being from ourselves, but our sufficiency is from God" (2 Corinthians 3:5).

Once you have confessed this sin to God, take the next step of acknowledging to your spouse that you need him (her). Admit your weaknesses, struggles, short-sightedness, and shortcomings to your partner. Ask your spouse to help you by honestly and lovingly telling you when you are acting prideful and self-sufficient. Then, learn to ask for your spouse's advice, opinion, and help. Remember: God has given you your husband or wife to be your completion. Choose to use this gift God has given you. Remember 1 Corinthians 12:20–21 about the Body of Christ: "But now indeed there are many members, yet one body. And the eye cannot say to the hand, 'I have no need of you'; nor again the head to the feet, 'I have no need of you.'" The human body is not just one big foot! Rather, it has different parts, each with distinct strengths and abilities. In like manner, God has given the Church, His Body, different parts, which work together for Him. God has brought together you and your spouse, with diverse gifts and skills, to work in unity (without pride) for His glory.

Romans 12:16 reminds us, "Be of the same mind toward one another. Do not set your mind on high things, but associate with the humble. Do not be wise in your own opinion (v.16)."

ROCKS OF SELF-CENTEREDNESS

Prison of self-interest. "I have to take care of #1!"

The third structure we find in the garden of marriage is built with the rocks of self-centeredness. These rocks block everyone out and create a type of prison. These rocks say, "I don't trust you. I have to watch out for my own interests. I won't let anyone take advantage of me. I have to take care of number 1!" These rocks often disguise themselves as self-pity, and indeed, they are related to self-centeredness. Whenever we focus solely on ourselves, the rest of the world around us becomes blurred. We fail to trust God or to believe that He

> *When we focus solely on ourselves, the rest of the world around us becomes blurred.*

is at work in our lives. We ignore the needs of our spouse because we are consumed by our own needs. These rocks prevent our partner from getting close to us, and eventually we find ourselves imprisoned by our own fears, selfishness, doubts, and despair.

King Saul provides a good example of this. God commanded King Saul to "go and attack Amalek, and utterly destroy all that they have, and do not spare them" (1 Samuel 15:3a), but Saul disobeyed and kept some of the spoil for himself. God sent the prophet Samuel to confront him:

> *"So Samuel said, 'When you were little in your own eyes, were you not head of the tribes of Israel? And did not the LORD anoint you king over Israel? Now the LORD sent you on a mission, and said, 'Go, and utterly destroy the sinners, the Amalekites, and fight against them until they are consumed.' Why then did you not obey the voice of the LORD? Why did you swoop down on the spoil, and do evil in the sight of the LORD?'" (1 Samuel 15:17–19)*

King Saul attempted to justify his actions and even to shift the blame. Finally, in verse 24, he says, "I have sinned, for I have transgressed the commandment of the LORD and your words, because I feared the people and obeyed their voice" (1 Samuel 15:24). King Saul stumbled on the rocks of self-centeredness—looking out for himself and his interests, which led to fear and disobedience.

The prophet Samuel delivered God's judgment on King Saul: God rejected him as king and declared that the kingdom would be torn from him and given to another. You would have expected King Saul to repent, but his next statement reveals the prison the rocks of self-centeredness had already erected in his life: "I have sinned; yet honor me now, please, before the elders of my people and before Israel, and return with me, that I may worship the LORD your God" (1 Samuel 15:30). Saul acknowledged his sin, but in the next breath, he begged to be honored before the people. It is evident in King Saul's next declaration that his relationship with God was broken: "...that I may worship the LORD *your* God." God was not *his* God. King Saul was only going through the motions to maintain his position in Israel.

Tracing the rest of King Saul's life, we discover a man who became paranoid, consumed with jealousy, fear, anger, and depression. His relationship with his own son was broken, and his life ended tragically. Sadly, the rocks of self-centeredness not only imprisoned him but also wrought much sorrow and pain in his kingdom.

How do we tear down the rocks of self-centeredness in our lives? We need an attitude adjustment. Dr. Dale Robbins, founder and president of Victorious Christian Ministries, provides an analogy: "Airplane pilots often use 'attitude' to describe their horizontal relationship with the runway when they land. If their attitude isn't aligned properly, the plane will make contact with the ground at the wrong angle and it will cause them to crash.... In essence, your attitude is your inward disposition toward other things, such as people or circumstances."[3]

Just as a pilot must keep the plane at the proper 'attitude,' so must we learn to maintain a proper attitude—one that keeps us in the right frame of mind: not too high, not too low, not crooked, but level, straight, and appropriate for the situation.

If our attitude is focused on ourselves, we will crash. How can we correct our 'attitude?' The best way is through a relationship with Christ and the work of His Holy Spirit. Romans 8:1 says, "There is therefore now no condemnation [no 'crashing'] to those who are in Christ Jesus, who do not walk according to the flesh, but according to the Spirit." Their 'attitude' is properly aligned.

Consider two aspects of Romans 15:6: "that you may with one *mind* and one *mouth* glorify the God and Father of our Lord Jesus Christ." If I want to align my attitude, then I need a *new mind*. Not only do I need to spend time in God's Word, but I also need to meditate on it and memorize it. I need to allow God's Word to burn away the dross of my self-centeredness and to purify my thoughts. Paul writes in Ephesians 5:26, "that He [Jesus] might sanctify and cleanse her [His Church] with the *washing* of water by the word."

Philippians 4:8 teaches,

"Finally, brethren, whatever things are true, whatever things are noble, whatever things are just, whatever things are pure, whatever things are lovely, whatever things are of good report, if there is any virtue and if there is anything praiseworthy—meditate on these things."

We need to stop meditating on the negative things—in our marriages, families, circumstances, and personal lives. Depression often arises as a direct result of the rocks of self-centeredness. Many people who are depressed claim they are not full of pride. But in reality, they are focused on themselves; thoughts such as "poor me," "my life is terrible," and "I have nothing to live for" are all indicative of pride.

2 Corinthians 10:5 commands, "Casting down arguments and every high thing that exalts itself against the knowledge of God, bringing every thought into captivity to the obedience of Christ." Negative thoughts do not belong in our hearts or marriages. Cast them out! Every time a negative thought rears its ugly head, take it captive and bring it to Christ.

> *Negative thoughts do not belong in our hearts or marriages. Cast them out!*

The second key word in Romans 15:6 is *mouth*. What comes out of your mouth? "And whatever you do in *word* or deed, do all in the name of the Lord Jesus, giving thanks to God the Father through Him" (Colossians 3:17). Giving thanks is one of the most powerful weapons we can use to destroy the prison of self-centeredness.

Romans 1:21 describes people who rejected Christ: "Because, although they knew God, they did not glorify Him as God, nor were *thankful,* but became futile in their thoughts, and their foolish hearts were darkened." What a tragic description! And yet what a perfect depiction of what happens when rocks of self-centeredness keep a person from thanking, glorifying, or even acknowledging God. The thoughts of such individuals become futile (empty, hopeless), and their hearts are darkened. But these characteristics do not have to describe your life or marriage.

Begin by thanking God *"in everything"* (Ephesians 5:20). Note: That does not mean that you thank God *for* everything (for example, one wouldn't thank God for sin). But you can thank God *in* everything—even in a difficult situation, focusing not on the problem but rather on God and His character. When you feel trapped in darkness, you can be thankful that Jesus is Light. "Be anxious [worried, fearful] for nothing, but *in everything* by prayer and supplication, *with thanksgiving,* let your requests be made known to God" (Philippians 4:6).

Continue to exercise an attitude of thankfulness with regard to your spouse. It may seem difficult at first to find some characteristic or act for which to be thankful, but as you seek the Lord and His perspective, you will find that He opens your heart, breaking through the prison of self-centeredness and changing YOU! Too often we are focused on changing our spouse. But being thankful for the partner God has given us redirects our focus away from ourselves and brings us to a new level of trust in the Lord. If I am truly thankful for the gift He has given me, I am acknowledging, "God, I believe this gift of my spouse is a good gift. I trust You."

Often, we fail to thank our spouse for anything. Or we mix our thanks with criticism: "Thanks for fixing that leaky faucet. But you really should have done that weeks ago, and you left such a mess behind," or, "My dinner was cold, and the meat should have been cooked longer. But thanks anyway." Why can't we just say, "Thank you?"

Some say, "My husband (or wife) knows I appreciate him (her). Why do I have to say 'thanks' all the time?" Apply that logic to your relationship with the Lord: Is it enough to tell Jesus "thank you" only once after you become a Christian? Why do we worship Him corporately week after week? Does Jesus really need our praise? No! But when we praise Him, we put Him in the proper place in our lives: first. In the same way, expressing thanks to your spouse is putting him or her in the proper place—a place of honor. And in so doing, you correct your 'attitude.' When you learn to shift the focus away from yourself, the rock walls of the prison of self-centeredness will tumble.

ROCKS OF SELF-GRATIFICATION
Fool's gold. "I want it all!"

These rocks scream, "I want it all! And I want it now!" In the gardens of our marriages, we place these worthless rocks in a treasure box or on display. The rocks of self-gratification are the lust of the flesh and the lust of the eyes. They are rocks of pride because we believe we deserve to have what we want when we want it. Hosea 13:6 states, "When they had pasture, they were filled; they were filled and their heart was exalted; therefore they forgot Me." They were *filled* (with stuff) and then *exalted* themselves (became proud) and *forgot* (rejected) God. A "pasture" is not evil, but seeking it and allowing it to become an idol leads to pride and, ultimately, to rejecting God. Jeremiah 49:4–5a asks, "'Why do you boast in the valleys, your flowing valley, O backsliding daughter? Who trusted in her treasures, saying, "Who will come against me?" Behold, I will bring fear upon you,' says the Lord GOD of hosts."

In the 1800s, thousands of people went to California in search of gold. People from every walk of life sacrificed everything in order to find the mother lode. They dreamed of striking it rich. Unfortunately, many of them were bitterly disappointed when they discovered that all they had actually found was "fool's gold." Fool's gold is a worthless, gold-colored rock (pyrite) that often is confused with real gold. How about you? Are you investing your time and energy in the pursuit of worthless fool's gold? Shakespeare wrote in "The Merchant of Venice," "All the glitters is not gold"; and yet we foolishly chase after these valueless rocks. Isaiah 55:2 poses the question, "Why do you spend money for what is not bread, and your wages for what does not satisfy? Listen carefully to Me, and eat what is good, and let your soul delight itself in abundance."

When is enough *enough?* No sooner have we bought the latest computer than we start looking at upgrades. We get a new cell phone but soon decide it isn't good enough; we need fashionable accessories for it. We purchase the latest kitchen appliance, but within a few months, it gets shoved to the back of the cupboard along with other unused gadgets. We are bombarded with advertising that urges us to buy the newest, latest, fastest, coolest products. But have you ever asked yourself, "Do I really need the newest, fastest, coolest stuff?" What's wrong with a 2gb mp3 player that plays 500 songs? Do you really need a device that plays 2,000 songs? How many songs can you listen to in a day? Too many people allow themselves to be defined by what they own. They have believed the lie that having a lot of stuff (especially cool and expensive stuff) makes them more valuable. "And He [Jesus] said to them, 'Take heed and beware of covetousness, for one's life does not consist in the abundance of the things he possesses'" (Luke 12:15).

How do we eliminate these rocks of self-gratification? In Chapter 7 ("Weeds: Lust of the Eyes") and Chapter 8 ("Fungus: Lust of the Flesh"), we described how to get rid of the weed and fungus that beset our marriages. We encourage you to review those chapters and apply them to the rocks of self-gratification. What are you planting (sowing) in your marriage?

"Do not be deceived, God is not mocked; for whatever a man sows, that he will also reap. For he who sows to his flesh will of the flesh reap corruption, but he who sows to the Spirit will of the Spirit reap everlasting life. And let us not grow weary while doing good, for in due season we shall reap if we do not lose heart. Therefore, as we have opportunity, let us do good to all, especially to those who are of the household of faith" (Galatians 6:7–10).

ROCKS OF SELF-RIGHTEOUSNESS
Weapons to wound. "I am right"; "I won't forgive."

We come to the final section of the garden, where we find a lot of rocks still buried in the soil and others gathered in small piles. The rocks that have been piled together have had their edges ground and shaped to form sharp tips. They are weapons. These are the rocks that say, "I am right, and you are wrong" and "I won't forgive you. You don't deserve my forgiveness." These "rock-weapons" are evidence that their creator is loath to admit that he or she is not perfect. They justify their creator's actions as he or she shifts blame to someone or something else.

In our marriages, these rocks sound like this:

- "If my wife would let me lead the family, we wouldn't be in the mess we're in. It's her fault that we are in debt. If she were more supportive, I could get a better job."
- "I have given my all to this marriage, and my husband just won't change. He doesn't allow me to serve God, and he keeps me from growing in my faith. He is a terrible example to our children. I'd be better off without him. I refuse to forgive him for the ways he has hurt me."

These rocks are weapons because we throw them at each other, blaming the other for the problem and refusing to accept any responsibility.

These rocks are also weapons of self-justification. Rather than humbling ourselves when we have offended our spouse, we pick up one of these sharp stones and hurl it: "I know I forgot to call, but you don't always call me when you should." Or, "You shouldn't be offended that I was friendly with my co-worker. After all, she doesn't mean anything to me. I was just being nice. I can't help it if she got the wrong idea." And "Well, you overcharged our credit card last month. What right do you have to yell at me for buying a new outfit?"

> *These rocks are the weapons of self-righteousness and self-justification.*

Isn't this exactly what Adam and Eve did? Caught in sin, Adam was quick both to blame God and to justify his actions: "It was the woman You gave me! She gave me the fruit. I just ate it." Eve followed suit: "I couldn't help myself. The Serpent tricked me. It's his fault." We are as adept with these weapons today as the first couple was in the Garden of Eden.

How can we stop throwing these rocks of self-righteousness at each other? Proverbs 30:32 provides the first step: "If you have been foolish in *exalting* yourself, or if you have devised evil, *put your hand on your mouth.*" Allow us to be blunt: *close your mouth!* James 3:5 explains, "Even so, the tongue is a little member and boasts great things. See how great a forest a little fire kindles!" How many times have you allowed your tongue to shoot a fiery blast at your partner? The tongue is such a little thing and yet it can destroy marriages! James 3:8–10 says, "But no man can tame the tongue. It is an unruly evil, full of deadly poison. With it we bless our God and Father, and with it we curse men, who have been made in the similitude of God. Out of the same mouth proceed blessing and cursing. My brethren, these things ought not to be so." How can we sing songs of praise at church on a Sunday morning and then attack our husband or wife with the poison of our tongue on the way home? "These things ought not to be so" (James 3:10)!

James 3:14–16 continues, "But if you have bitter envy and self-seeking in your hearts, do not boast and lie against the truth. This wisdom does not descend from above, but is earthly, sensual, demonic. For where envy and self-seeking exist, confusion and every evil thing are there." Wait… *demonic?* Isn't James exaggerating? No, we don't think so. Our words reflect what is in our hearts. Bitterness, envy, self-seeking, boasting, and lies: all of these come from the pit of hell.

We worked extensively with a couple who were experts at using their words as weapons. As they flung these rocks at each other, they rarely ever missed. Both knew exactly which words hurt the most and exactly when and where to aim them. Though the couple were not "demon-possessed," their actions surely caused much rejoicing among the demonic ranks. Their marriage was destroyed because they couldn't control their tongues.

But the last part of the passage in James gives hope: "But the wisdom that is from above is first pure, then peaceable, gentle, willing to yield, full of mercy and good fruits, without partiality and without hypocrisy. Now the fruit of righteousness is sown in peace by those who make peace" (James 3:17–18). Here is a prescription to cure a raging tongue: *Seek after the wisdom that comes from above, which is* "peaceable, gentle, willing to yield, full of mercy and good fruits, without partiality and without hypocrisy." If these characteristics are not in your marriage— and, even more specifically, not in your speech—then you are following the "wisdom" from below—that is, from Satan.

The next step in eliminating the rocks of self-righteousness from our marriage is to stop comparing ourselves to our spouse or to others. We often think, "I am not as bad as my spouse." Or, "I may not be a perfect husband, but I am not as terrible as that guy. He is a loser. At least I provide for my family." We have this idea that God will excuse our bad behavior because it is not as bad as someone else's. Beware: If you think you can stand before God on the basis of your own righteousness, then you are mistaken. God does not accept excuses—as, for example, "I would have served You, God, but my husband kept me from going to church" or, "God, you know I did the best I could. I worked hard to take care of my family, went to church, and even gave my tithe. Surely that is enough." God says, "For whoever shall keep the whole law, and yet stumble in one point, he is guilty of all" (James 2:10), and "As it is written: 'There is none righteous, no, not one; there is none who understands; there is none who seeks after God'" (Romans 3:10–11). "For they, being ignorant of God's righteousness, and seeking to establish their own righteousness, have not submitted to the righteousness of God" (Romans 10:3). You need to see yourself as God does.

Read what Paul wrote in Romans 3:1–3:

"Therefore you are inexcusable, O man, whoever you are who judge, for in whatever you judge another you condemn yourself; for you who judge practice the same things. But we know that the judgment of God is according to truth against those who practice such things. And do you think this, O man, you who judge those practicing such things, and doing the same, that you will escape the judgment of God?"

We must stop comparing ourselves with others and believing the lie that we can justify our actions because we are not "as bad as" someone else.

Begin by confessing your attitude of self-righteousness as sin. Ask God to forgive you and to help you see yourself as He does: as a sinner saved by grace. We cannot claim to be any better than our spouse because the truth is, we aren't! We all are sinners who have been offered the free gift of salvation; we did nothing to deserve or to earn our salvation. 2 Corinthians 5:2 reminds us, "For He [God] made Him [Jesus] who knew no sin to be sin for us, that we might become the righteousness of God in Him."

"Where is boasting then? It is excluded. By what law? Of works? No, but by the law of faith. Therefore we conclude that a man is justified by faith apart from the deeds of the law" (Romans 3:27–28). 1 Corinthians 4:7 says, "For who makes you differ from another? And what do you have that you did not receive? Now if you did indeed receive it, why do you boast as if you had not received it?" The rocks of self-righteousness and self-justification have no place in our gardens. Before we conclude this section, we want to consider forgiveness—as well as the path to reconciliation—in greater detail.

FORGIVENESS AND RECONCILIATION

Imagine another scene from the garden. This area is perfectly land-scaped, with lovely paths edged by lush, blossom-laden bushes. As you stroll through the garden, you discover a small patch of barren ground. You call to the gardener and ask him what is wrong. "Why isn't anything growing here?" He asks you if you'd like him to dig around and check it out, and you agree. It doesn't take long for him to discover the reason: rocks buried just inches beneath the soil. Nothing can grow in this rocky soil.

The gardener asks if you would like him to get rid of the rocks. "Of course!" you reply; you watch as He carefully removes them. But before he can haul them away, you say, "Wait! Just leave them here with me. I might need to throw them at someone in self-defense." The gardener sighs and grants your request, though he knows the rocks don't belong in the garden. He warns you that unless they are removed, the chances are good that they'll end up in the soil once again. These are the rocks of unforgiveness.

Many of us have been hurt in our marriage relationship. Our spouse comes to us, acknowledges the offense, and asks for forgiveness. But we are too hurt. The offense was too great. Many times, we refuse to grant forgiveness, and just like the analogy of the garden, the rocks of offense remain buried and prevent anything beautiful from growing.

How about you? You must invite the Gardener, Jesus, to work in the garden of your life. Start by showing Him an area of your life that is barren. Jesus will reveal what is causing the lack of growth. Most likely, it is a lack of forgiveness. Jesus is ready to dig up all the rocks. Will you allow

Him to work? The first step is to say, "I am ready to forgive my spouse."

"But wait!" you cry. "I will forgive my spouse, but I won't forget. I need to keep these rocks. I might need some evidence of what happened. I don't want to be hurt again. I intend to point to these rocks and remind my spouse of the ways I have been hurt in the past. I will forgive, but I won't forget!"

Jesus is sorrowful as you continue to make excuses for not letting go of the rocks. Perhaps you are thinking, "I might need these rocks to defend myself. Next time we have a disagreement, I can throw one in my spouse's face. After all, I am pretty sure my spouse will fail again, and I need to be prepared."

But Jesus admonishes, "This is not forgiveness. You can't just dig up the rocks and then keep them. Let me get rid of the rocks altogether. You will never be free to become all I intend you to be if you don't let go. I know you can't get rid of these rocks on your own; I am ready to help you. I will be your defense."

Forgiveness is not simply mouthing the words "I forgive you." It requires making the intentional choice—regardless of how we feel—to never mention the offense again. We must choose to destroy our "lists" of wrongs suffered. We all have them; in fact, we have amazing memories when it comes to hurts and offenses! Love is defined in 1 Corinthians 13:5: "It does not dishonor others, it is not self-seeking, it is not easily angered, it keeps no record of wrongs" (NIV). Love doesn't hang on to the rocks of offense or use them as weapons.

Forgiveness involves making a choice to never mention the offense again.

When God forgives us, does He really *forget* what we have done? God is not forgetful. Rather, He chooses to bury our sins in the deepest of oceans, to separate them from Himself as far as the east is from the west. He chooses to never mention them again. That is forgiveness. His forgiveness allows me to stand before Him pure and clean.

In the same way, He commands us to forgive one another. Jesus taught, "For if you forgive men their trespasses, your heavenly Father will also forgive you. But if you do not forgive men their trespasses, neither will your Father forgive your trespasses" (Matthew 6:14, 15).

We are so quick to ask God to forgive us when we do something wrong; yet we are so slow to forgive someone who has wronged us. Matthew 18:21–35 records a parable Jesus told about a king who had a servant who owed him 10,000 talents. *(A talent was a type of currency in Bible times.)* Depending on whether the talents were gold or silver, this

> *We are quick to ask God to forgive us ... yet slow to forgive someone who has wronged us.*

could have been the equivalent of a few million to several billion dollars! No matter which exchange rate you use, this was a lot of money! Obviously, Jesus was making a point here! The servant begged for mercy and asked the king for more time to repay his debt. In response, the king does something totally surprising: he forgives and *erases* the servant's debt.

But the story doesn't end there. The servant left the king's presence and went looking for a co-worker who owed him 100 denarii. *(One denarius was equivalent to a day's wage—perhaps $60 today).* Although the man pleaded for more time to repay his small debt, the servant refused and had him cast into prison.

When the king discovered how the servant had behaved toward his co-worker, he quickly apprehended him and said,

> *"'You wicked servant! I forgave you all that debt because you begged me. Should you not also have had compassion on your fellow servant, just as I had pity on you?' And his master was angry, and delivered him to the torturers until he should pay all that was due to him. So My heavenly Father also will do to you if each of you, from his heart, does not forgive his brother his trespasses"* (Matthew 18:32–35).

Do you realize how much you have been forgiven? Each of us owes a vast debt of sin that we cannot pay, and yet we can find complete forgiveness in Jesus. The king stood ready to forgive and to eliminate his servant's debt. So Jesus forgives us and expects us to forgive those who offend us.

Our good friend, Pastor Steven D. Felker provides insight into forgiveness and reconciliation:

"A sin event happens. The relationship is breached. The goal is reconciliation. However, each party must do his or her part: the offended must forgive, and the offender must repent. Until then, either can come himself into a right place before God, but reconciliation cannot happen. Once reconciliation happens, then trust can begin to be (re)built. Of course, a return to the sin event puts the process back at the beginning again."

The diagram illustrates the importance of forgiveness and repentance, which lead in turn to reconciliation and trust. Notice that rebuilding trust takes time; it requires a foundation of reconciliation, itself based on forgiveness and repentance. But don't confuse the order: forgiveness along with repentance must come first, leading to reconciliation and renewed trust. Often, individuals withhold forgiveness, believing they can't trust their partner anymore. But that is getting things backwards.

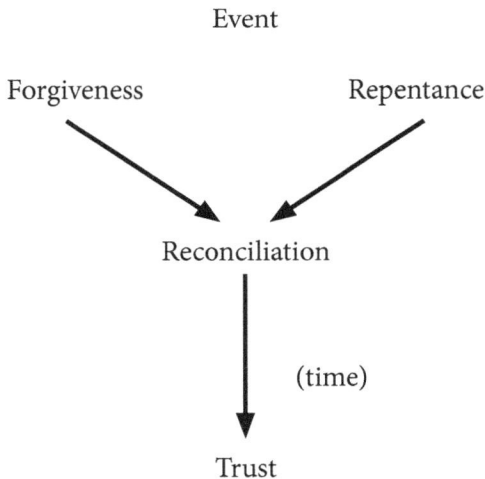

© (Steven Felker)

It is equally backward to attempt to be reconciled when there is not genuine repentance. Pastor Felker defines repentance as "the full ownership of my sin, and the exercise of all my faculties to not repeat it, and the meaningful pursuit of restitution of all that was lost." *This is not to say that forgiveness is conditional on the repentance of the offending party.* Rather, forgiveness is based on God's forgiveness of us—something we never deserved. Forgiveness must be offered freely. And reconciliation—restoration of the relationship—cannot take place until *both* forgiveness and repentance are offered. Trust—which may have been shattered by repeated offenses—requires time to be rebuilt.

How can we ever expect to become one in our marriages if we hold on to the rocks of offense, refusing to forgive and throwing these rocks at each other? Forgiveness is both an attitude and a choice. We choose to get rid of the rocks altogether. Do not keep the rocks as evidence of past wrongs! No more rock throwing!

STUDY GUIDE

Read Philippians 2:3–8; James 4:8; Daniel 4:29–37;
1 Samuel 15:3–30; Romans 15:6; Galatians 6:7–10;
James 3:5–18; Matthew 18:21–35

In this chapter we discussed five rocks of pride: self-exaltation, self-sufficiency, self-centeredness, self-gratification, and self-righteousness. This third enemy in the garden, the pride of life, reveals itself in these five ways. We need to learn how to identify these rocks and get rid of them. They hinder growth, waste space, and provide nothing of value in the garden. God wants the garden of your marriage to be filled with life—with growing and beautiful things—not dead rocks.

At the heart of pride and sin is the single word "I." We related these five rocks to key statements:

- "I am above all."
- "I don't need anyone."
- "I have to take care of #1."
- "I want it all."
- "I am right, and I won't forgive."

We want to rid these rocks from our garden, so grab your shovel and wheelbarrow, and let's dig a little deeper.

DIGGING DEEPER

1. What is the analogy we gave for each of the five types of rocks?

   a. Self-exaltation is like:

   b. Self-sufficiency is like:

   c. Self-centeredness is like:

   d. Self-gratification is like:

   e. Self-righteousness is like:

2. What is the definition of the Greek word for pride?

3. How do we get rid of the "rocks" of self-exaltation?

4. Which verse(s) do you find helpful with regard to the rocks of self-exaltation?

5. Which man from the Bible did we describe as portraying self-sufficiency? Summarize the man's story and what he learned.

6. What are two steps in tearing down the "wall" of self-sufficiency?

   a.

   b.

7. Which man from the Bible did we describe as portraying self-centeredness? Summarize his story and the result of the "rocks of self-sufficiency" in his life.

8. What are the two words we considered from Romans 15:6, and how do they help destroy the rocks of self-centeredness?

   a. _____

      A key verse is:

   b. _____

      A key verse is:

9. Paraphrase Galatians 6:7–10.

10. Finally, we considered the "rocks of self-righteousness." How do I get rid of the "rocks" that say "I am right?" What is a key verse?

11. "Rocks of unforgiveness" are a certain type of "rock of self-righteousness." What analogies did we give?

12. What does Matthew 18:21–35 teach?

13. How is the "garden" of your life? *(Check as many as apply.)*

- ☐ I have never invited the Gardener Jesus into my garden. My garden is a disaster. I need Jesus!
- ☐ I have invited Jesus into my garden, but I haven't allowed him to "dig around."
- ☐ I know there are barren spots where nothing is growing.
- ☐ I am afraid what the Gardener will discover if He starts digging around.
- ☐ I want the Gardener to remove the idols I have built in my garden.
- ☐ I know I have built walls of self-sufficiency in my garden.
- ☐ I want to be freed from the prison of self-centeredness I have built.
- ☐ I don't think I have any treasures to which I am clinging.
- ☐ I think I am right more often than my spouse is.
- ☐ I know my words are often weapons.
- ☐ I can forgive but not forget. I want to hold on to these rocks.
- ☐ I often throw these rocks at my spouse.
- ☐ I know I have to get rid of these rocks.
- ☐ I know these rocks have kept my spouse and me from becoming one.

CHAPTER TEN

ENEMIES IN THE GARDEN— MOLES AND MICE

Doubts and Lies

Remember Eve's encounter with the Serpent? In Genesis 3:1 he asked her, "Has God *indeed* said, 'You shall not eat of every tree of the garden?'" Allow us to paraphrase what the Serpent really was saying: "Are you sure God said that?" or "That can't be exactly what God meant…" or "Surely God wouldn't have said such a thing…." Was the Serpent just confused when he asked Eve to clarify God's instructions? NO! We are introduced to the Serpent as being "more cunning than any beast of the field which the LORD God had made" (Genesis 3:1). The Serpent knew exactly what God had said, but his tactic was to initiate **doubt, the fourth enemy in the garden**.

Once the Serpent had planted doubt in Eve's mind, he built on it: "Then the serpent said to the woman, 'You will not *surely* die. For God knows that in the day you eat of it your eyes will be opened, and you will be like God, knowing good and evil'" (Genesis 3:4, 5). The Serpent wanted both to discredit God and to cause Eve to doubt God's loving purpose. He began by first questioning the truth, then rejecting it, and finally accusing God's motives and character. Here we see **the fifth enemy in the garden: lies**.

The Serpent was saying, "You aren't really going to die. The truth is, God is withholding something good from you. God doesn't want to share His power. He doesn't really care about you. He is only looking out for His own interests. You need to start thinking about yourself." The Serpent, Satan, continues to use these weapons—doubts and lies— against our marriages today. He whispers, "God didn't really say it was wrong for you to get a divorce. God wants you to be happy. Your spouse doesn't care about you. Look out for your own interests."

Satan used five "enemies" to attack Eve in the Garden of Eden: the lust of the eyes, the lust of the flesh, the pride of life, doubts, and lies. In the last three chapters, we have considered the destructive nature of three of these enemies and how we can defeat them. Now we turn our attention to the last two enemies: **doubts and lies**.

DOUBT

Webster defines doubt as "to waver in opinion; inclined to disbelief; undecided; fearful or suspicious; lack of conviction; lack of trust or confidence."[1] The word derives from the Latin *dubius*, which is also the root of the English word 'duo,' or 'two.' Hence our understanding of doubt as "wavering between two options." The Old Testament highlights this meaning in 1 Kings 18:21: "And Elijah came to all the people, and said, 'How long will you falter between two opinions? If the LORD is God, follow Him; but if Baal [a false god], follow him.'" James 1:6 also presents this image of being tossed between faith and doubt: "But let him ask in faith, with no doubting, for he who doubts is like a wave of the sea driven and tossed by the wind." Eve was caught between two options: trust God and obey Him or believe the Serpent and disobey God. Her sin was not that she ate a piece of fruit; rather, her sin was that she disobeyed God. Doubt opened the door to an act of disobedience. (See Chapter 15 for a more in-depth exploration of doubt.)

IS DOUBTING SIN?

This is a highly debated topic. Certainly the meaning of the word 'doubt' is clouded by misuse and misunderstanding. Modern-day colloquialisms further cloud our understanding. For example, a judge can acquit a person on the basis of "reasonable doubt." Or a teacher may give her student the "benefit of the doubt" when he says he couldn't study because he was ill. And then there is the statement "I doubt I can finish this on time." But what does the Bible say about doubt? Romans 14:23 is often cited as "evidence" that doubt is sin: "But he who doubts is condemned if he eats, because he does not eat from faith; for whatever is not from faith is sin." If we fail to read this verse carefully, we may come to the conclusion that doubt is sin. But the key to right understanding of this verse is in the action it describes—that is, *whatever is not from faith*, or *"whatever we DO that does not come or proceed from faith is sin."* The verse goes on to say, "But he who doubts is condemned *if he eats…*" The sin was that the person acted on the basis of his doubts. Eve was confronted with doubt, but the real question has to do with what she "did" with her doubt. Eve allowed doubt to take root in her heart, and she *took* the fruit. She *acted* on her doubt; that was her sin. We believe that doubt is not sin; but what we *do* in response to our doubt can lead to sin.

> *Sin comes when we act on doubt.*

John the Baptist had a season of doubt when he was imprisoned. Hoping to get some answers, he sent messengers to Jesus: "And when John had heard in prison about the works of Christ, he sent two of his disciples and said to Him, 'Are You the Coming One, or do we look for another'" (Matthew 11:2–3). Why would John the Baptist, of all people, have doubts? Before he was born, John had been appointed as the prophet who would prepare the way for the Messiah. John himself had proclaimed that Jesus was the Lamb of God when he met Him by the Jordan River: "The next day John saw Jesus coming toward him, and said, 'Behold! The Lamb of God who takes away the sin of the world'" (John 1:29). Although we might expect Jesus to have condemned John for his doubts, Jesus' response was gentle: "Jesus answered and said to them, 'Go and tell John the things which you hear and see: The blind see and the lame walk; the lepers are cleansed and the deaf hear; the dead are raised up and the poor have the gospel preached to them. And blessed is he who is not offended because of Me'" (Matthew 11:4–6). John had his doubts, but what did he *DO* with them? John took them to Jesus.

Jesus was clear about the danger of what we allow in our minds: "For out of the heart proceed evil thoughts, murders, adulteries, fornications, thefts, false witness, blasphemies" (Matthew 15:19). The word translated "thoughts" is *dialogismos*. We could translate it 'evil doubts.' If we allow these thoughts or doubts to go unchecked, they can grow into evil doubts and sin.

Let's apply Matthew 15:19 to our marriages. We could paraphrase the verse as follows:

> *If we allow doubts to go unchecked, they can grow into evil doubts and sin.*

An evil doubt—for example, doubting your spouse's love for you—forms in the heart, leading you to entertain thoughts of adultery. Or "I doubt my spouse can take care of this problem correctly. I need to handle it myself"—which leads to 'theft'—stealing from your spouse the responsibility that God gave them to do. Or "I don't have any proof that my spouse is being unfaithful to me, but I have a strong feeling"—which leads to 'false witness'—telling your friends about what you imagine your spouse might do."

Doubt is a dangerous enemy in the garden of marriage. We can compare doubt to another enemy in your backyard: the mole. Learning about this animal can help us understand how doubt attacks our marriages. We also want to discover how we can eliminate this enemy.

MOLES

Moles are fascinating—and highly destructive—creatures! Although they are blind, they can discriminate between light and darkness. These small creatures live underground and are active day and night. Contrary to popular belief, they do not eat plants but rather are insectivores. Moles have a high metabolism and an insatiable appetite. Their two large front feet make them amazing diggers: One mole can dig up to an 18-foot-long tunnel in an hour and a 150-foot-long tunnel in a day!

Some people view moles as cute little critters and even welcome their presence in the yard. They claim that because moles eat unwanted insects and because their tunneling aerates the soil, they should be left alone. Yet moles can severely damage a garden. As they tunnel around plants and search for food, they often inadvertently uproot the plants or strip nutrients away from the roots. Some commercial bulb growers and farmers experience significant crop loss because of damage caused by these animals.

Moles' tunnels also have been known to undermine concrete slabs, patios, driveways, pools, and other shallow foundations. The damage can be irreparable. Moles' burrowing can also leave bare spots on the lawn and can create mounds that can result in injury to a person walking through the yard as well as to lawn equipment. Other rodents such as field mice that do eat plants can also use moles' tunnels. The result can lead to serious damage as the rodents gain easy passage into the garden.

So how are moles like doubts? Consider these similarities:

MOLES...	DOUBTS...
— are blind and prefer the dark.	— are often blind to truth and prefer ignorance.
— have insatiable hunger.	— feed on lies, fears, and imaginations.
— are active day and night.	— can consume a person's thoughts day and night.
— are unsociable.	— withstand offers of help from others.
— can tunnel quickly.	— can burgeon quickly.

A MOLE'S TUNNELS

While it is rare to see a mole at work, his handiwork is quite evident: veins of tunnels visible on the lawn and mounds of dirt can appear overnight. Plants may be uprooted, and cracks may appear in your patio. You may think an army of moles has moved into your yard, but the reality is that it only takes one, and that is probably all there is. But oh, the damage one little mole can do! Like a mole, doubt often lurks below the surface. In our marriages, doubt can feed on a single misspoken word, a careless act, a bad choice, or a whisper of gossip. Something small can grow into a sizable problem, and before you know it, the garden of your marriage is filled with unsightly tunnels and mounds.

Moles dig two types of tunnels: The first is close to the surface and is used for feeding. These are the tunnels that will destroy your plants as the mole burrows around plant roots in search of grubs and worms. Doubt has a similar habit: some couples constantly "dig around" for evidence of anything their spouse *might* have done; they interpret every action through a filter of doubt. Because doubt lives below the surface of their marriage, offenses come easily, and misunderstandings occur frequently. It is exhausting to live with a partner who doubts everything you do. In a marriage, "tunnels" can undermine trust and respect. These are the tunnels close to the surface.

When you interpret every action through a filter of doubt, you will be easily offended.

The deeper tunnels are even more critical. These are where the mole stores its food, builds its nest, breeds, and lives. In our marriages, these deep tunnels are hard to reach, but they are often the source of doubt—they are where doubt really "lives," where it stores its "food." What does your doubt feed on? Is the source of your doubt a deep hurt from childhood, a dysfunctional family, erroneous teaching, bitterness, or lack of forgiveness? If we never get to the deep tunnels, then we won't be able to get rid of the doubt. For it is in these deep, dark tunnels that more doubts are bred. It is to our peril that we ignore doubt or attempt to bury it deeper. We must deal with it.

These tunnels are dangerous: an innocent person may trip on the resultant mounds of dirt or stumble in a hole. Doubt works in the same way; often, children are the unsuspecting victims of their parents' doubts. Children need to feel secure in their parents' relationship. Doubt undermines that security. Doubt is messy, leaving piles of "dirt" everywhere. Your doubts—whether on the surface or farther below—will affect those around you.

These tunnels are also dangerous because other rodents can use them to enter your garden. Rodents will eat your plants and cause serious damage. In the same way, doubt opens the way for lies, fear, disbelief, rebellion, and despair. Consider the similarities between moles' tunnels and doubts:

A MOLE'S TUNNELS...	DOUBTS...
— can be extensive.	— can grow out of proportion.
— are connected to one another.	— can affect other areas of life.
— feeding tunnels are shallow.	— feed even on small, superficial offenses.
— living tunnels are deeper.	— can have deep-rooted causes.
— store food.	— can store past hurts and unforgiveness.
— can destroy foundations.	— can destroy core beliefs and stability.
— can provide other rodents access.	— can open a person to lies, fear, and disbelief.
— can uproot plants.	— can uproot trust.
— can strip away nutrients.	— can lead to unhealthy relationships.
— can cause injury to others.	— can injure other people.
— can destroy a garden.	— can destroy a marriage.

RICK AND AMANDA

Rick and Amanda's marriage was overrun with tunnels of doubt. It started before they were married. They were sexually active when they were dating, and this resulted in a pregnancy. Their relationship was wrought with guilt, shame, blame, accusations, and lack of forgiveness. Their child was born before they married. Rick refused to believe the child was his until a paternity test confirmed that he was the father. Amanda was deeply hurt by his accusations. He later claimed that he married her only because of their child. Shortly after their marriage, both Rick and Amanda recommitted their lives to Christ. And while this should have resulted in a new beginning for them, it did not. The tunnels of doubt ran deep.

Rick often became angry with Amanda over small offenses. When she accidentally misplaced a gift he had given her, he perceived it as rejection. Although the gift eventually was found, Rick constantly scolded her for having lost it. When Amanda asked a male friend of theirs to help with a building project, Rick became furious when he found that the friend had arrived at the house when Rick was not there. Although nothing inappropriate happened, Amanda admitted to having had poor judgment and asked for forgiveness. But Rick wouldn't forgive her and instead accused her of trying to seduce their friend. Even when their friend told Rick that nothing of the sort had happened, Rick wouldn't believe it. Rick had deep "storage tunnels" of doubt and had filled them with hurts, offenses, bitterness, and anger.

In counseling this couple, we found that Rick often refused to hear truth. He preferred living in his dark tunnel of doubt. He called his wife horrible names and accused her of terrible wrongs. And although Amanda was not an angel, neither was she guilty of everything of which he accused her.

We believe that Rick was unable to deal with the deep doubt that started before he and Amanda were married. The sin of their child being born out of wedlock was burdensome to Rick. He was defeated by Satan's weapon: doubt. Rick doubted God would forgive him. This doubt opened him up to believe lies. Because Rick wouldn't accept God's forgiveness, he shifted his guilt to his wife. This led him to believe another lie: that he wasn't responsible for the sin. He claimed she seduced him: "She was the sinful one." Living in a dark tunnel of doubt, Rick allowed lies, bitterness, and despair to enter his marriage. Ultimately, as a result of these doubts and lies, his and Amanda's marriage was destroyed.

Tragically, their daughter was deeply wounded as a result of these tunnels of doubt. Often caught in the middle of her parents' arguments, she grew increasingly insecure. She felt she had to choose sides. She was unable to function well in school and acted aggressively toward other children. She blamed herself for her parents' problems. Fear, anger, deceit, and despair were all evident in her young life. It broke our hearts to see the damage done in this young girl's life—all because of tunnels of doubt that opened her up to lies.

ALEX AND AUDREY

When Alex and Audrey came for counseling, it was difficult to get to the truth. Audrey had been hurt in the past by Alex's actions and habits. But Alex had confessed and was making efforts to change. Audrey claimed she had forgiven Alex, but their problem now was that she couldn't trust him. Everything he did went through her filter of doubt. As we sat with this couple, it became clear that Audrey was overwhelmed by her imagination. The mole of doubt doesn't like light, and Audrey seemed to prefer living in the dark. Confronted by the truth, she would "run back to her dark tunnel" by expressing her fear that Alex might fail again. Alex felt that no matter what he did, Audrey was apt to misconstrue it. Her tunnels of doubt were undermining trust, to the point that Alex felt that their marriage had lost its foundation. The biggest problem seemed to be Audrey's fear of what might happen—the "what ifs." Doubt had tunneled into her garden, and fear had crept in. Trust was destroyed because Alex might do something wrong again!

Miles of tunnels had been built, and because they were so interconnected, Alex couldn't do anything right. We encouraged Audrey to verbalize her doubts and Alex to learn to listen to her. Because he perceived her doubts as false and even ridiculous, he wasn't very understanding. Alex and Audrey needed to learn better communication skills. Alex also needed to become more "transparent" with his wife. Because Audrey was always suspicious, Alex had started hiding even small things from her; he was afraid she would make mountains out of molehills. But his lack of openness and honesty was hindering healing in their marriage.

Audrey needed to confront her doubts and fears honestly. There will always be things in our lives that we cannot control. In spite of our partner's good intentions, he or she will disappoint and hurt us—as we will him or her. We all are human, and we all make mistakes. But we cannot allow doubt to rule in our hearts, for this only opens us up to fear and despair. For these reasons, we challenged Audrey to give her doubts and fears to Jesus—to place her complete trust in Him and to commit her husband fully into His hands.

GETTING RID OF MOLES

A quick Internet search turns up some interesting and even humorous remedies for getting rid of moles. Our favorite is: put chewing gum into the mole's hole. Supposedly, the mole will chew the gum, blow a bubble and suffocate itself! The truth is that it is extremely difficult to get rid of them. Even if you rid your yard of one, another is likely to move in and take over. (Some farmers have been known to catch as many as 100 moles in a year!)

When I was a boy, we had moles in our backyard. My dad would go outside and stomp down all the mounds and surface tunnels in an effort to smooth the lawn. But the reality was that he didn't get rid of the moles. By the next morning, new mounds would have popped up, and out my dad would go again, attacking the mounds with relish but accomplishing nothing. Many couples treat doubt the same way: They attack its symptoms but do nothing to eliminate doubt itself.

Getting rid of moles—and doubts—requires radical action. Moles—and doubts—must either be captured or killed. They cannot merely be repelled or scared away. And as my dad discovered, you can't just stomp down the symptomatic mounds of dirt and ignore the underlying problem. Moles—and doubts—must be removed completely.

It is important to repeat that *doubt is not sin*. Doubt can be a "signpost" in our relationships. For example, a wife may sense that her husband is getting too friendly with a woman at work. She may begin to doubt his actions and his explanations for working late. What should she do in response to her doubts? Lovingly and directly, she should share them with her husband. She should openly communicate her concerns but without making unsubstantiated accusations. The Lord may be giving the wife insight into a possibly dangerous situation. It is a wise husband who will listen to his wife's concerns and address them.

Mary Lou and I learned the hard way how important it is to deal openly with our doubts. A number of years ago, we had the opportunity to buy a piece of land that was supposed to be a good investment. Mary Lou had serious doubts about the wisdom of this purchase, especially because we didn't have the finances we needed. But she didn't share her doubts with me because she thought it would be disrespectful. We purchased the land on credit, and it turned out to be a terrible investment.

The property value plummeted soon after we bought the land, and we lost a lot of money. This was a difficult but important lesson for us as it changed one of our core values: We agreed that we never would purchase anything or make any major decision unless we were 100 percent in agreement and were "doubt free." The Lord had given Mary Lou insight that I didn't have. Her doubt should have been a red flag for us. So how should we deal with doubts?

The first step in getting rid of doubts is to face them head-on: speak the truth. Talk about it. Share your doubts with each other. Do not ignore them or pretend they don't exist. Communication is not easy, but it is vital that you learn to communicate properly with each other. It is possible that your partner is lacking some basic information that will help clear the air. Paul writes in Ephesians 4:14, 15 "that we should no longer be children, tossed to and fro and carried about with every wind of doctrine, by the trickery of men, in the cunning craftiness of deceitful plotting, but, speaking the truth in love, may grow up in all things into Him who is the head—Christ." Be truthful with each other. Be honest about doubts. But speak the truth in love! Truth should never be a weapon. But it also should not be buried in tunnels of doubt.

First, face doubt head-on!

Keep short "lists." Don't allow days to go by without addressing problems, concerns, or doubts. When you sense that something is wrong, talk about it right away. If you find yourself doubting something your spouse did, then ask questions. (I wish I could say that Tim and I always ask nicely, but sometimes our emotions get in the way!) Make it your goal to address doubts and not allow any other enemies to attack your marriage. It is not always easy, but the effort, discomfort, and hard work are well worth it. Face your doubts head-on and speak the truth.

The next step in getting rid of doubt is to look deeper. Is there something in your past that is allowing doubts to breed? Have you failed to obey the first rule of marriage *(leave father and mother)* and so carry a lot of emotional baggage? Perhaps your father or mother was not trustworthy, and now you find it difficult to trust your spouse. You may have experienced some trauma during your childhood. You may need to prayerfully re-examine your past to determine if there are situations you have not let go of. You may need to ask your husband or wife to help you process some of these memories in order to identify the source of your doubt. (Remember: If you are trying to help your partner resolve deep-

Second, look for deeper tunnels.

seeded doubts, the best thing you can do is to just ask questions and listen. You don't need to "fix" the problem. Rather, allow your spouse to talk about past struggles. Often, healing comes as a result of honestly examining the past and then choosing to let go of it.) You or your spouse also may need to seek professional help—a Christian counselor or pastor—to help resolve doubts. Remember that moles capture their food close to the surface in feeding tunnels, but they store the food in the deeper tunnels, where they build their nests and live. If you are struggling with unreasonable doubts, then it is quite possible that you need to look deeper.

The third step is to capture and eliminate doubt. Once you have spoken the truth, sought and identified any missing information that might resolve the problem, and addressed any underlying issues from your past, then it is time to make a choice. You don't have to live with doubt. Doubt is an emotion. You can choose to take it captive. In 2 Corinthians 10:5, Paul writes, "Casting down imaginations, and every high thing that exalteth itself against the knowledge of God, and bringing into captivity every thought to the obedience of Christ" (KJV). The Greek word translated 'imagination' is *logismos,* which is related to the Greek word *dialogismos.* Paul uses strong imagery: "casting down" (don't allow doubt to have a position of power in your life) and "bringing into captivity" (when doubt rears its ugly head, capture it!). This requires making a choice. But simply relying on will-power is not sufficient: **Where do you take these captured thoughts? You take them to Jesus!**

This verse has become my (Mary Lou's) call to action. I don't sit by and allow moles to tunnel into my marriage or personal life. I take doubts captive and bring them to Jesus in prayer. When a thought pops up its head, I grab it, and take it to Jesus in prayer. I might pray, "Jesus, I don't want this thought in my life. I know it is wrong. I am struggling with getting rid of it. But I am choosing to bring it to you now. And the next time it comes to mind, I will bring it to you again. I choose not to dwell on this thought but to rebuke it. I don't want this thought to take

Your place in my life. Help me, Jesus. Amen." And when that thought comes to mind again, I pray again! Sometimes I have spent hours praying, "capturing," and praying again. The great thing is that my prayer life has been enriched! But I also discovered that as I faithfully continued to bring my doubts to Jesus, they slowly lost their hold over me.

Imagine what might have happened in the Garden of Eden had Eve taken her doubts to God.

> *Third, capture and eliminate doubt.*

"Casting all your care upon Him, for He cares for you. Be sober, be vigilant; because your adversary the devil walks about like a roaring lion, seeking whom he may devour. Resist him, steadfast in the faith, knowing that the same sufferings are experienced by your brotherhood in the world" (1 Peter 5:7–9). When we "cast all our care upon Him," we bring Him our doubts and fears and worries. We submit to His authority in our life. We acknowledge our trust in His loving care. That is how we get rid of moles!

LIES

The Serpent started by presenting Eve with a doubt: "Did God *really* say that?" And once Eve had opened the door to doubt, Satan boldly announced lies. Eve probably wouldn't have believed the Serpent had he started by saying, "You won't really die if you eat this fruit." The Serpent used doubt to undermine the authority of God in Eve's life, which led her to listen to the lies. In the same way, we are not usually confronted with a bold-faced lie in our marriages. Lies enter subtly. For example, a man who has an affair typically doesn't wake up one morning and decide to cheat on his wife. Chances are good that he has been wrestling with doubts for some time. "Does my wife really love me? Is it really wrong to be 'just friends' with my female co-worker? Doesn't God want me to be happy?" Rather than doing something about his doubts, he ignored them and the "tunnels" grew. Lies took hold of his thinking: "My wife never loved me. My co-worker is the only one who understands me. I have the right to be happy at any cost."

Jesus calls Satan the father of lies in John 8:44b: "He [Satan] was a murderer from the beginning, and does not stand in the truth, because there is no truth in him. When he speaks a lie, he speaks from his own resources, for he is a liar and the father of it." From the beginning of time

Satan has used the weapon of lies. We compare this enemy with another enemy of the garden: mice.

MICE

Field mice are one of the most destructive rodents in the garden. Mice will eat plants, seeds, fruit, bark—anything. They are fast and clever nocturnal scavengers. They can squeeze through even a well-built fence and are able to blend in with their surroundings. Mice gnaw constantly. They can chew through even hard wood or plastic. They are prolific breeders. Mice not only will destroy your garden, but they also can contaminate your food as they can carry parasites and disease.

Mice are more damaging to a garden than moles! (Moles are not rodents and do not eat plants.) But moles' tunnels often provide mice with the means of entry into a garden. Consider the similarity to doubts and lies: Where moles provide points of entry for mice, so Satan attacks marriage partners first with doubts, which open the way to lies. There are numerous parallels between mice in a garden and lies in a marriage:

- *Lies enter our lives through the "tunnel" of doubts.*
- *Lies often are small and seemingly harmless.*
- *Lies can "squeeze through" even small cracks in our defences.*
- *Lies are prolific: one breeds another.*
- *Lies prefer the dark; the light of truth exposes them.*
- *Lies can masquerade as something "good."*
- *Lies can contaminate everything.*
- *Lies bring illness and disease.*
- *Lies are destructive.*

How can we defeat this fifth enemy in the garden? Allow us to reiterate that we must deal first with doubt because it is the "tunnel" through which lies often enter. (The majority of this chapter is focused on doubt because it is often Satan's first means of attack.)

Paul spoke to the church at Ephesus about how to defeat Satan:

"Finally, my brethren, be strong in the Lord and in the power of His might. Put on the whole armor of God, that you may be able to stand against the wiles of the devil. Therefore take up the whole

armor of God, that you may be able to withstand in the evil day, and having done all, to stand. Stand therefore, having girded your waist with truth, having put on the breastplate of righteousness, and having shod your feet with the preparation of the gospel of peace; above all, taking the shield of faith with which you will be able to quench all the fiery darts of the wicked one. And take the helmet of salvation, and the sword of the Spirit, which is the word of God; praying always with all prayer and supplication in the Spirit, being watchful to this end with all perseverance and supplication for all the saints" (Ephesians 6:10–11,13–18).

How do we protect our marriages with this "armor?" Let's examine Satan's lies and replace them with God's truth.

Principle 1: Find your strength in the Lord and in His power.
Satan's lie: *"It's too late. You've tried before and failed."*
God's truth: *"In your weakness, I am strong"* (2 Corinthians 12:9).
When you replace Satan's lies with God's truth, you acknowledge that you cannot fight for your marriage in your own strength or power. Humbly ask the Lord to help you, confess your need to rely solely on Him, and repent of your self-reliant attitudes.

Principle 2: Use the defensive weapons God has provided.
Satan's lie: *"God's ways don't work. You should take a 'self-help' course."*
God's truth: *"I have given you all you need; now use it"* (2 Peter 1:3).
The key is to use the "weapons" God has already given you. Shiny armor on display in the corner of your house won't protect you in battle! Put it on!

Principle 3: Take all the armor of God.
Satan's lie: *"God doesn't expect you to obey everything He says. Some of that Bible teaching doesn't really apply to you."*
God's truth: *"If you love Me, you will obey Me"* (John 14:23).
Don't pick and choose: Take all God has prepared for you! Decide to fight for your marriage. Not only will you use the armor God has provided, but you will use all of it.

Principle 4: Truth is like a belt.

Satan's lie: *"There are no absolutes, no rights or wrongs. Do what you think is right for your marriage. You don't need to be truthful with your spouse."*

God's truth: *"My Son, Jesus, is the source of real truth. The truth I give you will bring freedom and light"* (John 14:6, John 8:32, 1 John 1:6).

When a Roman soldier went into battle, he gathered up the edges of his toga and tucked them into his belt to keep from tripping on his skirt. This is the analogy of the belt of truth: It keeps us from "tripping." It should be ever-present, surrounding us and keeping us from falling. Proper use of the belt of truth requires spending time in God's Word reading, meditating on, and memorizing verses for the express purpose of replacing the lies of Satan. Surround yourself with truth, and refuse to accede to the world's standards. This might require not watching TV shows that promote ungodly values about marriage. You may need to break off relationships with friends who encourage you to disregard God's ways. In their place, intentionally seek godly friends and fellowship, which will draw you closer to God. You also must be willing to listen to your spouse about the truth of your actions. Even when it is painful or difficult, lovingly seek after truth.

Principle 5: Righteousness is like a breastplate.

Satan's lie: *"You are not as bad as your spouse. Your spouse doesn't deserve forgiveness."*

God's truth: *"You are a sinner saved by My grace. Be merciful. Forgive others as I have forgiven you"* (Matthew 6:14, Romans 5:8).

The Roman soldier used a breastplate to protect his chest, including his heart and other vital organs. Our hearts are protected by the righteousness we have received from Jesus: Through His death and resurrection, Jesus covers us with His righteousness and brings us into a righteous relationship *(right standing)* with God. When you place yourself under the righteousness of Jesus, you will find yourself equipped to be merciful toward and forgiving of your spouse. You didn't earn the breastplate of righteousness; it is God's gift to you. Growing in your understanding of God's grace and mercy will help you be more patient and merciful toward your spouse. When your emotions are exposed and vulnerable, choose to cover yourself with the breastplate of His righteousness.

Principle 6: Put on the "shoes" of the Gospel of peace.

Satan's lie: *"You need to think about yourself first. Do what makes you happy."*

God's truth: *"You have been bought with the blood of Jesus. I have a job for you to do. Go and share this Gospel of peace with others"* (Romans 12:1, 1 Corinthians 6:20).

Proper footwear enables a soldier to march, run, or fight. When a soldier is in battle, he doesn't kick off his shoes and relax! Similarly, we must put on our shoes and get moving! Our motivation for action must be to share the Good News with others. The real purpose of your marriage is to model Jesus' love for the world and to share this good news *(literally, "Gospel")* with others. When you embrace the purpose of your marriage, you will be able to focus on a common objective of glorifying God. More important, you'll stop listening to Satan's lie that you should "only think of yourself."

Principle 7: Take up the shield of faith.

Satan's lie: *"You can't trust God to help you. God doesn't hear your prayers."*

God's truth: *"I will never leave you nor forsake you. I keep My promises"* (Hebrews 13:5-6, Psalm 105:8).

A shield can be positioned to protect any vulnerable part of the body from attack. Our faith needs to be like that: alive and active. Faith cannot be passive. In the midst of a failing marriage, it is hard to believe that anything can ever change. Yet God is the God of the impossible. There may be times when you can't see God at work, but faith believes that God is able to do above and beyond what you ask or even think. "Now to Him who is able to do exceedingly abundantly above all that we ask or think, according to the power that works in us" (Ephesians 3:20). Faith is based not on what our eyes see or on what our emotions feel. Instead, believing and trusting in the power of God to save, redeem, and restore, we hide behind the shield of faith.

Principle 8: Wear the helmet of salvation.

Satan's lie: *"Your little daydreams are harmless." Or, "You need to think like the rest of the world."*

God's truth: *"My ways are not your ways, and My thoughts are not your thoughts"* (Isaiah 55:8).

Satan loves to manipulate our thoughts, especially with regard to marriage. We must not allow negative thoughts about our spouse to go unchecked. We must learn to fill our minds with thankful, worshipful, uplifting thoughts (Philippians 4:8). Jesus said, "But I say to you that whoever looks at a woman to lust for her has already committed adultery with her in his heart" (Matthew 5:28). "For as he thinks in his heart, so is he" (Proverbs 23:7a). If you have allowed sinful fantasies to roam wild in your mind, then you already are caught in a deadly snare. The chances are good that you will fall. Protect your thoughts by putting on the helmet of salvation! Allow God to renew your mind (Romans 12:2). Take every thought captive and bring it to Jesus (2 Corinthians 10:5).

Principle 9: The sword of the Spirit is the Word of God.

Satan's lie: *"You don't need to study the Bible. It is outdated. Modern psychology is more applicable for today."*

God's truth: *"My Word is powerful. My Word never changes. My Word can change you"* (Psalm 119).

The best defense against Satan is a good offense! For every temptation that Satan threw at Jesus in the wilderness, Jesus counterattacked with God's Word. The best way to defeat the lies of Satan is to replace them with God's truth. You must know God's Word and use it correctly if you are to win the battle against Satan and his lies. It is not enough to simply tell Satan he is wrong. God's Word must become a priority in your marriage. It must be the standard for your actions. The sword of the Spirit is an offensive weapon. Don't leave it sitting on a shelf covered with dust.

Principle 10: Prayer.

Satan's lie: *"God doesn't care about your little problems. You don't need to ask God what to do. Try to figure it out yourself. God helps those who help themselves."*

God's truth: *"Bring me your burdens—big or small—because I care for you. Commit your ways to Me. I delight in helping you"* (1 Peter 5:7, Philippians 4:6).

Pray for your spouse—not a critical, judgmental prayer—but rather pray for him/her to grow strong in Jesus. Pray for God to open your eyes to see the truth about your mistakes and responsibility. Be willing to confess and repent. Choose to pray together for your marriage. It may be difficult at first, but together, through prayer, you and your spouse can defeat Satan's lies. As you draw near to God together, Satan will flee (James 4:7–8)!

PREVENTATIVE MEASURES:

Slow Down!

Most garden experts will tell you that preventative measures go a long way toward ensuring that your garden remains free of moles and rodents. A garden that is overwatered may attract moles because the soil is easier for them to tunnel through. And moist soil means an abundant food supply. An overgrown garden provides plenty of places to hide, build nests, and reproduce.

An overwatered or overgrown garden is out of balance. Too much of anything can be unhealthy. "Overwatered" or "overgrown" marriages may be the result of too much busyness. When our schedules are so overloaded that we don't have time to talk, doubts can take root simply because we haven't spent time with each other. As doubts grow, lies may gain a foothold.

> *Don't overwater your marriage with busyness.*

We live in an age when everything seems to be instant, high speed, and automatic. Unfortunately, our marriages often bear the brunt of the frantic pace we keep. Neither instant nor automatic, good marriages require the investment of time. We hear couples say, "We may not have much quantity of time for each other, but we do have quality time." That is just plain wrong! Both quality and quantity of time with your spouse are needful. What good is it to live in a luxurious home that necessitates both of you working overtime if you are never there at the same time to enjoy it? You are overwatering your garden! You are letting it become overgrown! Doubts and lies can arise readily when you don't have time to connect with each other.

245

Slow down! Make time for each other. Be sure you take a day off. Play together. Eat together. Laugh together. You may need to radically adjust your lifestyle—and perhaps even get rid of some "stuff"—but investing in your marriage is worth it!

WHEN TRUST IS BROKEN

As we conclude this chapter on doubts and lies, we want to address an important issue: broken trust. For example, perhaps you trusted your husband but discovered that he is addicted to gambling. Perhaps he lost all of your savings. Does this mean you should allow him to take more money from the family, even knowing that he most likely will gamble it away? No: It is legitimate to tell your spouse, "I doubt I can trust you. You have repeatedly broken my trust. I love you and forgive you, but this does not mean that I can permit this destructive behavior to continue." Love does what is best for the other—and it is not "best" when you allow harmful, abusive, or addictive behavior to continue.

Some situations demand firm responses. For example, if your husband is an alcoholic and becomes abusive when he is drunk, it is correct and proper to seek protection and legal advice. Although we do not suggest a divorce, a separation may be necessary in order to protect your children or yourself from injury. A separation also may be important for your husband to realize the seriousness of his actions. It is important in these situations to stop enabling his addiction. You must confront him and establish clear boundaries. At times, love must be tough. Love says, "I love you so much that I cannot allow you to continue to destroy yourself and our marriage."

But what do we do when our spouse has repeatedly broken our trust and then asks us to trust him again? How do we restore broken trust? How do we keep doubts and lies out of our garden but at the same time walk wisely through a difficult situation? Both partners must take certain steps in order to rebuild a "house" of trust. It is difficult but not impossible.

The partner who has broken trust:
- Must lay a **foundation of honesty and openness**. Deceit has played a pivotal role in breaking trust. You must confess your sin without

shifting blame or accusing anyone else. Allow the injured party to ask questions. Hiding the truth can result in doubt cracking the foundation. This does not mean you need to provide vivid details about your sin. Nevertheless, you must be willing to answer questions truthfully.

- Must erect **walls of accountability**. You must be willing to be accountable to your spouse. This may mean sacrificing things you enjoy. For example, if gambling is the sin of which you are guilty, you should give your spouse control of all bank accounts and credit cards. If you are serious about rebuilding trust, then you have to be willing to change old habits—even some you perceive as harmless. It is also a good idea to have another close friend or pastor as an accountability partner.
- Must build a **roof of affirmation**. Your partner needs to hear words of reassurance. This will take time. Remind your spouse of your love and of your earnest desire to change. Be patient with your partner's apprehension.

The partner who has been injured:
- Must **build a foundation of forgiveness.** It will be difficult to do so, but relying on God's love and mercy and remembering that you, too, are a forgiven sinner may help you extend grace to your spouse. Forgiveness is a choice, not an emotion. Once you and your spouse have engaged in honest discussion about the past, choose not to bring it up again. Let it go. Reminding your spouse of what he or she has done will undermine forgiveness.
- Must erect **walls of faith.** Only God is worthy of our complete trust. Our faith must rest on Him alone. It is vitally important to commit your partner to God. However, you also must choose to believe the best about your partner and not automatically assume the worse. Earnestly seek the good in your partner, and focus on positive changes. Communicate your faith in your partner and in his or her ability to change. He will need to know you haven't given up on him...or he may give up on himself.
- Must build a **roof of affirmation**. "Above all things have fervent love for one another, for 'love will cover a multitude of sins'" (1 Peter 4:8).

Communicate your love and support to your partner. Time is necessary to heal deep wounds, but choose to show acts of love.

These three steps are only the beginning. It is critical to remember that rebuilding trust takes time. Demanding forgiveness or making statements such as "Just get over it. I said I was sorry" will never allow for healing. It also may be necessary to take specific action steps: make restitution, join a support group, break off unhealthy relationships, perhaps even change jobs. Often, the hurt and betrayal are so deep that a biblical counselor or pastor may need to be enlisted to help bring healing. Be willing to take whatever steps are necessary to restore trust in your marriage.

DOUBTS AND LIES

It starts with Doubt hissing in your ear "Maybe we shouldn't have gotten married in the first place." Then the Lie turns up the volume: "It's too late. Divorce is the only option." You can almost hear the Serpent's sneering laugh as he incites you to question the power of God and the Holy Spirit to do a new work in your marriage. The Serpent repeats that same old doubt: "Did God really say that?" And he follows it up with a lie: "God doesn't care about you." It's time you grab these critters by their tails and cast them out of your garden!

STUDY GUIDE

Read 1 Kings 18:21; James 1:6; Romans 14:23;
Matthew 15:19; 2 Corinthians 10:5;
Ephesians 6:10–11 and 13–18

William Shakespeare wrote, "Our doubts are traitors and make us lose the good we oft might win, by fearing to attempt."[2] We learned in this chapter that doubt is an enemy we must address. Doubt is not sin in and of itself, and it can be a motivator to seek truth. But it is something we must deal with because it opens the door to another enemy: lies.

In Deuteronomy 28:65–67, we read the curses that would befall the children of Israel if they refused to follow God:

> "And among those nations you shall *find no rest*, nor shall the sole of your foot have a resting place; but there the LORD will give you a *trembling heart, failing eyes, and anguish of soul*. Your *life shall hang in doubt* before you; you shall fear day and night, and have no assurance of life. In the morning you shall say, "Oh, that it were evening!" And at evening you shall say, "Oh, that it were morning!" because of the *fear which terrifies your heart*, and because of the sight which your eyes see."

This is an apt description of what can happen when doubt is not addressed correctly. (Reread the italicized words.) In this passage we read the curses that would come upon the nation if its people started to doubt God—His power, His goodness, and His authority in their lives. Doubt provides the "tunnels" through which lies can enter the gardens of our marriages. Doubts and lies are destructive when we ignore them, bury them, or adopt the mindset that they aren't so bad. Let's dig a little deeper.

DIGGING DEEPER

1. Write your own definition of doubt.

2. The Latin word for doubt is *dubius,* which is related to the words 'duo' and _____.

   a. What two things are referred to in 1 Kings 18:21?

   b. What two things are referred to in James 1:6?

   c. What two things was Eve wavering between in the Garden?

3. What is the key point in Romans 14:23?

4. Provide some examples of how Jesus addressed doubt.

5. What warning does Jesus give in Matthew 15:19? Apply this verse to marriage.

6. Choose five comparisons between moles and doubts that you can relate to.

    a.

    b.

    c.

    d.

    e.

7. What two types of tunnels do moles dig?

    a.

    b.

8. How do these two tunnels relate to marriage?

    a.

    b.

9. Tunnels can be dangerous because:

    a.

    b.

    c.

10. What other enemies can the tunnels of doubt allow to enter your marriage?

11. What foundations in marriage can be destroyed by tunnels of doubt?

12. Who else can be injured by tunnels of doubt?

13. What are three steps for eliminating doubt?

    a.

    b.

    c.

14. Paraphrase 2 Corinthians 10:5.

15. What recurring doubts do you struggle with? Are they rooted in deeper sources (e.g., your past, false teaching, lack of forgiveness, etc.)? What is your action plan for dealing with these doubts?

16. Perhaps you believe that doubt is not a problem in your marriage. Read the following list and check as many as apply:

☐ I have secretly looked in my spouse's computer/phone/etc. to check on his or her activities.

☐ I have browsed Facebook (or another social network) to look up a former boyfriend or girlfriend.

☐ I have thought it was a mistake to marry my spouse.

☐ I find myself seeking to live in the past and have many regrets (e.g., "if only," "I should have," etc.).

☐ I have inwardly or outwardly considered divorce.

☐ I feel insecure when my spouse and I are with friends—especially if we are with someone I perceive as being more attractive or desirable than I am.

☐ If my spouse is late in calling or coming home, I often assume the worst.

☐ My spouse thinks I am untrustworthy.

☐ I think my spouse is untrustworthy.

☐ My spouse thinks I make mountains out of molehills.

☐ My thoughts are often consumed with worry about money.

☐ Without constant reassuring and approval, I feel like a failure.

☐ I am often suspicious of my spouse's motivations.

☐ I don't really believe God can save my marriage.

☐ I usually view life negatively—i.e., "the glass is half empty."

☐ I am afraid to tell my spouse how I really feel.

☐ I keep secrets from my spouse.

17. What are some of the comparisons between mice and lies to which you can relate?

18. According to Ephesians 6:10–11 and 13–18, what are the ten principles for defeating Satan?

   1.

   2.

   3.

   4.

   5.

   6.

   7.

   8.

   9.

  10.

19. Name one of Satan's lies that you have struggled with in your marriage. How can you fight it?

20. If broken trust is an issue in your marriage, reread the steps to restoring trust. Devise a plan of action and specify steps you and your spouse will take together.

CHAPTER ELEVEN

MAN AND WOMAN
IN THE GARDEN

Submission

SUBMIT! We can almost hear the sound of women everywhere gritting their teeth and sneering. How can one word cause so much turmoil? This word is greatly misunderstood in our culture today, and Christianity is often held in contempt because of unbiblical teaching about submission in marriage. Critics and antagonists point their finger at Christians, calling them intolerant, brutish, and tyrannical.

We suspect that many who read this chapter will have preconceived notions of what it means to submit. Your opinions may have been formed by your family values, religious traditions, cultural mores, and personal experience. Unfortunately, there has been a lot of bad teaching about submission by Bible-thumping extremists who love to take verses out of context and create their own biased theology.

Don't misunderstand us: We are unashamedly and radically committed to the Bible. However, we firmly believe in the importance of teaching all of God's Word in context.

In this chapter, we examine Biblical submission. We challenge you to set aside any preconceived notions about submission that you may have. We invite you to prayerfully consider what God has to say about submission and to align yourself and your marriage with His ways.

Certainly, submission is a difficult topic. Nevertheless, let us begin by jumping into the pool of controversy with both feet, with eyes wide open, *and perhaps holding our breath!*

WHAT SUBMISSION IS NOT

Before we define submission, we want to clarify what submission is NOT!

Submission is not: slavery – abuse – tyranny – dictatorship – bullying. It is a clear distortion of God's Word to claim that a wife must submit like a slave to an abusive husband. A man who demands that his wife gratify his every whim is treating her like a possession. This is not God's plan for marriage, and it is not Biblical submission! Submission is also not dictatorship or tyranny. We believe in the roles of leadership within the family, but a leader according to God's design is never a dictator! Jesus is the head of the Church, and Jesus NEVER beat His Church! Indeed, the concept of "beating someone into submission" is completely unbiblical.

Submission is not: repression – abandoning intellect – rejecting godliness. God's Word is consistent throughout: our first allegiance is to God and God alone. When the behavior of any leader or government is contrary to God's Word, we are to obey God first. This is equally true in the family. Should a wife silently follow her husband as he leads the family into obvious sin? NO! Should she repress her God-given knowledge and insights, keeping her mouth shut under the guise of being submissive? NO! Should a wife offer her husband a "blank check" to sin as much as he wants to because she must submit? Absolutely not!

Submission is not: based on inequality or inferiority – demeaning – one-sided. The Biblical mandate to submit is not based on the idea that one person has more worth than the other. It is erroneous to claim that the wife must submit to her husband because he is superior to her in strength, intellect, or spirituality. This does NOT describe Biblical submission! God's Word is clear regarding the equality of man and woman. Anyone who attempts to claim otherwise perverts God's Word. If we embrace Biblical submission, we will not find ourselves in a demeaning situation; rather, we will enjoy real freedom.

WHAT SUBMISSION IS

When Christians discuss submission, they most often refer to Ephesians 5:22: "Wives, submit yourselves unto your own husbands, as unto the Lord" (KJV). You may react to this verse with disdain, disbelief, or disregard, or you may feel justified in your practice of demanding that your wife obey.

First, we want to caution against taking any verse out of context. Far too often, when a disgruntled husband comes to us complaining that his wife is not submissive, he flips open his Bible to this passage and jabs his finger at verse 22. "Tell my wife she must obey me," he barks. The problem is that he isn't reading the verse in context. We typically suggest that he begin reading a few verses earlier in Ephesians 5, at verse 17:

"Therefore do not be unwise, but understand what the will of the Lord is. And do not be drunk with wine, in which is dissipation; but be filled with the Spirit, speaking to one another in psalms and hymns and spiritual songs, singing and making melody in your heart to the Lord, giving thanks always for all things to God the Father in the name of our Lord Jesus Christ, submitting to one another in the fear of God" (Ephesians 5:17–21).

Consider these verses one phrase at a time:

"Therefore do not be unwise, but understand what the will of the Lord is." This passage teaches about wisdom and understanding. (So far so good!)

"And do not be drunk with wine, in which is dissipation; but be filled with the Spirit." Being 'drunk' refers to the condition of allowing something else to control you. In this passage, wine is the explicit example, but 'being drunk' applies to anything that controls us, be it drugs, sex, money, or power. History is littered with the horrific results of men "drunk" on power. The King James Version uses the word 'excess' rather than "dissipation." Excessive alcohol, drugs, or power leads to disaster. A husband who is a tyrant in his marriage exerts excessive power and so is out of control. The antithesis of such behavior is to be filled with the Holy Spirit. The point we want to underline here is that the Holy Spirit is to control us.

"Speaking to one another in psalms and hymns and spiritual songs, singing and making melody in your heart to the Lord, giving thanks always for all things to God the Father in the name of our Lord Jesus Christ." Most abusive husbands who demand absolute servitude from their wives could never be described as speaking to their wives in this way. Most men who bully their wives are anything but thankful. Our homes—not just churches— should be filled with worship! Now read the phrase that comes next:

"Submitting to one another in the fear of God." "In the fear of God" reveals our motivation for submitting. Submission shows our respect for God and brings Him—and only Him—honor and glory! When submission is misunderstood, one partner gets glory while the other is downtrodden. In contrast, proper submission, in which God is exalted—is pleasing to God.

> *Submission shows our respect for God and brings Him— and only Him—honor and glory!*

"Submitting to one another" is an interesting phrase. Before wives are admonished to submit to their husbands, *all* believers—male and female—are commanded *to submit to one another.* The command to submit is not just for wives. In fact, the same Greek word translated "submit" that is used in Ephesians 5:21 is also used in the following verse (vs. 22): "wives, submit yourselves to your own husband."

The same Greek word is used as well in 1 Peter 5:5: "Likewise you younger people, *submit* yourselves to your elders. Yes, all of you be *submissive* to one another, and be clothed with humility, for 'God resists the proud, but gives grace to the humble.'"

Wives are *not* singled out for submission. Rather, submission is a Biblical principle required of all believers, men, women, and children. Men with chauvinistic tendencies and women with stubborn independent streaks must consider carefully the admonition for *all* believers to submit to one another.

What does it mean for believers to submit to one another? Five definitions for submission are as follows:

1. I allow you to do for me what your responsibility is to do.
2. I place myself under the command of a leader.

3. I choose to voluntarily surrender my rights and self-interests.
4. I freely offer my gifts, talents, abilities, and knowledge.
5. I must obey God first.

Submission means:
I allow you to do for me what your responsibility is to do.

Tim loves the first definition, which we believe puts submission into the proper perspective. Now apply this definition in the context of several situations. For example, when you go to church and listen to your pastor, you submit to him. You allow him to do for you what his responsibility is to do: to teach you God's Word. When your doctor prescribes medication for an illness you have and you follow his treatment plan, you submit to him. You allow him to do for you what his responsibility is to do: to treat you when you are ill.

We can apply this same definition to many different relationships. Imagine that you are a salesperson for a company that produces computers. You submit to the designers who develop the computers you sell in so far as you allow them to do their jobs (as a salesperson, you don't take over product development). Similarly, you submit to the bookkeeper who manages the accounts and pays the invoices (as well as your salary!). You submit as well to the shipping department, which is responsible for distribution.

This may seem simplistic, but we want to demonstrate that submission is *not* based on one individual being more "valuable" than another. Peter continues, "and be clothed with humility" (1 Peter 5:5). Often, we are unable to submit to one another because of pride. Unwilling to allow another person to do for us what he is supposed to do, we try instead to be a "one-man show." Usually this is based on the egotistical attitude described by the thought, "I can do it better myself! I don't need any help!" But this attitude is not in line with the Biblical concept of submission. God has placed other people in your life who can contribute much to you if only you allow them to! Whether at church, in the workplace, or in our marriages, unwillingness to submit to another can destroy relationships and can result in ineffectiveness and even chaos.

Nature provides evidence of the perfection of God's design. He created a natural order. From the symbiotic relationships of various species to the beautiful harmony of our own human bodies, God demonstrates Himself to be a God of order. So it is not surprising that He established order in marriage. (In the following two chapters, we consider in greater detail the roles and responsibilities within marriage; we hope this will clarify God's design.)

Submission means:
I place myself under the command of a leader.

The New Testament Greek word translated 'submit' is *hupotasso*, which means "to arrange under, to subordinate, to subject, to obey, to submit to one's control, to yield to one's admonition or advice."[1] Further understanding derives from an understanding of Greek culture: *Hupotasso* is also "a Greek military term meaning 'to arrange [troop divisions] in a military fashion under the command of a leader.' In non-military use, it was 'a voluntary attitude of giving in, cooperating, assuming responsibility, and carrying a burden.'"[2] Just as military troops are organized according to a chain of command, so our marriages must be built upon a structure of responsibility and leadership. This does not presume dictatorship; rather, it refers to an understanding of roles and responsibilities.

The problem many encounter when they read this definition of submission is that their understanding of leadership is warped. Too many leaders are guilty of abusing their power and authority. We need to review what the Bible says about leadership if we are to understand this definition of submission.

1 Peter 5:1–4 teaches about Biblical leadership:

"The elders who are among you I exhort, I who am a fellow elder and a witness of the sufferings of Christ, and also a partaker of the glory that will be revealed: Shepherd the flock of God which is among you, serving as overseers, not by compulsion but willingly, not for dishonest gain but eagerly; nor as being lords over those entrusted to you, but being examples to the flock; and when the Chief Shepherd appears, you will receive the crown of glory that does not fade away."

"Shepherd" is the key word that stands out in this text. In the Old and New Testaments, the word was often used figuratively to mean 'leader.' Ezekiel 34:2–4 says,

"Thus says the Lord GOD to the shepherds: "Woe to the shepherds of Israel who feed themselves! Should not the shepherds feed the flocks? You [shepherds] eat the fat and clothe yourselves with the wool; you slaughter the fatlings, but you do not feed the flock. The weak you have not strengthened, nor have you healed those who were sick, nor bound up the broken, nor brought back what was driven away, nor sought what was lost; but with force and cruelty you have ruled them."

Here we learn God's expectations for leaders: They are to feed the flock, strengthen the weak, heal the sick, bind up the broken, bring back what was driven away, seek the lost, and never rule with force or cruelty. In short:

1. The leader should put the needs of others above his own.
2. The leader should be committed to strengthening, healing, and restoring those in his care.
3. The leader should not rule with force or cruelty.

Think about these standards with regard to submission. Wives, would it be difficult to submit to the loving care of this kind of leader? Of course not! These are the requirements God sets for leaders, whether of the church or of the home. Women often struggle with the concept of submission because their husbands do not understand the concept of Biblical leadership.

The Bible is replete with descriptions of the shepherd who lovingly leads his sheep. Isaiah 40:11 compares God to a Shepherd: "He will feed His flock like a shepherd; He will gather the lambs with His arm, and carry them in His bosom, and gently lead those who are with young." Psalm 23:1 reminds us, "The Lord is my Shepherd." In John 10:11 Jesus says, "I am the good shepherd. The good shepherd gives His life for the sheep."

Jesus instructed His disciples about proper leadership:

"But Jesus called them to Himself and said to them, "You know that those who are considered rulers over the Gentiles lord it over them, and their great ones exercise authority over them. Yet it shall not be so among you; but whoever desires to become great among you shall be your servant. And whoever of you desires to be first shall be slave of all. For even the Son of Man did not come to be served, but to serve, and to give His life a ransom for many" (Mark 10:42–45).

Husbands, the next time you demand that your wife submit to you, it would be wise to ask yourself, "Am I following God's standard of leadership?" Ask yourself how Jesus modeled leadership. Jesus came to serve and to give His life. If you want to be "great" in God's hierarchy then you must be the greatest servant of all.

Submission means:
I choose to voluntarily surrender my rights and self-interests.
The Greek word *hupotasso* is in the reflexive tense. What does that mean? Here is a quick grammar review: if I say: "I cut the paper," this is not reflexive; it is an action I do to something else. But if I say: "I cut myself with the paper," this is reflexive; it is an action I do to myself. In the first case, the paper gets cut; in the second case, I get cut! Submission, as it is described in the verses where the word *hupotasso* is used, is reflexive. The King James Version therefore reads, "Wives, submit yourselves." The reflexive tense indicates free choice. I choose to voluntarily submit myself. Submission is not to be forced upon another individual.

Submission is not to be forced upon another individual.

In Philippians 2:5–8, Paul reminds us,

"Let this mind be in you which was also in Christ Jesus, who, being in the form of God, did not consider it robbery to be equal with God, but made Himself of no reputation, taking the form of a bond-servant, and coming in the likeness of men. And being found in

*appearance as a man, He humbled Himself and became obedient to
the point of death, even the death of the cross."*

Jesus humbled Himself (reflexive). He freely gave Himself for us.
Jesus chose to lay down His life for us: "Therefore My Father loves Me,
because I lay down My life that I may take it again. No one takes it from
Me, but I lay it down of Myself. I have power to lay it down, and I have
power to take it again. This command I have received from My Father"
(John 10:17–18).

In the same way, we are exhorted to surrender our rights and self-
interest to others. In Philippians 2:3–4 we read, "Let nothing be done
through selfish ambition or conceit, but in lowliness of mind let each
esteem others better than himself. Let each of you look out not only for his
own interests, but also for the interests of others."
Romans 12:10 teaches, "Be kindly affectionate to
one another with brotherly love, in honor giving
preference to one another." A few chapters later,
Paul continues this theme: "Let each of us please
his neighbor for his good, leading to edification. For even Christ did not please Himself; but
as it is written, 'The reproaches of those who
reproached You fell on Me'" (Romans 15:2–3).

> *Submission
> means that
> we choose to
> surrender our
> rights and
> self-interests
> for the good of
> someone else.*

Submission means that we choose to surren-
der our rights and self-interests for the good of someone else. Allow us to
share more about this aspect of submission by giving you a glimpse into
the lives of two of our children.

Our oldest daughter, Julianne, was extremely submissive. She obeyed
us readily. Even as a toddler, she would repent instantly in response to
a mere disapproving look. Because she voluntarily obeyed us, it was not
necessary to impose many external boundaries or rules.

Lest you get the wrong impression, it is worth mentioning that
Julianne was strong willed. She held passionate opinions about right and
wrong, and she was not swayed by other people's opinions. Her siblings
even accused her of being stubborn. How could a strong-willed child be
submissive? Julianne chose to submit to her parents; and when Julianne
chose to do something, she did it wholeheartedly. Julianne submitted to

the "spirit of the law" and never required strict rules or regulations.

Our third child, Janna, had a very different personality. I will never forget one experience we had when she was a toddler. She discovered the electric wall socket and was determined to put her finger into it. I tried in vain to distract, dissuade, discourage, and discipline her. Nothing worked. She gave voice to her annoyance that I had hindered her from attaining her goal of electrocution. She looked right at me and attempted again to stick her finger into the socket. Janna had no intention of submitting, with the result that none of the "external" pressures I applied convinced her to change her course of action. (I finally won that particular battle, but it certainly wasn't our last conflict!) Her personality required that we impose many more rules and guidelines during her early years. Both our daughters were strong willed. But unlike Julianne, Janna's idea of submission was to submit to the "letter of the law" rather than to the spirit of the law. She was quick to say, "I didn't disobey you. You didn't say I shouldn't eat *those* cookies." (And she might have been right! I didn't think I had to name the cookies specifically when I told her she couldn't have any snacks!) Janna was great at interpreting the law as she saw fit. She might obey external rules (particularly when Mom was looking), but her submission was not voluntary; neither did her submission indicate that she had surrendered her rights.

Voluntary submission actually contributes to greater freedom and openness in marriage.

Biblical submission is voluntary. You should never force or demand your spouse to submit. Rather, submission must be an act of love and free will. Voluntary submission actually contributes to greater freedom and openness in marriage. Just as our daughter Julianne experienced far more independence and very few constraints in her relationship with us, so it is in a marriage relationship when submission is offered freely, without reservations. Trust is abundant. Love is unconditional. Power struggles are rare.

Submission means:
I freely offer my gifts, talents, abilities, and knowledge.

Valerie earned her master's degree in economics. She worked for several years for an investment firm and was a highly respected and capable

eral years for an investment firm and was a highly respected and capable employee. Valerie met Marcus at church and knew she was making the best investment of her life when she married him. Within a few years, Valerie happily resigned in order to stay home and care for their new baby. Marcus was an entrepreneur who dreamed of starting his own company. But he was clueless about how to develop a realistic business plan. He could see the big picture and could motivate others to join him in pursuit of his vision, but he was challenged by organizational details— and financial details, in particular.

Valerie watched her husband struggle through the paperwork required to start a new business, as well as through numerous meetings with bankers and investors. She often caught herself biting her lip, as she avoided offering any helpful advice. She believed that being submissive meant that she needed to allow Marcus to be the man of the house and do this himself. Marcus became increasingly discouraged and overwhelmed. He was utterly unprepared and ill-equipped for the organizational aspects of managing his new company, but he couldn't afford to hire a manager or consultant.

Marcus knew that Valerie was highly qualified, capable and better trained than he was to manage the business aspects of his company, but he was reluctant to ask for her help. He felt insecure and feared that if he failed to get his company off the ground, his wife would no longer respect him.

Valerie misconstrued the meaning of submission. Submission does not mean keeping your mouth closed because you are afraid that offering your advice might be perceived as being disrespectful. In fact, Valerie's failure to offer her husband the talents, skills, and gifts she possessed was a failure to submit. In essence, she withheld from him something he desperately needed. Valerie needed to humbly and respectfully offer her skills to her husband. Had he chosen not to accept her help, then she would have had to accept his refusal. But she needed to offer to help.

Participating in a Bible study helped Valerie understand the true meaning of submission. She realized she could use her talents and skills to serve her husband, and she gently offered to help. Marcus was thrilled. A good leader openly acknowledges that he cannot do it all, and Marcus was more than convinced that he was not up to the challenge. Marcus immediately handed Valerie a stack of paperwork and then swooped up their six-month-old son. Marcus cared for the baby while Valerie happily re-organized the company's financial and business structure. She skillfully resolved in a few days what Marcus had struggled with for months.

Marcus realized that Valerie was perfectly qualified to serve as his company's financial consultant and bookkeeper. Together, they agreed on a plan whereby Marcus would stay home with the baby and Valerie would work for the company once each week. The business thrived, and this young couple learned a great lesson about submission.

In 1 Peter 4:10, Paul writes, "As each one has received a gift, minister it to one another, as good stewards of the manifold grace of God." You have certain gifts, talents, skills, knowledge, and wisdom. God calls you to be a good steward of the gifts He has given you. Wives, submission means that you freely (and respectfully) offer these to your spouse for him to use as he sees fit. Be aware, however, that he may refuse your offer. Submission means that we offer our help but do not force it.

Many women are afraid to offer their opinions. God has gifted many women with insights and wisdom that their husbands do not possess. It is a wise man who seeks counsel from his wife. And it is a sign of submission when a woman respectfully shares her insights with her husband.

Everything a wife possesses—her knowledge, intellect, insights, skills, talents, and abilities—she is to freely offer her husband. If a woman sees her husband heading down a path that she suspects will be harmful to him but refuses nevertheless to warn him because she doesn't want to tell him he might be wrong, is that really being submissive? No! God has given the wife to the husband to be his completion, his helpmeet. There is nothing unbiblical about warning your husband if he is going the wrong way.

Of course, the key here is *how* to offer your knowledge. If you are disrespectful, demanding, belittling, nagging, or condemning, then you are not in fact being submissive. Submission means that you make available all you have for your husband to use, not that you use what you possess as a weapon against your husband! We will discuss this in more detail as we examine our roles and responsibilities.

Submission means:

I must obey God first.

What if a husband asks his wife to do something sinful or illegal? Must she still submit to him? Christian women who are married to non-believing husbands often ask this question. While submission means, "I choose to voluntarily surrender my rights and self-interests," we also assert that as believers, our first and foremost allegiance is to God.

Scripture teaches that we are to obey and submit to our government and yet we see the Apostle Peter and the other disciples openly and boldly disobeying the law of the land. Peter and John were arrested because they had been preaching and teaching about Jesus. During their trial, they were warned to cease their activities. But they continued their ministry. Soon they were arrested again. During their interrogation, the high priest reminded them of the previous command to stop preaching and teaching about Jesus. "But Peter and the other apostles answered and said: 'We ought to obey God rather than men'" (Acts 5:29).

> *Our first and foremost allegiance is to God.*

Does God hold a wife responsible if she remains silent and does not confront her husband's sin? Consider the account of Ananias and Sapphira: "But a certain man named Ananias, with Sapphira his wife, sold a possession. And he kept back part of the proceeds, his wife also being aware of it, and brought a certain part and laid it at the apostles' feet" (Acts 5:1–2). The first church was growing rapidly. Acts 2:44–45 describes this amazing time: "Now all who believed were together, and had all things in common, and sold their possessions and goods, and divided them among all, as anyone had need." The needs were great, and the believers willingly shared with each other.

Ananias and Sapphira sold a piece of property and brought a portion of the proceeds to the disciples to share with the new church. They were not required to give a gift, and they would have been within their rights to give just a portion. The problem was that Ananias lied: He wanted the apostles to think he was making a great sacrifice when in fact he was giving just a portion of the sum he had received. Peter confronted him with the lie, and God instantly struck Ananias dead.

Because the verse reads, "...he [Ananias] kept back a part of the proceeds" (Acts 5:2), we understand that it was Ananias's idea to falsify the amount he had received from the sale of his land and to present to the church only a portion of the money. The next phrase is key: *"his wife also being aware of it...."* Sapphira knew about the deception. It may not have been her idea, but she was aware of it.

When Ananias was struck dead, Sapphira was not present. Three hours later, Sapphira arrived at the church meeting, unaware that her husband had died. Peter asked her, "'Tell me whether you sold the land for so much?'" She replied, "Yes, for so much." Sapphira should have obeyed God rather than her husband, but she didn't. She had an opportunity to do what was right, but instead she continued in the sin. "Then Peter said to her, 'How is it that you have agreed together to test the Spirit of the Lord? Look, the feet of those who have buried your husband are at the door, and they will carry you out.' Then immediately she fell down at his feet and breathed her last" (Acts 5:9–10a).

The account of Ananias and Sapphira makes it clear that God held Sapphira responsible for her choices. But wasn't she supposed to submit to her husband? Wasn't the deception his idea? Wasn't Sapphira just being obedient? She should have obeyed God. Her husband sinned willfully. Biblical submission is always to God first.

In 1 Samuel 25:4–42, we read the story of Abigail, who disobeyed her husband in order to obey God. At this time in Israel's history, King Saul was ruling and had sworn to kill David. David and his followers had fled from Saul and were hiding in an area known as Carmel. Although David and his men were on the run, they had provided extensive protection for certain shepherds who had been working in that area. These shepherds tended the flocks belonging to a foolish and wicked man named Nabal. When it came time for the sheep to be sheared, David sent messengers to humbly ask Nabal for a gift. The shepherds agreed that David and his men deserved a reward. But Nabal refused.

Upon learning of Nabal's response, David became furious. He and his men prepared to kill Nabal and the members of his household. But when Nabal's wife Abigail learned of the injustice and insults her husband had heaped upon David, she ordered her servants to deliver a large gift of food to David and his men. Then she risked everything to come in person to plead for the life of her husband.

Abigail met David's small army as it advanced toward Nabal's home. She bowed before David and took responsibility for not having acted sooner to meet the needs of David and his men. She begged for forgiveness and acknowledged David's future as the next king of Israel. She offered David wise counsel as she encouraged him not to avenge himself upon Nabal.

David was impressed by Abigail and her wisdom. He agreed not to seek revenge. He praised Abigail and blessed her, recognizing that God had used her to protect him.

Abigail returned home to find her husband drunk. The next morning, she explained all that had happened the day before. She did not conceal the part she had played. In verses 37 and 38 we read, "So it was, in the morning, when the wine had gone from Nabal, and his wife had told him these things, that his heart died within him, and he became like a stone. Then it happened, after about ten days, that the LORD struck Nabal, and he died." David rejoiced at God's protection and justice. Subsequently, he proposed to Abigail, and she became his wife.

We may not think at first that Abigail is a good example of a submissive wife. After all, she disobeyed her husband. She knew how her husband had treated David yet she defied his example. Nevertheless, we believe Abigail exemplified godly submission in that *she chose to obey God first*. Her husband acted sinfully, and she refused to follow his example.

We can speculate about what Abigail's marriage might have been like with Nabal. He had a reputation for being a foolish and wicked man. Even his servants confirmed this assessment. We can only imagine how terrible it must have been for a godly woman like Abigail to live with such an evil man. When the servant came to Abigail and told her what Nabal had done, he also declared to her that David was bent on revenge. Abigail could have easily gotten rid of her husband by doing nothing! She could have just allowed David to charge in and murder Nabal. But this is not what she did.

Abigail took a great risk to save her husband's life (and the lives of the men in their household). In the culture of that day, a woman had very little authority. Abigail acted bravely in riding out to meet David, a man with revenge on his mind. She could easily have been killed before she even had a chance to speak. Abigail acted in accordance with our third definition of submission: "I choose to voluntarily surrender my rights and self-interests."

It is worth considering what her honesty might have cost her when she told her husband what she had done. Nabal is described as "such a son of Belial, that a man cannot speak to him" (1 Samuel 25:17). "Belial" literally means 'the son of Satan' (not the kind of man I would want to defy!). Abigail acted despite the possibility of abuse or retaliation.

Remember our fourth definition of submission: "I freely offer my gifts, talents, abilities and knowledge." Abigail freely offered her wisdom, insight, and discernment in support of her husband (though he was unaware of her doing so). Abigail also submitted to David in that she placed herself "under the command of a leader." She acknowledged his anointing as the future king of Israel and wisely cautioned him against acting in vengeance and thereby tainting his reign as king.

But let us be clear: You must be very careful to discern when it is acceptable to disobey your spouse. Many women have told us, "My husband isn't saved. I can't respect him and don't believe I should submit to him." We often discover, however, that the husband is not demanding that the wife do anything sinful. (He may be living a less than holy life, but it would be unrealistic to expect him to adhere to God's righteous standards when he is not a follower of God.

For example, he may have bad habits such as gambling or drinking. Certainly, these habits can affect the family. But unless he is demanding that his wife rob a bank to support his bad habits, she needs to submit to him and show respect. What if he wants her to get drunk with him? She does not have to obey him in this case. (Of course, she should lovingly and respectfully offer wisdom and practical help to end his addictive behavior.) But refusing to submit is not an option *unless the husband is asking his wife to disobey God.*

What about the husband who refuses to allow his wife to go to church? Many women are quick to quote Hebrews 10:25, "not forsaking the assembling of ourselves together…" and then suggest that they have to disobey their husbands so they can obey God and go to church. We do believe in the truth of this verse. But note what it doesn't say: It doesn't say how often we are to assemble together, where we are to assemble, or on which day we are to do so.

When we hear that a husband refuses to let his wife attend church, we ask several questions: First, why is he refusing to let her go? Is Sunday the only day he has free? Perhaps he wants to spend that day with his wife and family. In that case, the wife needs to show respect to her husband and ask if he would be opposed to her attending a Bible study while he is at work. This would not disrupt his free time, and it demonstrates submission. After all, the command to "assemble together" doesn't specify on which day.

Second, we ask if something else has caused him to become embittered against the church. Has his wife nagged at him and condemned him for not going to church so often that he has rejected it completely? If so, she needs to repent and ask for his forgiveness. Her behavior and disrespect may have caused his antagonism.

Finally, we inquire about how often the wife attends church. Some women believe they must be at church every time the door is open. A husband can become resentful when his wife is never (or rarely) home. The wife who is guilty of this would be wise to apologize to her husband for putting church events ahead of him. Notice, that we didn't say that she is guilty of putting God ahead of him. Attending church events does not make a person "spiritual" and is not a sign of obedience. God has given the wife the responsibility to minister to her husband. Ultimately, this is not an issue of obeying God and disobeying one's husband. Many women who suggest that it is are self-righteous hypocrites: they are quick to point out their husbands' spiritual flaws but blind to their own rebellious actions and lack of love.

Consider the story of a woman we met a number of years ago. Although her husband was a believer, she believed he was spiritually immature. She was convinced that she needed to take over the spiritual leadership of their home. He never measured up to her standard of a spirit-filled life. Yet whenever we discussed the Bible with her, her decidedly unbiblical beliefs betrayed her true spiritual condition. Rarely could she support her opinions with sound Biblical teaching.

One day she told us that she believed God was calling her to the mission field. She believed she must leave her husband and young son and go alone. Because her husband wasn't "spiritual," she didn't believe his opinion mattered. She believed that her "calling" outweighed the authority of God's Word. She was convinced she had the right to ignore Biblical teaching on the sanctity of marriage and her responsibilities as a mother. She belittled us as "unspiritual" and "unwilling to hear God's voice."

When we say "submission means that I must obey God first," we are *not* saying that this is an excuse to disobey one's spouse or to act disrespectfully. With very few exceptions, the two are not mutually exclusive: submission to God is usually synonymous with submission to our spouse.

PUTTING IT ALL TOGETHER

Five definitions of submission discussed in this chapter are:
1. I allow you to do for me what your responsibility is to do.
2. I place myself under the command of a leader.
3. I choose to voluntarily surrender my rights and self-interests.
4. I freely offer my gifts, talents, abilities, and knowledge.
5. I must obey God first.

The scenario that follows depicts how each of these definitions can be exemplified in marriage. (The numbers below correspond with the definitions above.)

Ted's responsibility is to provide for the needs of his family. He is to be the overseer or manager. (1) One morning his wife Miriam noticed that the milk in the refrigerator wasn't cold and that the meat smelled bad. Because she accepted Ted's role as the family manager, she called him at work and told him about the problem. She submitted to his responsibility to provide for the family's needs.

(2) But that afternoon, Miriam's father came to visit. When Miriam poured him a glass of juice, he noticed it wasn't cold. Realizing that the refrigerator wasn't working properly, he did what many well-meaning fathers would do: he offered to buy them a new one. He suggested they buy the same kind he had and as he was reaching for the phone to place the order for a new refrigerator, Miriam stopped him: "Dad, thank you for the offer. But Ted will have to make the decision about what we buy. I appreciate your willingness to help. I can tell Ted that you might have

some suggestions. But I need to let him decide what is best for us."

(3) That afternoon, Miriam looked through stacks of advertisements and catalogs, researching various makes and models of refrigerators. By the time Ted arrived home from work, she had identified her favorite. She loved the color and the features. Miriam thought they might splurge and get a good one. Ted was less than enthusiastic; he wanted a more basic model. Miriam was annoyed. After all, she was the one who took care of the kitchen. Shouldn't she have the right to make the final choice? Slowly, Miriam relented and relinquished her rights. She knew her husband was looking out for their best interest. She told him she would be happy with whatever he thought was best.

(4) Ted poured himself a glass of lukewarm juice and sat with his wife to make a final decision. Ted noticed the stack of catalogs and realized his wife had done more research than he had. "It looks as though you have done your homework. I would like to hear what you learned about the pros and cons of these refrigerators. Which ones are more cost effective in the long run?" Miriam proceeded to highlight which used less energy, which had better warranties, and which had the best service records.

(5) Miriam could tell that Ted was trying to determine the best course of action. Suddenly he said, "We have some money we have been saving for our tithe. Why don't we take that money, buy the fridge, and pay back our tithe account later?" Miriam was uneasy: Their tithe account contained money they set aside each month to give to the Lord. At times the account would accrue, as when they were saving for a mission project. But they had made a commitment that this money belonged to God and never would be used for personal needs. "Ted, I don't believe we can violate our commitment to the Lord in this way. I want to follow your leadership, but it would be wrong for us to do this. I cannot agree with you in this area." Ted shook his head slowly. "I know you are right. I am sorry I suggested this. We need to pray about this need." Together they committed their need to the Lord and asked Him to provide. That evening, Ted received a call from a friend at work who needed some help on a building project. He was willing to pay Ted quite well for five days of labor—and the amount proved just sufficient to buy a new refrigerator!

Not all decisions are so easy. But God's design for submission in marriage works! In order to facilitate harmony and unity in our marriages, we also must understand and embrace the roles and responsibilities God has given husband and wife. In the next two chapters we will delve into the roles for men and women.

STUDY GUIDE

Read Ephesians 5:17–22; 1 Peter 5:5; Ezekiel 34:2–4;
Philippians 2:5–8; John 10:17–18; 1 Peter 4:10;
Acts 5:1–2; 1 Samuel 25:4–42

The brutal warrior standing with one foot planted firmly on the face of a defeated peasant while his glistening sword is thrust high in the air: this is the image that comes to mind when we hear the word "submission." To some, it is synonymous with conqueror and slave. Others find it archaic and old-fashioned. Your family, traditions, culture, and faith likely have shaped your view of the word. We hope this chapter has challenged you to set aside preconceived notions as well as misunderstandings and to discover what God has to say about submission.

Biblical submission will always bring God—and God alone—glory. Thus, it will never contradict God's Word. Let's dig a little deeper…

DIGGING DEEPER

1. List a few of the key words that describe what submission is *not.*

   a.

   b.

   c.

   d.

   e.

   f.

2. Paraphrase Ephesians 5:17–21.

3. What are the five definitions of 'submission' provided in this chapter?

   a.

   b.

   c.

   d.

   e.

4. What is the key point related to pride in 1 Peter 5:5?

5. The Greek word for submission *(hupotasso)* means:

6. What are the three standards for leaders that God gives in Ezekiel 34:2–4?

   a._

   b.

   c._

7. What are some other standards for leaders that are articulated in the Bible? (Include the reference.)

8. Why is it important to understand the reflexive tense of *hupotasso,* the Greek word for submission?

9. How is the reflexive tense used in Philippians 2:5–8 and John 10:17–18?

10. How does 1 Peter 4:10 relate to the fourth definition of submission?

11. What does the story about Ananias and Sapphira reveal about submission? (Reread Acts 5:1–2.)

12. Of the five definitions of submission that are given in this chapter, which four are exhibited in the life of Abigail? Give specific examples. (Reread 1 Samuel 25:4–42.)

    a.

    b.

    c.

    d.

13. How well does your spouse submit?
    ☐ Very well.
    ☐ Usually well.
    ☐ Just ok. Could do better.
    ☐ Needs a lot of improvement.
    ☐ My husband is a tyrant.
    ☐ My wife is rebellious.

14. *Ask your spouse*: "In what area of our relationship do you have the most trouble submitting?" Pray together about your mutual ability to submit.

15. Reflect on your last disagreement with your partner. *Discuss together* how it might have gone differently had you implemented Biblical submission.

CHAPTER TWELVE

MAN IN THE GARDEN

Roles For Men

"Tell my wife I am supposed to be the head of this marriage! Tell her to start obeying me!" We can't tell you how many times we have heard men bellow this demand. (The fact that these men are asking us to talk to their wives about this indicates a huge problem already—on both sides!) Men, if you truly understood your role as head of your marriage, you might not be so quick to insist on fulfilling it! Being the head of your marriage is not an easy job; certainly, it is not a simple matter of "conquering" your wife and standing over her, your foot on her back, your fist raised in victory.

Some men position themselves at the other extreme: they prefer to sit in their easy chairs and let their wives take the lead. Perhaps these men tried to lead their family at some point but failed. Their failure led them to relinquish leadership altogether. Other men have grown weary of struggling with their wives for control and have resigned themselves to letting their wives have their way.

Neither of these extremes—dictatorship and resigned subservience—are God's plan for man's role in marriage. Some men start reading Ephesians 5:23—"For the husband is head of the wife..."—and stop there. One type of man says, "Yeah! That's right! I'm the boss!" Another type mumbles, "Actually, I have no desire to be the head. Let my wife do it!" But that is not the verse in its entirety; what follows is crucial for husbands to understand: "…as also Christ is head of the church; and He is the Savior of the body." If men are to understand their role as "head of the wife," then they must understand Christ as head of the church as well as His role as Savior. The little word that many overlook in this verse is the word "as." Husbands are to be the head of their wives *as* Christ is the head of the church—that is, in the same way!

So how is Christ the head of the church? Debate about the meaning of the word "head" in the Bible is extensive. Some interpret "head" to mean "authority;" others believe the word is more accurately translated "source;" still others assert that it means "top ranking," as in the "top-ranking" player on a team.

Lest we, too, become bogged down in this controversy, let's consider each of these definitions as possible. Thus, "head" may be defined as:

1. authority
2. source
3. top ranking

AUTHORITY

If we interpret "head" as "authority," we need only to review Jesus' teaching about authority to understand that He would never condone oppression, abuse, or self-centered behavior. (Review Mark 10:42–45.) Jesus taught, "But whoever desires to become great among you shall be your servant. And whoever of you desires to be first shall be slave of all. For even the Son of Man did not come to be served, but to serve, and to give His life a ransom for many" (Mark 10:44–45).

Husbands, if you believe the meaning of "head" is "to be in authority," then you must look at Christ and His style of leadership. Jesus was a servant leader—hence, this first role for husbands:

Be the head servant: Serve your wife.

If Jesus is our standard, how are men to serve their wives? Reread Ephesians 5:25: "Husbands, love your wives, just as Christ also loved the church and gave Himself for her." How did Jesus love the church? By giving Himself through His death on the cross. In Philippians 2:5–8, we read,

"Let this mind be in you which was also in Christ Jesus, who, being in the form of God, did not consider it robbery to be equal with God, but made Himself of no reputation, taking the form of a bondservant, and coming in the likeness of men. And being found in appearance as a man, He humbled Himself and became obedient to the point of death, even the death of the cross."

The Amplified Bible provides additional insight into verse 6 of this passage:

> "Who, although being essentially one with God and in the form of God [possessing the fullness of the attributes which make God God], did not think this equality with God was a thing to be eagerly grasped or retained, but stripped Himself [of all privileges and rightful dignity], so as to assume the guise of a servant (slave), in that He became like men and was born a human being."[1]

Let's "pull together" these two thoughts from Ephesians 5:25 and Philippians 2:5–8: Husbands, love your wives as Christ also loved the church and gave Himself for her—in that He willingly stripped Himself of His rights and privileges and became a servant. Husbands, if you want to be the head of your home, it means you must be the head servant. You must be willing to sacrifice what you want—your rights, privileges, and desires. You must be willing to serve your wife before you serve yourself.

Husbands, if you want to be the head of your home, it means you must be the head servant.

Jesus modeled servanthood. At the Last Supper, before He went to the cross, Jesus washed His disciples' feet. This was a dirty job. And yet we see the Lord of the universe humbling Himself to serve.

"So when He [Jesus] had washed their feet, taken His garments, and sat down again, He said to them, "Do you know what I have done to you? You call Me Teacher and Lord, and you say well, for so I am. If I, then, your Lord and Teacher, have washed your feet, you also ought to wash one another's feet. For I have given you an example, that you should do as I have done to you" (John 13:12–15).

Continue reading Ephesians 5:28: "So husbands ought to love their own wives as their own bodies; he who loves his wife loves himself." Many times we hear wives say, "My husband only cares about himself. He never thinks about my needs. He comes home from work, plops down in front of the TV, and expects me to wait on him like a slave. He never even considers that I have also worked hard all day." Men, this is *not* loving or serving your wife as you would love or serve your own body. Do you want to be head of your home? Then follow the Biblical mandate: Be a servant leader.

My husband is a pastor and a leader in our church, and I have been astonished by the ways in which he willingly serves me. He brings me a cup of coffee each morning (and he doesn't even like coffee). When he notices that my clothes are looking worn, he insists that I go and buy whatever I need—even if it means he won't get to purchase something he wants. Tim watches movies with me that most men would run away from; he has been willing to sacrifice his preferences to serve me. Countless times Tim has changed his schedule to accommodate mine, to include giving up a nap because he realized I had a need. This is servant leadership. It is not difficult for me to submit to his leadership. I know that he is constantly putting me first. The result? As his wife, I am more than willing to serve him and sacrifice for him. My heart is full of respect for him, and I look for ways to honor him.

It is important to stipulate that being a servant to your wife does *not* mean giving her everything she may want. Indulging her every whim is not doing what is best for her. Lovingly serving your wife requires that you carefully consider what she needs. Sometimes, the most loving thing may be to gently say, "No. This is not good for you. I love you too much to give you something that will harm you." Again, the emphasis is on what she needs—not on what you need.

In essence, serving your wife is love in action. Jesus didn't merely shout from heaven, "Hey, I love you!" He came to earth to minister, to serve, and to give His life for us. *That* is the kind of love you are commanded to have for your wife. And it is a command, not a suggestion.

Serving your wife means placing her needs—physical, emotional, and spiritual—before your own. The next aspect of the husband's job description ties in closely with this one.

SOURCE

The second meaning of 'head,' "source," directs us to consider another passage. Ephesians 4:15 says, "But, speaking the truth in love, may grow up in all things into Him who is the head—Christ—from whom the whole body, joined and knit together by what every joint supplies, according to the effective working by which every part does its share, causes growth of the body for the edifying of itself in love." This verse indicates that the "source" of nourishment, unity, and growth is the "head," Christ. Accordingly, the second element of a husband's job description is:

Be the source: Supply what your wife needs.

In Ephesians 5:28-29, we read, "So husbands ought to love their own wives as their own bodies; he who loves his wife loves himself. For no one ever hated his own flesh, but nourishes and cherishes it, just as the Lord does the church." Two key words are 'nourishes' and 'cherishes.' Husbands, are you 'nourishing' your wife, not just by providing food for the table, but more important, by providing spiritual and emotional 'food?'

Spiritually. Men, you are to be the spiritual leaders in your families. It is not your wife's job to oversee the spiritual training of your family. Jesus provides spiritual nourishment for His bride, the church, through the Holy Spirit, His Word, and spiritual gifts. Husbands, you should be the source of spiritual growth for your wives. Through your example and leadership, your wives should be challenged in their spiritual walks with Christ.

Husbands, you should be the source of spiritual nourishment for your wives.

We have heard men say, "My wife is very unspiritual. She doesn't even want to go to church." We also know of men who have used this as an excuse to divorce their wives. However, if the spiritual climate in your home is cold or carnal, you must go to the "source"— yourself! Men are to be the "sources" of nourishment in the home. Are you truly living as a godly husband? Are you serving your wife according to the Biblical model? Are you healthy spiritually? You cannot give what you do not have. If you don't spend time in God's Word or in prayer, then you have nothing to offer your wife. The job of nourishing the family spiritually is the husband's.

Are you praying for your wife? Are you praying with her (read James 5:16)? Are you sharing God's truths with her—not preaching at her but rather helping her discover all the Lord has planned for both of you? Are you setting an example for your wife in your own quiet time and prayer life? Are you encouraging and supporting your wife to use her spiritual gifts? Are you guarding your home against any influences that would corrupt your family? These are all aspects of the husband's job. It should not fall to the wife to suggest family devotion time or that the family go to church.

Years ago, a woman in our church came to me (Tim) with a theological question. I love to teach and to share from God's Word, but this time, I felt a greater issue was at stake. I responded, "You need to go and ask your husband this question." Her stunned look and loss for words didn't surprise me. She had been a Christian for a long time and was far more knowledgeable about the Bible than her husband, who often showed little interest in spiritual things. After composing herself, she explained that her husband was not very interested in the Bible. Nevertheless, I repeated my admonition: "You need to ask your husband." Flustered, the woman left.

Later, I received a call from the woman's husband. "Pastor, why did you tell my wife to ask me about the Bible? I have no idea about this stuff." I allowed him to rant for a while about his inadequacies, and when he finally took a breath, I said, "That may be true. But you are called to lead your family spiritually. If you don't know the answers, I will be happy to meet with you and we can study it together." This man finally took responsibility for leading his wife spiritually, and he was changed. His wife was astounded at the insights he later shared with her. By meeting the requirements of his job description, he grew spiritually himself.

Physically. Being the "source" also includes meeting your wife's physical needs. Your wife should not be afraid to ask you for anything she genuinely needs. We know of too many wives who go behind their husbands' backs because they do not trust their husbands to take care of them—or they are afraid to ask. This ought not to be. We know of women who started working because their husbands were not providing for the family. Men, it is not your wives' job description to be the sole financial provider for the family! We believe strongly that God has given this role to men. As we read in Ephesians 5, husbands are to "nourish" their wives. This is reiterated in 1 Timothy 5:8: "But if anyone does not provide for his own, and especially for those of his household, he has denied the faith and is worse than an unbeliever."

Did Jesus expect or require us to pay part of the price for our sins? No! He paid it all; and He continues to provide all we need. In the same way, a man is to provide for his family. We are not saying that it is wrong for a wife to work, but the full responsibility to provide financially for the family is the husband's. Any monies that the wife earns should be used for extras or for savings—not to meet the basic budget. Emergency situations—e.g., sickness, injury, loss of employment—may compel a wife to work in order to help meet the family's basic needs, but we believe this must be the exception and not the rule. It may become necessary for a family to sacrifice the standard of living to which it is accustomed, but the principle is for the husband to be the main provider.

Our son Josiah married Elke a few years ago. Although both of them are earning good wages, they have learned to live on only one salary. The other salary they have put into savings. This shows tremendous wisdom on their part. They have built their lifestyle on one income so when they decide to start their family, it will be easy for Elke to quit her job and stay home with the baby. They are making sound financial decisions, and Josiah is providing for the family.

Emotionally. The other aspect of nourishing your wife is emotional. Have you taken time to really know your wife? Do you listen to her heart? Do you ask her what she needs? Do you communicate your love for her in a manner she can recognize? Do you take care to nourish her spirit, or are you constantly tearing her down and "starving" her through your cruel jokes, belittling comments, critical attitudes, and harsh words?

In 1 Peter 3:7, Peter teaches, "Husbands, likewise, dwell with them [wives] with understanding, giving honor to the wife, as to the weaker vessel, and as being heirs together of the grace of life, that your prayers may not be hindered." Husbands are to understand their wives! This may seem like the impossible dream, and yet God has commanded it. Men, read James 1:5: "If any of you lacks wisdom, let him ask of God, who gives to all liberally and without reproach, and it will be given to him." God has promised to give you wisdom if you ask honestly and with a sincere heart. God would not command you to do something that is impossible to do.

The idea of the "weaker vessel" is controversial. Many women are deeply offended at being referred to in this way. Another passage helps put this language into perspective. In 1 Corinthians 12:21–23, Paul used an analogy to explain the spiritual principle of working together in unity:

"And the eye cannot say to the hand, "I have no need of you;" nor again the head to the feet, "I have no need of you." No, much rather, those members of the body which seem to be weaker are necessary. And those members of the body which we think to be less honorable, on these we bestow greater honor; and our unpresentable parts have greater modesty...."

In this passage, Paul uses the same Greek word for "weak" (or "weaker") as is used in 1 Peter. Following the analogy, we could compare women to the eyes. Compared to other parts of the body, the eyes are weak: they cannot walk, they can't hammer a nail, and they certainly can't digest food. We protect our eyes from dust and bright sunlight. We rest our eyes when they get weary. Our eyes can be injured more easily than our feet. Skin protects almost the entirety of the body, but the eyes are vulnerable. Even a tiny splinter can cause blindness.

But are the eyes less valuable than feet? Certainly not. Are they "weaker?" Yes, but they have a different function. Similarly, a woman typically is "weaker" than a man. The typical woman can't lift as much, run as far, or endure such heavy labor as a man. (The military acknowledges physiological differences by requiring women soldiers to meet a different standard of physical competence than her male counterparts.[2]) Emotional differences also distinguish men from women (see Chapter 5 of this book). Emotional differences can result in a woman being far more vulnerable to deep hurts and offenses.

While we believe that these differences contribute to women being the "weaker vessel," we do not believe that this is at all degrading to women. Mary Lou doesn't feel she is less of a person because she is not as physically capable as I am. The truth of 1 Peter 3:7 is often lost on chauvinistic men and insecure women who get stuck on the phrase "weaker vessel" and fail to read it in context: "giving honor to the wife, as to the weaker vessel, and as being heirs together of the grace of life." Peter makes it clear that husbands and wives are equal heirs of the grace of life. Being "weaker" does not denote inequality.

Men, ask yourselves, "What is God asking me to do with this information?" The answer is "giving honor to the wife, as to the weaker vessel" (1 Peter 3:7). The word "honor" comes from the Greek word *time,* which means "to value, esteem highly, or to be precious."[3] When you honor something, you treasure it, value it, appreciate it, take pleasure in it, and esteem it highly. Husbands, your wives

> *Honor means "to value, esteem highly, or to be precious."*

should feel they are the most important things in your lives (after the Lord). No wife should doubt that she is a top priority for her husband.

Whenever we hear of men who are physically or verbally abusive toward their wives, we know they have not learned to honor them. No one abuses something he honors.

Perhaps you are thinking, "I have never been abusive to my wife in any way." But do you put your job, career, car, sports, entertainment, or personal interest ahead of her? Does she feel she must compete for your time? If so, then you are not honoring her.

We believe this connects beautifully with Ephesians 5:29 and the word "cherish." "…no one ever hated his own flesh, but nourishes and cherishes it, just as the Lord does the church." Cherish can be translated from the Greek: *to warm,* to cherish with tender love, to foster with tender care."[4] In his letter to the Thessalonians, Paul uses the same Greek word: "But we were gentle among you, just as a nursing mother *cherishes* her own children" (1 Thessalonians 2:7). What a beautiful image! Men, if you understand that your wives are "weaker vessels," then you will cherish, protect, foster and care for them. A wife should feel protected by her husband.

We have identified the first two aspects of the job description of a husband who is the "head" of his family: *servant* and *source.* Now we consider the third and final aspect of the job description.

TOP-RANKING

Given the definition of "head" as "top ranking," consider 1 Corinthians 9:24: "Do you not know that those who run in a race all run, but one receives the prize? Run in such a way that you may obtain it." Paul taught about the importance of giving and doing our best. The top-ranking player on a team sets the example for the rest of the team. He gives 100 percent and is willing to sacrifice everything to win. Thus, the last element of a husband's job description is:

Be the best "head": Strive for mastery.

In 1 Timothy 3:2a, Paul clarifies for Timothy the qualifications required of a leader in the church. Paul instructs, "A bishop then must be blameless, the husband of one wife…" What does he mean by "husband of one wife?" The emphasis we like to draw from this verse is on the word "husband." Paul is exhorting men to *be* a husband to one wife— not simply on paper—but actively fulfilling the requirements of *being a husband* to her.

We like to use the English word: "husbandry" to illustrate what being a husband means. Years ago, while we were living in Kansas, we were introduced to the field of study at Kansas State University called *"animal husbandry."* (now commonly called "animal science") It includes the study of breeding, raising, managing, and caring for animals—usually farm animals. The term here *"husbandry"* is linked etymologically to the word *"manager or overseer."*

A man who has studied animal husbandry knows what is necessary to keep his livestock healthy. He doesn't lie around all day, demanding that his cows serve him! He serves his animals, often sacrificing his own sleep and personal comfort in order to provide what his animals need. Years of study and experience give him the tools he needs to ensure that his animals remain disease free and productive. If he is wise, he will stay abreast of the latest findings and techniques. He will maintain the animals' stalls and protect the animals from predators.

Now, we aren't calling your wife an old cow! But, in the same way a farmer or rancher practices animal *husbandry*, a man should be a *husband* to his wife. He must study how to care for his wife. His goal must be to become an expert on his wife. It will require more than a haphazard approach to learning. A husband should strive for excellence. The more he learns, the better his marriage will function and the healthier it will be.

A Christian husband has a high calling. Ephesians 5:25–27 sets forth the goal:

> *"Husbands, love your wives, just as Christ also loved the church and gave Himself for her, that He might sanctify and cleanse her with the washing of water by the word, that He might present her to Himself a glorious church, not having spot or wrinkle or any such thing, but that she should be holy and without blemish."*

In the same way in which Christ sanctifies and cleanses His Bride, the church, so, too, a husband's goal is to present his wife—cleansed, set apart, without spot or wrinkle—to the Lord. He must never "throw mud" on her, injure her, ignore her, or care for her half-heartedly.

In order to fulfill this calling, a man must commit himself to "husbandry": first, he must learn how to be a good husband; then, actively and selflessly, he must manage his marriage. "And whatever you do in word or deed, do all in the name of the Lord Jesus, giving thanks to God the Father through Him" (Colossians 3:17). There is no allowance for sloppy or careless management. A good farmer knows that if he doesn't give 100 percent to the care of his animals, they will become sick, unproductive, and die. The Lord calls men to excellence, regardless of whether their wives are perfect, deserving, respectful, or even loving.

The Lord calls men to excellence, regardless of whether their wives are perfect.

Ephesians 5:15–18 reminds us, "See then that you walk circumspectly, not as fools but as wise, redeeming the time, because the days are evil. Therefore do not be unwise, but understand what the will of the Lord is. And do not be drunk with wine, in which is dissipation; but be filled with the Spirit."

Husbands: if you truly understand the requirements, sacrifice, and hard work inherent in your job description, you might be tempted to quit! But the last part of Ephesians 5:18 offers hope: "but be filled with the Spirit." The Holy Spirit is the ultimate source of wisdom, strength, power, and endurance. He will enable you to become the husband God has called you to be as you fulfill these three job requirements:

Be the head servant: Serve your wife.

Be the head source: Supply what your wife needs.

Be "top ranking": Strive for mastery.

MEN, LOVE YOUR WIVES!

"Owe no one anything except to love one another, for he who loves another has fulfilled the law. For the commandments, "You shall not commit adultery," "You shall not murder," "You shall not steal," "You shall not bear false witness," "You shall not covet," and if there is any other commandment, are all summed up in this saying, namely, "You shall love your neighbor as yourself." Love does no harm to a neighbor; therefore love is the fulfillment of the law." (Romans 13:8–10)

Substitute the word "wife" for "neighbor" in this passage, and we have a great guideline for marriage:

You shall love your wife as yourself.

Love does no harm to your wife;

therefore love is the fulfillment of the law.

This passage contains the summation of all three aspects of a husband's job description:

Love your wife by serving her.

Love your wife by supplying for her.

Love your wife with excellence.

"Husbands, love your wives, just as Christ also loved the church and gave Himself for her" (Ephesians 5:25). This is the standard for determining whether you are truly loving your wife. It is not enough to say the words "I love you." Love is an action.

Did Jesus ever beat His followers? Did He ever humiliate them or make cruel jokes about them? Did Jesus ever selfishly assert His rights? Never! In stark contrast to Christ's example, many men treat their wives in unloving ways.

Jesus showed His love for us while we were still sinners. A husband may say, "If my wife would just respect me, then I would love her." But this is not the kind of love Jesus models; His love is unconditional. So a man's love for his wife must also be unconditional.

I know a man who only does nice things for his wife when he wants to have sex with her. He will buy her flowers and other presents, expecting her to stop whatever she is doing and meet his physical needs. But if she does not respond immediately to his demands, he becomes angry and verbally abusive. She doesn't feel loved; she feels used. Is her husband showing unconditional love? No. Does Jesus ever love us like that? Absolutely not!

Most (if not all) men who read this book truly do love their wives. But you yourself may sense that your wife doesn't feel loved, perhaps because that is what she keeps telling you. You want to love her, but somehow your best efforts seem to fall flat. I (Tim) had the same problem. I knew I was to love my wife like Jesus loves us, but I kept failing. My marriage suffered because Mary Lou felt unloved. Let me tell you my story.

WHAT LANGUAGE ARE YOU SPEAKING?

It was Christmas morning. I was feeling pretty pleased with myself: I had bought a lot of presents for Mary Lou and had even wrapped them myself. As she opened the first present, I expected her to jump into my arms. Instead, she responded with a less than enthusiastic smile and "Oh, thank you." The scene repeated itself as she opened each present. I didn't understand what the problem was! I thought that perhaps she was tired. But as the day progressed, it became increasingly clear that she wasn't happy.

I had bought her some new pots and pans, dishes, and kitchen towels. I thought she would be thrilled with these practical gifts. But as I watched her wash the dishes and pots and put them in the cupboards (with what I deemed excessive slamming and banging), I knew I had done something wrong. But what?

The temperature between us remained cold for several days. I felt unappreciated and didn't understand why she was acting so distant. Then I came across an article by Gary Chapman about the "five love languages." As I read, I began to understand. When I came home from work, I handed Mary Lou the article and an apology. I said, "I just realized that I've been speaking another 'love language.' I have been trying to express my love for you, but I was going about it all wrong." We spent the next few hours talking about the article and the very different ways in which we communicate and understand love.

When I was growing up, my family had expressed love in very practical ways. It was not uncommon for me to get socks for Christmas or for my birthday. Mary Lou, on the other hand, had a father who had bought romantic presents for his wife. As a result, Mary Lou expected love to be expressed through the giving of romantic gifts.

In giving Mary Lou practical gifts that Christmas morning, I was trying to say "I love you." But I was speaking my own love language. Mary Lou longed for a personal gift—something just for her, not something the whole family would use (or that she would use to serve us!). She needed to feel that I loved her as a person, not just as my housekeeper or cook!

When Mary Lou realized that practical gifts constituted an expression of love in my "language," she realized in turn that the gifts she had been giving me were missing the mark in a similar way. Typically, she would buy me something sentimental—a framed picture or some knick-knack inscribed with "I love you." I would shrug my shoulders and set her gifts aside, not sure what to do with such "impractical" items. Our mutual realization that we were speaking two different love languages was revolutionary.

When Valentine's Day rolled around, I finally got it right: I bought Mary Lou a two-cup coffee maker. That time she did jump into my arms! This was not a "practical" gift at all because Mary Lou was the only one in our family who drank coffee. We hadn't bought a coffee machine previously because it hadn't seemed practical to have a machine for just one person. But when I found this small coffee maker, I realized that it would "speak" her love language.

Learning to speak your wife's love language is necessary if you are to fulfill your job requirements. How can a man serve his wife if he does not communicate his love in a way she can understand? She will perceive her husband's service as self-serving or manipulative. When I bought Mary Lou only practical gifts, I was really thinking of myself: I preferred to spend money on practical things. In reality, I was serving my own interests.

How can I supply what my wife needs if I do not speak her love language? Mary Lou didn't need new pots and pans. She was content with the old ones! What she did need was reassurance that I loved her as a person—as my wife, not just as my cook. She needed to feel that I *knew* her. I have learned that she will be thrilled if I buy her even a single flower. For Mary Lou, the cost is not what matters; it is the personal touch.

How can a man strive for excellence if he doesn't take time to learn his wife's love language? Just like the farmer learns to properly interpret the "language" of his animals, husbands, must learn what communicates love to their wives. (We urge you to read *The Five Love Languages* by Gary Chapman. We include in "Tools for the Garden" some resources to help men and women identify their love languages.)

Husbands, we are to love our wives as Jesus loves His church. Did Jesus speak the five love languages? Yes! Using the five love languages Gary Chapman presents, *(quality time, acts of service, words of affirmation, physical touch, and gifts)* [5] let's examine how Jesus communicated His love to us.

1. **Quality time**
   a. Jesus spent time alone with His disciples (Mark 6:30–32).
   b. Jesus promises to be with us always (Matthew 28:20).
2. **Acts of service**
   a. Jesus came to serve (Mark 10:45).
   b. Jesus modeled servanthood (John 13:14–15).
3. **Words of affirmation**
   a. Jesus spoke words of joy (John 15:11).
   b. Jesus spoke words of peace (John 16:33).
4. **Physical touch**
   a. Jesus touched the children (John 19:13).
   b. Jesus often touched people when He healed them (John 20:34).
5. **Gifts**
   a. Jesus explained that the Father gives good gifts (Matthew 7:11).
   b. Jesus is the Bread of Life (John 6:34–35).
   c. Jesus gives eternal life (John 10:28).
   d. Jesus gave His own life (John 3:16).

We were speaking with a young man one day about love languages and he replied incredulously, "My wife needs to understand me. That is her job. It is her problem if she doesn't speak my love language. I don't see why I need to change at all." Our answer was very simple: "Jesus came and spoke your language. He willingly sacrificed everything in order to communicate the love of the Father to you. This is the kind of love you are to have for your wife."

Jesus could have looked down on all of us from heaven and said to God, "Father, I know these people you created don't understand our love for them, but I am Your Son. I don't need to go down to their level and try to communicate with them. They are lost, and they can stay that way!" But that is not what Jesus said. Rather, Jesus came to earth in the flesh to "speak our language." He came to reveal the Father's love for us and to pay the price for our redemption.

Men, Jesus set the standard for us to follow: We are to love our wives as He loved the church and gave Himself for her. Jesus' love is unconditional: "But God demonstrates His own love toward us, in that while we were still sinners, Christ died for us" (Romans 5:8). Jesus didn't wait for us to respect Him or obey Him or respond to Him with love. No, Jesus died for us while we were still sinners. Learn to love your wife unconditionally, in the same way in which Christ loves us.

Men, we offer the following Scripture as our closing prayer for you:

"Therefore be imitators of God as dear children. And walk in love, as Christ also has loved us and given Himself for us, an offering and a sacrifice to God for a sweet-smelling aroma" (Ephesians 5:1–2).

"And this I pray, that your love may abound still more and more in knowledge and all discernment, that you may approve the things that are excellent, that you may be sincere and without offense till the day of Christ" (Philippians 1:9–10).

"But above all these things put on love, which is the bond of perfection" (Colossians 3:14).

STUDY GUIDE

Read Mark 10:42–45; Philippians 2:5–8; Ephesians 5:25–29;
John 13:12–15; 1 Peter 3:7; 1 Timothy 3:2

We began this chapter on the roles of men by carefully avoiding the controversy over the various meanings of "head" (as, for example, in the phrase "head of the wife.") Our solution? We applied each of three possible meanings of the word to man's roles in marriage. We believe the Bible has a great deal to say about each one of these valuable definitions.

If you read this chapter carefully and understood the immense responsibility you have as a husband, you might be thinking, "This is impossible! How can I ever fulfill my role as husband?" Don't despair! Remember: God doesn't ask us to do anything that is impossible. But one thing is certain: it is impossible to do alone! You need the power of the Holy Spirit.

Because men are to follow the example of Jesus' love for His Bride, the church, it is vital that men understand this important aspect of their job description: Love your wife! We concluded this chapter by discussing the importance of learning to speak your wife's love language. Men, you could say to your wives, "Ich liebe dich!" ("I love you!") a thousand times a day, but if she doesn't speak German, she'll never get the message. Make the effort to learn to speak her "love language." Men, let's roll up our sleeves and dig a little deeper.

DIGGING DEEPER
1. Three possible meanings of "head" are:
   a.

   b.

   c.

2. What is the first job description for husbands?

3. How did Jesus model leadership?

4. What is the second aspect of the job description for husbands?

5. What are the two key words from Ephesians 5:28–29?

   a.

   b.

6. How are you to "nourish" your wife?

7. What do you find difficult about "nourishing" your wife?

8. Paraphrase 1 Peter 3:7.

9. Explain the Biblical meaning of "weaker vessel."

10. Explain the Biblical meaning of "giving honor."

11. What is the third aspect of the job description for husbands?

12. What is the key point of 1 Timothy 3:2?

13. How do you typically communicate your love to your wife?

14. What does your wife usually do, to communicate her love for you?

15. Ask your wife to rate on a scale of 1 to 10 (10 being the highest) how well you communicate love to her.

16. Take the love language test with your wife. (See the resource section.) What is your wife's primary love language? What is your primary love language?

17. Ask your wife to tell you three things you could do that would clearly communicate your love for her.

CHAPTER THIRTEEN

WOMAN IN THE GARDEN

Roles For Women

L et's go back to the Garden of Eden and re-examine the first days of creation. Remember that after God created man, He said, "It is not good that the man should be alone" (Genesis 2:18). God didn't suddenly discover that man was alone and decide that it wasn't good; He knew all along what man needed. It was always part of God's divine plan to create woman. God gave woman her first job description: "And the LORD God said, 'I will make him an help meet for him'" (Genesis 2:18 KJV).

Some read the word "help" and believe that it infers a person of lower standing, as in "kitchen help" or "house help." Although the term sometimes is used to refer to an uneducated person who has little or no training and who is hired for menial jobs, this is not how the word is used in the Bible.

The Hebrew word for "help," *"ezer,"*[1] is used both to describe a woman's role and to describe God's role in our lives. God Himself is often referred to as our "help." In Psalm 115:11, we read, "You who fear the LORD, trust in the LORD; He is their help and their shield." Psalm 33:20 reminds us, "Our soul waits for the LORD; He is our help and our shield." If the God of the Universe refers to Himself as "our Help," then we can be sure that the word is in no way demeaning.

In fact, this little word incorporates so much truth that we think of it as an acronym that describes God's role for women in marriage.

Honor and Respect

Encourage

Love

Pray

HONOR AND RESPECT

Often, these two words are used synonymously. Webster's defines 'honor' as "high respect;"[2] 'respect' is defined as "to feel or show honor."[3] So what's the difference? The Greek word for "respect" (translated "reverence" in the KJV) is *phobeo*. A direct translation carries the idea of "fear," but it also means "to reverence, venerate, to treat with deference."[4] Thus, "respect" can focus on outward actions in response to a person's position. In contrast, the Greek word for "honor" means "to value, esteem highly, or to be precious."[5] Thus, "honor" focuses more on emotions toward something or someone perceived to be of value. Think of it this way: Respect is in response to a person's position or authority; honor relates to how I value the person. Both respect and honor result in positive actions, but the motivation for those actions is different.

> *Respect is in response to a person's position or authority; honor relates to how I value the person.*

Consider this example: I *respect* a policeman who directs me to stop my car. I acknowledge his position and I obey him, but I do not necessarily *honor* him. But imagine that the policeman is my father: Not only do I respect his authority, but I also honor him because of who he is in my life.

Another example may be a soldier who has acted heroically and is honored with a medal. The military honors him because they value his actions. Perhaps he is a low-ranking soldier and therefore he won't be given respect as a commander – but he is given honor for his heroic deeds.

Honor and respect go hand in hand. Wives are to respect their husbands because of the position of leadership God has given them. Wives are to honor them because they are a gift from God.

RESPECT

Ephesians 5:33 says, "Nevertheless let each one of you in particular so love his own wife as himself, and let the wife see that she respects [reverences] her husband." This is a command, not a suggestion. Notice that this verse does not say:

- Respect your husband IF he deserves it;
- Respect him IF he is loving;
- Respect him IF he always makes the best choices; or
- Respect him IF he earns it.

No, a wife's respect for her husband is to be unconditional. We are to respect our husbands out of respect for God, who placed our husbands in a position of leadership. Sadly, many women fail miserably in this area. Hurt by the actions of our husbands, we lash out in disrespect. Perhaps our husbands have done something that has caused us to lose trust, and with that loss of trust comes a loss of respect. Nevertheless, the truth of God's Word remains. Regardless of culture, society, or experience, we are commanded to respect.

> *We are to respect our husbands out of respect for God.*

Unconditional respect does not mean that we allow our husbands to do whatever they want, especially when their actions are sinful or abusive. Rather, unconditional respect means that we confront our husbands when we see areas of sin or when their actions are not righteous. But even when we confront, we do it respectfully, not nagging, yelling, pointing a finger, being sarcastic, or backbiting.

Some women have said, "My husband is not a believer. He does not deserve my respect." But 1 Peter 3:1 and 2 say, "In the same way, you wives, be submissive to your own husbands so that even if any of them are disobedient to the word, they may be won without a word by the behavior of their wives, as they observe your chaste and respectful behavior" (NASB).

Peter is writing in this passage about disobedient husbands—whether unsaved or unfaithful to the Lord—and how their wives are to respond. Women, do you want to win your husbands for Christ? Here is the key:

Your behavior needs to be characterized by purity and respect. This is to be your testimony at home. No scheme to change your husband will ever be as effective as simply being obedient to what God has commanded: Respect your husband.

Men need to be respected. There was a recent survey that helps illustrate this point. In this survey men were asked if they would rather:

- Feel alone and unloved in the world or...
- Feel inadequate and disrespected.

Three out of four men said they'd rather feel alone and unloved than feel disrespected.[6] This doesn't mean that men don't need love. But it does reveal what many men value more: respect. Respect is not based on what men do but rather on who they are. Every man wants to be a hero. They long for admiration, appreciation, and esteem.

Imagine that you manage a small company. You are responsible for the success of the business, so you have issued clear guidelines designed to keep things running smoothly and avoid chaos. But no one in your office respects you. Your employees act as though they are the bosses. They ignore your instructions, belittle your leadership, and do whatever they want. How would you feel? Would you enjoy this kind of work environment? Day after day of arguing with your employees, defending your decisions, and guarding against backstabbing might prompt you to quit!

Isn't this what happens in many marriages? Women refuse to respect the position of leadership God has given their husbands. They are defiant, rebellious, and disrespectful toward their husbands. Is it any surprise that so many husbands "quit?"

Many men have fallen into the sin of adultery. A lack of respect is often a contributing factor. Perhaps a female co-worker shows the man respect. Unlike the man's wife, she doesn't yell at him for leaving his socks on the floor. She doesn't criticize every decision he makes. She doesn't belittle him in front of her friends. She may think he is amazing! She laughs at his jokes and compliments his appearance. She praises his abilities. She shows him respect.

As counselors, we have become aware of numerous situations in which men have had affairs with women not nearly as beautiful or as attractive as their wives. What attracted them to this adulterous affair?

Often, the "other" women showed respect, something every man needs and longs for and something their wives failed to do.

Although we do not excuse these men's sinful actions, we believe that every wife needs to acknowledge this reality: if your husband doesn't feel like the king of his castle when he is at home, he may be tempted to build his castle somewhere else.

It is not always easy to show respect, especially to a husband who is cruel and hurtful. But wives are commanded to respect their husbands, and every command brings blessing if we obey it. If you ask Him to, the Lord will give you the wisdom and strength to show your husband respect.

How can you respect your husband?

1. Acknowledge that God has given him—not you—the role of leading the family.

2. Ask him to be the leader of your home. If he is reluctant, it may be because you undermined him in the past. He may feel insecure. Or he may have resigned his role as leader because he has grown weary of trying to assert his leadership. Let him lead. Invite him to take leadership, and then step back and let him do it.

3. Allow him to explain his choices. Don't be so quick to assume that you know what his motivations are. If you don't understand or like what he is doing, don't tell him he is wrong. You might say instead, "I am confused about your decision. Can you please explain your thinking?"

4. Avoid phrases such as "I knew you were wrong." "Why do you always do that?" "Why can't you be more like …" and "What's wrong with you?"

5. Accept the fact that you might not always agree with your husband's final decision. You have the responsibility to share (respectfully) your insights and wisdom, but allow your husband to make the final decision. Leave the results in God's hands. After all, your husband—not you—will have to answer to God.

6. Abstain from criticizing him in front of your children, family, or friends. Even if you don't agree with him, keep your mouth shut! Women must learn to keep their critical words to themselves.

7. Admit it openly when you have acted disrespectfully. There have been times when I was angry with Tim and lashed out at him in front of our children. After I apologized to him, I apologized to our children for treating their father disrespectfully.

8. Absolutely never undermine your husband's authority. (We are not speaking here of situations in which a wife or her children may be in danger because of an abusive husband or father.) Too many women boast of going behind their husbands' backs: They sneak money, lie about where they are going or what they are doing, and encourage their children to disobey their fathers' guidelines. Not only is this disrespectful, but it is sin. How do you feel when your husband goes behind your back, deceives you, or undermines your role? You feel disrespected. Do not treat your husband this way!

This list does not describe every aspect of respect, but it is a starting point. The important thing to remember is that respect is acknowledging the husband's position of authority in marriage.

HONOR

Honor involves placing value and great worth on who your husband is. Even as respect is not contingent on your husband's performance, so honor is not afforded according to the worthiness of his accomplishments. Honor considers the man, not the things he has done. Honor says, "I choose to value you because you are valuable to me."

> Honor says, "I choose to value you because you are valuable to me."

I am often amazed when I visit art galleries and see the high cost of certain paintings. Why does one painting sell for thousands of dollars and another for only a few? As we often say, "Beauty is in the eye of the beholder."

Honor is much the same. Whatever I value, I honor. For example, Tim once bought a small, framed painting for me. To anyone else, it probably seems rather ordinary—certainly not a treasure. But I love it and have hung it in a place of honor in our home. It is something I cherish. Every time I see it, it evokes sweet memories. I dust it and make sure it hangs straight. I honor it because I value it.

Women, we are to honor our husbands not because they are amazing or handsome or intelligent or romantic but because they are our husbands. Our husbands are gifts from God, and we must learn to think of them as a priceless treasure.

Proverbs 31 describes a godly woman. Verse 23 says, "Her husband is known in the gates, when he sits among the elders of the land." Why does her husband sit in such an honorable place? I believe it is because his wife has treated him with honor. We know far too well the power of our words to destroy. But our words also have power to build up. The wife who treats her husband with honor will find that he will live up to her image of him. In the same way, the wife who constantly nags and tells her husband he is foolish will find that her husband "lives down" to her expectation. If we honor our husbands with our words and actions, we will be amazed at the men our husbands will become.

How can you honor your husband?

The wife's job is to be her husband's "help meet." One of the greatest ways to help your husband is to honor him. Consider the analogy of the priceless possession and how we honor that which we cherish.

1. We keep it safe. We protect it from harm or damage. Honor your husband by protecting him from harmful words (especially yours!), negative influences, and exposure to temptation (for example: filter through magazines to guard your husband from being exposed to explicit material).

2. We show it off. We tell others about our treasure. Honor your husband by bragging about him. Tell your friends how thankful you are for your husband. Tell your children how blessed they are to have the father they have. If your husband is truly your priceless treasure, then you will not belittle or ridicule him in front of your family or friends. Rather, you will look for ways to build him up and "show him off."

3. We place it in a position of honor or prominence. Give your husband a position of honor in the home. Put his interests above your own (for example: buy foods he likes and plan activities he enjoys).

4. We take care of it. We keep it clean and maintain its condition. Honor your husband by maintaining your relationship. Make it a priority to spend time together. Don't give him the "leftovers" of your time and energy. If an important person were to come to your home, you would treat him with honor. You would dress your best, make the house spotless, prepare good food, and give him your undivided attention. Does your husband deserve any less? If he is your priceless treasure, then treat him that way!

Both honor and respect are unconditional. Do not say, "My husband is a jerk! He doesn't deserve my respect" or "My husband has failed me so many times. There is no way I will honor him." Respect is based on his role as husband; honor is based on who he is. Do not withdraw honor or respect because of failure on your husband's part. Wives are to honor and respect their husbands—regardless of whether we think they "deserve" it—out of obedience to Christ,. It is not our responsibility to see that our husbands do their jobs correctly. They (and we) are answerable to God. Our responsibility is to ensure that we are doing our job: giving honor and respect. God will not excuse our bad behavior because we considered our husbands to be losers. We each must stand before the Lord and account for our actions. Choose to honor and respect!

Respect is based on his role as husband; honor is based on who he is.

ENCOURAGE

The second letter in HELP, "E," stands for *encourage.* Again let's return for a moment to the Garden of Eden. After sin entered the world and God pronounced His punishments, Adam gave his wife her name. This powerful interjection in the narrative reveals Adam's faith. In

Genesis 3:20 we read, "And Adam called his wife's name Eve, because she was the mother of all living." Despite the curses—most significantly the reality of death having entered their lives—Adam calls his wife "the mother of all living." God promised that from the seed of woman, Jesus the Savior would come to give eternal life. But we also see Adam's recognition of a second aspect of his wife's role – mother of all living. The Hebrew word for Eve, *Chavvah,* is translated "life giver."[7] Women, do

Am I a "life giver?"

you bring "life" to your family, or do your actions destroy and instead bring death? "The wise woman builds her house, but the foolish pulls it down with her hands" (Proverbs 14:1). Ask yourself: "Am I building up my home (filling it with life), or am I tearing it down with my own hands (bringing destruction)? Am I a "life giver?"

Webster's defines *encourage* as "to give courage, hope, or confidence; to hearten; to give support, to foster, to help."[8] Eve's name suggests that she encouraged her family (that is, she brought hope, courage, and confidence). Do you encourage your husband? Do you give courage, hope, confidence, support, and help?

In the King James Version of the New Testament, the word 'encourage' is translated "comfort." The Greek word *parakaleo* stems from the words *kaleo*[9] ("called") and *para*[10] ("besides"), thus meaning "to call to one's side."[11] Consider that the root word *Parakletos*[12] is used to describe the Holy Spirit, the Comforter, the One who comes alongside to encourage.

Isn't this a beautiful picture of a wife's role? We are called to *come alongside* our husbands. We are to be life givers, not life takers! Paul wrote to the church about his concern for its growth. Colossians 2:2 says, "that their hearts may be encouraged, being knit together in love, and attaining to all riches of the full assurance of understanding, to the knowledge of the mystery of God, both of the Father and of Christ."

Encouragement emanates from our words and actions. Proverbs 18:21 teaches, "Death and life are in the power of the tongue, and those who love it will eat its fruit." Proverbs 10:11 says similarly, "The mouth of the righteous is a well of life, but violence covers the mouth of the wicked." In Ephesians 4:29, we read, "Let no corrupt word proceed out of your mouth, but what is good for necessary edification, that it may impart grace to the hearers."

Ask yourself: What comes out of your mouth most often? Do you speak words that build up—that edify—your husband? Do your words impart grace? Or do "corrupt words proceed out of your mouth?" When something is corrupt, it is rotten or decaying. It is the opposite of life giving.

Proverbs 31 describes another attribute of the godly woman: "She opens her mouth with wisdom, and on her tongue is the law of kindness" (Proverbs 31:26). This verse iterates several key characteristics:

- She speaks words of wisdom.
- She doesn't open her mouth unless it is to speak wisdom.
- She rules her tongue by the law of kindness.

This woman has learned the power of an encouraging word. Having experienced the power of kind words, it should be the goal of all wives to offer them, particularly to our husbands.

Our actions also can encourage our husbands. Do we welcome him when he comes home? Do we strive to make our home a "sanctuary," a place where our husband feels safe, relaxed, and revived? Continue reading Proverbs 31:27: "She watches over the ways of her household and does not eat the bread of idleness." Taking care of your home is not just about cleaning the floors or picking up the trash. It is about providing an environment of encouragement. If you have allowed your house to fall into complete disarray, your husband probably will not feel that it is a welcoming or restful place. Most men appreciate a home that is in order. Whether you live in a one-room apartment or a mansion, you can create a place of sanctuary by ensuring that your home is clean and organized. This is a great way to encourage your husband.

Titus 2:5 instructs older women to teach younger ones "to be discreet, chaste, *homemakers,* good, obedient to their own husbands, that the word of God may not be blasphemed." Consider the word "homemakers." This does not mean that a wife must stay at home and not have a career. The honorable woman described in Proverbs 31 is industrious inside as well as outside her home (Proverbs 31:16, 20, 24). The point is that she makes her home a home. Regardless of whether a wife is a stay-at-home mom or works full time outside the home, she must ensure that her house is a home. That is what a "homemaker" does. Doing so encourages her husband as well as her family.

Throughout our marriage, our finances have been limited. I (Mary Lou) wanted to be a good homemaker but found myself frustrated by limited funds. How could I create a sanctuary for my husband, a home of which he would be proud? I learned that the most important thing is to pray! The same God who created the universe full of beauty, color, and elegance can inspire me to be creative in making my home an encouraging place. I have often spent hours praying over a room or project, asking God to help me find good deals, to conceive of ingenious and innovative ideas, and to provide me with skill to bring plans to completion. Sometimes the Lord has surprised and thrilled me through an unexpected gift from a friend. When we first moved to Austria, I found some incredible deals at the thrift store. Our house wasn't fancy, but it was a home!

When children are young, it is challenging to keep the house clean and in order. It is unrealistic to expect to receive the *"Good Housekeeping* seal of approval" when you have three children under the age of four! But even when our children were young, I set a standard for our home that proved helpful, particularly in later years. I taught our children from the time they were toddlers that the living room was not a playroom and that it needed to be kept clean. Their toys belonged in their rooms.

Create a sanctuary that is a blessing to your husband.

Because Tim was a pastor, it was important that people be able to visit without tripping over toys and trash. Tim was encouraged when he came home from work and walked into an orderly home. Because the living room was the first room he saw, I focused my energy on keeping just this one room presentable. Not everything was perfect (especially when our children were small), but I was able to create a sanctuary that was a blessing to my husband. You situation may be different than ours, but it is important for your husband to feel blessed when he walks in the door.

Being an encouragement to your husband in words and in deeds is an important role.

LOVE

Titus 2:4a urges "that they admonish the young women to love their husbands...." The Greek word translated "love" in this verse is *philos,* meaning "friend or companion."[13] Tim is my best friend. I love doing things with him, sharing my secrets with him, and spending hours just talking with him. There is no one else with whom I would rather be. I have close girlfriends who mean a great deal to me, but Tim is my best friend. It is important that we learn to be friends with our husbands.

How do we cultivate a friendship? We make it a priority to spend time together. Even after years of marriage, Tim and I cherish our date nights: We still love to go to the movies, out to dinner, or just for walks.

A number of years ago we met Jeff and Tanya. They had two children, a 12-year-old boy and a 10-year-old girl. I'll never forget the afternoon I spent with Tanya. She confided in me that she and her husband had grown apart. She admitted that all her attention and energy was spent on their children. They were her world. Her husband had his job and other interests. Jeff and Tanya lived in the same house, but theirs had become a marriage of convenience. Tanya flatly stated her expectation that once the kids were out of the house, her husband would be gone. She had despaired of anything changing and had resigned herself to living a lonely, empty life.

Tanya's mistake was making her children the center of her universe. She had pushed her husband out of her life. She never had time for him and wasn't interested in his job or hobbies. Everything in her world revolved around their kids. The reality was that Tanya was not loving her husband; her children had become her idols.

I am a passionate mom. I love all five of our children, and they would tell you how readily I would sacrifice anything for them—anything, that is, except my relationship with their father! Our children learned early on that mom and dad's time together was sacred. Sometimes they whined and cried when we left them with a babysitter, but we lovingly reminded them that their parents needed time alone together.

Now four of our five children are married. My role in their lives has changed. We still enjoy close relationships with one another, but they don't need me to be "mom" anymore. I am still their advisor and friend. But we have entered a new season of life. It is dangerous to build your world solely upon your identity as "mom." Sooner or later, your role as mother will change. If you invested all your time, energy, and priorities in your children, you will find yourself empty as they grow and leave your home. Your marriage is for life. You must learn to invest in your friendship with your husband. This is the first aspect of "love your husband."

Invest in your friendship with your husband.

We discussed the second aspect of loving your husband in the previous chapter, "Roles for Men," in the sub-section entitled "What Language Are You Speaking?" We encourage wives as well as husbands to read that section, and we commend *The Five Love Languages,* by Gary Chapman, to you.

As wives, it is of utmost importance that we understand what communicates love to our husbands—that is, what "love language" our husband speaks. We often communicate in the love language we understand best and then feel offended when our husbands don't understand us. Far too often, husbands feel unloved by wives who truly do love them but who fail to communicate their love in ways the husbands understand.

One of Tim's primary love languages is "quality time." Often, he will go shopping with me just because he wants to be together (he *really* doesn't enjoy shopping!). I cuddle up next to Tim as he watches movies because I know that just being beside him communicates love to him. Many times I have given up doing something I would rather do because I have made it my priority instead to communicate my love to my husband. It took me years to learn this—in fact, I still am learning—but it is well worth the effort.

I also have had to learn to interpret the ways in which Tim communicates his love to me. It is not uncommon for Tim to clean the kitchen for me, to do some laundry, and to take out the trash—all without being asked. He will give me that little boy grin and say, "Look! I did all the cleaning for you." What he really is saying is "I love you so much that I wanted to serve you."

The challenge for me is that "serving" is not my primary love language. (I am not fluent in that dialect!) For years, I would glance at the work Tim did and would say "Thanks!" and then go about my business. Tim would sit there, dejected, not understanding why I hadn't jumped into his arms! I have learned to recognize why he serves me and now can "translate" his meaning. Gaining this understanding has enriched our relationship!

SEX

For many men, physical touch is a primary love language. Many women do not understand that most men have a strong sex drive. Generally speaking, men and women are wired very differently sexually. This can lead to significant misunderstandings between man and wife. The wife may not understand why her husband wants sex all the time; she may feel that he is using her. Meanwhile, her husband feels rejected and frustrated.

It is important for women to understand that God has given man his sex drive. His need for sex is very different from hers. (We acknowledge that we are making generalizations; certainly there are men and women who don't fit this description.) A man's need for sex is physical as well as emotional. Physically, a man experiences relaxation and restoration as a result of the sex act. No matter how tired a man is, he desires sex because it actually helps him relax and sleep better. But when a woman (especially a young mom) is tired, all she wants to do is sleep. The stage is set for conflict! The husband thinks, "We are both tired, but sex will help us sleep better!" even as the wife turns away, thinking, "Can't you leave me alone? I am exhausted!"

Emotionally, a husband's need for sex involves several key facts: **First, sex may be the only way he knows to express intimacy.** Remember that women typically are better at expressing their emotions. Women have many ways to express intimacy. Many men, however, struggle in this area, and they view sex as the primary way to enjoy closeness with their wives. When a man's wife rejects his sexual advances, the man feels frustrated and hurt. Unfortunately, the wife doesn't understand her husband's attempt at intimacy and thinks he is just being an animal.

Because a husband may believe sex is the best (or even the only) way to express intimacy, he may suggest having sex after he and his wife have an argument. He feels the need to restore and heal their relationship in the primary way he understands: sex. For the husband, having sex says, "Our relationship is good again." His wife, on the other hand, may view his advances as manipulation. She may think that he only apologized so he could have sex with her. Women, we need to gain a better understanding of our husband's emotional needs.

Second, your husband's need for sex involves his masculinity and self-worth. When you reject your husband sexually, you reject him. He may question his masculinity, his ability to satisfy you, and his identity. Many wives simply tolerate sex with their husbands. This can be as harmful as outright rejection. When a husband sees that his wife enjoys sex and that he has satisfied her needs, he feels rewarded and experiences a boost to his self-esteem. Too few women understand how profoundly important their sexual response is to their husbands. A wife who shows her pleasure and enjoyment sexually communicates her love and acceptance to her husband in a powerful way. By the same token, an indifferent, unenthused, unmotivated attitude toward sex can destroy his self-worth.

The Bible gives some clear guidelines for a woman's sexual relationship with her husband:

"Let the husband render to his wife the affection due her, and likewise also the wife to her husband. The wife does not have authority over her own body, but the husband does. And likewise the husband does not have authority over his own body, but the wife does" (1 Corinthians 7:3–4).

God designed sex to portray sacrificial love. Women's bodies belong to their husband; men's bodies belong to their wives. But one person cannot demand that the other perform in a certain way. We give up our natural rights to our spouse. We look to the needs of our partner without insisting on our own needs being met. The marriage bed is to be defined by mutual submission. Is this always easy? No! Is it right? Yes! Learning to meet your husband's needs before your own means that you must take your eyes off yourself and focus on him.

> *God designed sex to portray sacrificial love.*

I can almost hear you saying, "Wait! My husband never thinks of me! He only cares about himself." This may be absolutely true, but we aren't talking to husbands right now: We are talking to wives! You must do what is right, even if your husband does not. Allow God to work in his life, and ask God to give you strength to do what He has asked you to do.

In light of the teaching of 1 Corinthians 7:3–4 regarding mutual submission and sacrificial love, we are reminded that wives must NEVER use sex as a weapon against their husbands. Sex is an expression of love and service; it should never be used to manipulate, punish, humiliate, or control your husband.

It is important to acknowledge that sexual sins (especially pornography addiction) can lead to significant problems in the bedroom. Many men with this addiction demand that their wives behave in ways that are not pure. They may have expectations that are unrealistic and even sinful. Some men ask their wives to view pornographic films with them. This is sin. Sexual addiction can lead to a decrease in normal sexual activity with their wives; this is also problematic.

Although we cannot address all these problems in this book, we encourage you to seek godly counsel if your sexual relationship is dysfunctional. Many women have been sexually abused, with consequent dysfunction in their marriages. Prayerfully ask the Lord to lead you to a person who can provide godly guidance and healing to you and your husband. (See the resource section for a list of books that provide more specific help in this area.)

Women, remember: your husband is wired differently than you are. He is not wrong, but he is different! His need for sex is physical and emotional. Sex is often his primary means of expressing love and intimacy. Stop thinking of him as an animal. Learn to recognize his desire for closeness. Remember, too, that sex is extremely important to your husband's self-worth. Love your husband emotionally, mentally, spiritually, and physically.

PRAY

I used to think Tim wasn't such a great preacher. He was a young pastor at a small church, and I thought it was my responsibility to "help" him grow in his ministry. Honestly, I was quite critical! Every Sunday over lunch, I dished up huge servings of negative comments and suggestions. While I was ostensibly trying to "help," the reality was that I was tearing him down. I felt frustrated when he didn't welcome my recommendations and even more annoyed when he made the same "mistake" over and over.

I don't remember what finally made me realize that my approach wasn't working, but something clicked and I realized I needed to keep my mouth shut and just pray for him. I am sure that first Sunday following my decision, he was bracing himself for the customary barrage of criticisms I usually flung at him. But none came. I just kept praying for him, week after week.

Then a truly miraculous thing happened: Tim became an amazing preacher! Each Sunday I was thrilled by the messages he gave. I learned so much, and I grew in my faith. I couldn't believe the change! But the truth was that Tim hadn't changed all that much; I had! God had adjusted my perspective as I had prayed for my husband. As I had spent time in prayer, my heart had become "soft" and open to hearing from the Lord. *My prayer didn't change Tim's preaching; instead, it changed my hearing!*

I thought it was Tim who needed to change but as I was praying for him, God was changing me. Prayer does that. I often meet women who are very critical of their husbands. Quick to point out their husbands' every flaw, they fail to see their own shortcomings. Prayer adjusts our thinking.

Prayer adjusts our thinking.

"Draw near to God and He will draw near to you. Cleanse your hands, you sinners; and purify your hearts, you double-minded" (James 4:8). When we draw near to God in prayer, we notice our filth as we stand in the Light of His holiness. This is where God wants to begin: with YOU! To be "double-minded" means to be unable to decide what is right or wrong. But as we seek the Lord intently and honestly, He will purify our hearts.

We are so bold as to suggest that the majority of the problems in marriages today could be solved if prayer became a top priority. Humble, God-seeking prayer redirects our focus away from the problem and to the Solution. That said, it is not enough to mutter some self-righteous prayer, asking God to change your "sinful" husband. Jesus condemned those who prayed self-serving prayers: "These people draw near to Me with their mouth, and honor Me with their lips, but their heart is far from Me" (Matthew 15:8). James 4:3 explains why we may experience unanswered prayer: "You ask and do not receive, because you ask amiss, that you may spend it on your pleasures." Why are you asking God to change your husband? What is your real motivation? Is it for his benefit or for yours? Are you embarrassed by the way your husband behaves? Are you unwilling to sacrifice your "rights" even as you pray that your husband will stop being so bossy? Are you rebelliously refusing to follow God's design for marriage and yet insisting in prayer that God change your husband?

God wants to change you—to give you His perspective, His wisdom, His strength, and His love. "Seek the LORD and His strength; Seek His face evermore" (1 Chronicles 16:11).

The first thing you need to do is to ask God to open your eyes to the truth about yourself. Be willing to really listen to what God wants to say to you. I needed to confess my critical spirit toward Tim and his ministry. As I spent time in prayer, my negative attitudes gave way to a heart ready to hear God's voice and His Word.

Pray: God, what part have I played in this problem? Where are my blind spots? Show me what I have been doing wrong and what I have failed to do right.

"If My people who are called by My name will humble themselves, and pray and seek My face, and turn from their wicked ways, then I will hear from heaven, and will forgive their sin and heal their land" (2 Chronicles 7:14).

The second thing you need to do is to ask God for knowledge and wisdom. Knowledge has to do with "facts"; wisdom is knowing what to do with the facts. If you are confronting a significant problem in your marriage, the problem may not be with you. Perhaps there is another underlying factor. Ask God for the knowledge to understand what is really happening and then pray for wisdom that you will use the knowledge correctly.

Pray: God, my husband and I have been struggling with this problem for some time. I want to understand the root cause of the problem. I also need to know what steps I should take in response to the knowledge You will give me.

"If any of you lacks wisdom, let him ask of God, who gives to all liberally and without reproach, and it will be given to him. But let him ask in faith, with no doubting, for he who doubts is like a wave of the sea driven and tossed by the wind" (James 1:5–6).

"And though I have the gift of prophecy, and understand all mysteries and all knowledge, and though I have all faith, so that I could remove mountains, but have not love, I am nothing" (1 Corinthians 13:2).

In other words, you may know exactly what the problem is and have all the knowledge you need, but without love, your knowledge is like a clanging cymbal: It is worthless if you lack the wisdom to share your knowledge with love and in the correct way.

The third thing to remember is to not give up. God's timetable is not ours. Perhaps you have been praying for your unsaved husband for years. Don't quit! Psalm 37:7 reminds us, "Rest in the LORD, and wait patiently for Him; do not fret because of him who prospers in his way, because of the man who brings wicked schemes to pass." We don't always understand why God does things the way He does, but we can trust Him. It could be that "learning to wait" is the lesson He is trying to teach you!

Pray: Lord, I feel weary, and at times I want to give up. I have prayed for my husband for years yet it seems he never changes. I know my ways are not Your ways and that You have called me to be faithful and persevere. Lord, give me Your strength. Teach me to wait on You.

"Pray without ceasing, in everything give thanks; for this is the will of God in Christ Jesus for you" (1 Thessalonians 5:17–18).

"As for me, I will call upon God, and the LORD shall save me. Evening and morning and at noon I will pray, and cry aloud, and He shall hear my voice" (Psalm 55:16–17).

"Lead me in Your truth and teach me, for You are the God of my salvation; on You I wait all the day" (Psalm 25:5).

Finally, pray daily for your husband. This is such an important aspect of your job description! We love the Old Testament story of Moses, Aaron, and Hur: As the Israelites fought the Amalekites, Joshua led the army and Moses stood on a hill in view of his people. Whenever Moses held up the rod of the Lord, the Israelite army would succeed; but when his arms grew tired and he lowered the rod, they would start to lose. Aaron and Hur came alongside Moses to help: They stood on either side of him and held up his arms! Israel won the victory that day, and God provided a beautiful reminder of how we need one another.

Take your job seriously: Stand beside your husband in prayer.

Women, through prayer, you can "hold up your husband's arms!" He needs you! Daily he is subject to temptation, stress, worry, and weariness. Take your job seriously: Stand beside him in prayer.

Tim and I love to "pray the Scriptures"—to "pray a passage back" to God. We have been amazed at how the Lord has spoken to us through His Word during these times of prayer. It is especially meaningful to personalize the Scripture. We encourage you to find verses that you can pray for your husband. We conclude this section on prayer with some examples. But please, ask God to show you specifically how you should pray for your husband. *(I have personalized this for Tim. You may wish to insert your husband's name.)*

Lord, I bow my knees in worship and adoration to You, the Father of our Lord Jesus Christ. Thank You for allowing Tim and me to be part of your family and for calling us by Your name. Lord, I pray that You would grant Tim, according to the riches of Your glory, to be strengthened with might through Your Spirit in his inner man. Jesus, I pray that Your presence would dwell in his heart through faith; that he would be rooted and grounded in love—for You, for his family, and for others. I pray that Tim may be able to comprehend with all the saints what is the width and length and depth and height of Your love—that he would know Your love which passes knowledge. I ask that Tim may be filled with all Your fullness—that he may be full of Your power to do the work You have called him to do; full of Your strength; full of Your wisdom. God, I know that You are able to do exceedingly abundantly above all that I ask or think, according to Your power that works in us. Lord, I pray that you would be glorified in our marriage and family, through Christ Jesus. Amen (from Ephesians 3:14–21).

HELP!

"And the LORD God said, I will make him [Adam] an help meet for him" (Genesis 2:18 KJV). Women, what an incredible job God has given us to do! Just as Eve was the mother of all living—the woman who brought life to her family—so should we be the ones who bring life to our families.

Proverbs 31 describes one more aspect of a godly woman. In verses 11 and 12 we read, "The heart of her husband safely trusts her; so he will have no lack of gain. She does him good and not evil." Her husband lacks for nothing! His wife is an asset to him. He trusts her! He feels secure with her. She does good things for him. In short, she helps!

We close this chapter with one final thought: Why is it important for women to follow God's design? Consider this: Marriage is a "picture" of Jesus and His relationship with His Church (Ephesians 5:32). The husband's job is to represent the way in which Jesus loves the Church. In the same way, the wife's job is to represent the Church's relationship to Jesus. Are you a good "representative?" What picture are you painting for the world to see?

Ephesians 3:10 gives us our goal: "to the intent [purpose] that now the manifold wisdom of God might be made known by the church to the principalities and powers in the heavenly places."

God wants the church to reveal His multi-faceted wisdom to principalities and powers in the heavenly places. God's plan is to use the Church—believers like you and me—to communicate His attributes to "principalities and powers."

Women, our role in marriage is to represent the way the Church should be in relationship to Jesus. We should be revealing to the world the "manifold wisdom of God." Talk about a huge responsibility! Our marriages should speak volumes to the world. If we are doing our jobs well, then the world should be able to see God's wisdom, love, grace, mercy, truth, patience, faithfulness, kindness, power, and redemption.

STUDY GUIDE

Read Ephesians 5:33; 1 Peter 3:1, 2; Proverbs 14:1;
Colossian 2:2; Proverbs 10:11; Ephesians 4:29; Proverbs 31;
Titus 2:4–5; 1 Corinthians 7:3–4

"HELP!" No, we don't mean a desperate cry for assistance. Rather, this simple word can be considered an acronym for a wife's job description. In the Garden of Eden, God gave woman her first job: to be the "help meet" for her husband. We have presented the word HELP as an acronym, which we believe summarizes the role of woman.

We explained that the same Hebrew word for "help" that is used to describe a woman's role in marriage is also used to express God role as our "help." If the Lord of lords and King of kings refers to Himself as our "help", then surely it is not degrading for women to be charged with being "help" for their husbands. Let's dig a little deeper.

DIGGING DEEPER

1. The acronym HELP stands for:
   a.

   b.

   c.

   d.

2. What is the difference between honor and respect?

321

3. According to 1 Peter 3:1–2, what is the best way to witness to an unsaved or disobedient husband?

4. Summarize the eight ways in which a woman should respect her husband.

   a.

   b.

   c.

   d.

   e.

   f.

   g.

   h.

5. Bearing in mind the analogy of ways in which we honor a priceless possession, how can you show honor to your husband?

   a.

   b.

   c.

   d.

6. What is the significance of the meaning of Eve's name, particularly as it applies to wives?

7. Paraphrase Colossian 2:2.

8. Encouragement is communicated through our _____ and _____.

9. Which verses speak about "encouraging words?"

10. Which verses speak about "encouraging actions?"

11. What is the meaning of "love" in Titus 2:4, and how can we apply it to marriage?

12. Generally speaking, two key aspects of a man's emotional need for sex are:

    a.

    b.

13. Apply 1 Corinthians 7:3–4 to your marriage.

14. Why is prayer such an important part of a woman's role as "help?"

15. Find a verse that you can "pray for" your husband. Personalize it and write it here as a prayer for him.

CHAPTER FOURTEEN

GOD IN THE GARDEN

The Redeemer

All of creation seemed to hold its breath as God pronounced the curses on mankind. Adam and Eve stood before God with their eyes downcast. Shame and guilt had entered the Garden. The Serpent had been right about one thing: Man had gained the ability to know the difference between right and wrong. But what had this knowledge brought them? A broken relationship with their Maker, curses, and death: These were the price of their disobedience. Adam and Eve had known God as their Creator, Provider, and Companion; now they were introduced to God as Judge. Fortunately for us all, they were introduced to still another aspect of God: Redeemer. God did several things for Adam and Eve that are equally important for us today: *He gave them hope; He covered their sin; and He protected them.*

First, we see **hope** shining through, even in the midst of the curses. When God cursed the Serpent, He included a promise for all mankind: "And I will put enmity between you [the Serpent] and the woman, and between your seed and her Seed; He shall bruise your head, and you shall bruise His heel" (Genesis 3:15). Here, in the wake of Adam and Eve's sin, is the first prophecy that tells of the Redeemer, the One who would come to end the power of Satan. The prophetic reference to the "bruised heel" points to Jesus' death on the cross. God did not leave Adam and Eve without hope. A few verses later, in Genesis 3:20, we read, "And Adam called his wife's name Eve, because she was the mother of all living." The Hebrew word we translate 'Eve' means "life-giver."[1] Adam made a declaration of faith in giving his wife this name. Although death was now a reality, Adam affirmed his trust in God that a "Seed" would come to defeat Satan and death.

Second, God **covered** Adam and Eve, literally and figuratively. "Also for Adam and his wife the LORD God made tunics of skin, and clothed them" (Genesis 3:21). God sacrificed an animal, took its skin, and made clothing for Adam and Eve. God was proactive in providing a solution—albeit a temporary one—to Adam and Eve's sinful state. God established the practice of a blood sacrifice for sin. In this symbolic act, God revealed His plan to sacrifice the Lamb of God, Jesus. Throughout the Old Testament, even prior to the giving of the Law, God's people understood the need for a blood sacrifice for sin. We rejoice because Jesus fulfilled God's requirement once and for all through His death on the cross.

Finally, God **protected** Adam and Eve. One of the most loving acts God did was to expel them from the Garden. How was this loving? Genesis 3:22–23 says, "Then the LORD God said, 'Behold, the man has become like one of Us, to know good and evil. And now, lest he put out his hand and take also of the tree of life, and eat, and live forever'—therefore the LORD God sent him out of the Garden of Eden to till the ground from which he was taken." God did not want to condemn Adam and Eve to their sinful state for all eternity. Instead, He protected them from eating from the tree of life. To have eaten from the tree of life would have meant eternal damnation. God's plan was to send Jesus to pay the price for mankind's sin. Through Jesus' death and resurrection we have the promise of eternal life. In this final chapter, we focus on God's work as Redeemer. In every chapter, we have discussed the importance of making God the center of our marriages. We have covered a lot of material. But one fact underscores it all: we can do nothing without God. He is the Redeemer, and He makes all things new.

THE REDEEMER IN THE GARDEN

In this chapter, we consider the three things God did in response to Adam and Eve's sin and apply them to our marriages.

- God gave them HOPE.
- God gave them COVERING.
- God gave them PROTECTION.

Perhaps you have sung the song "There is a Redeemer" but never truly considered its meaning. Webster's defines 'redeem' as "to buy back."[2] Two Hebrew words and two Greek words in the Bible are translated "redeem." The Old Testament uses the Hebrew word *ga'-al,* which means "to purchase, deliver, or ransom."[3] This word is also used to describe the "kinsman redeemer" so beautifully portrayed in the story of Ruth and Boaz. The other Hebrew word is *padah,* which means "to release, rescue, or preserve."[4] The New Testament uses the Greek words *lutroo* and *exagorazo. Lutroo* means "to ransom"[5] and *exagorazo* "to buy up, ransom, or rescue from loss."[6] These words have three ideas in common: someone or something is in bondage, someone has to pay a ransom, and only then will deliverance come. The imagery in the New Testament is of the slave market, a common scene at the time in which it was written. A slave is helpless to free himself: He needs a redeemer to pay his ransom and set him free.

Many marriages today find themselves on the slave market. Husbands and wives are in bondage to fear, distrust, hurt, disillusionment, despair, and sin. Using every human resource available, they have tried to escape their bondage. Perhaps a couple has spent hundreds of dollars on counseling and has purchased numerous self-help books. Perhaps the couple has attended marriage retreats and promised each other to "try harder." But the chains remain. Neither husband nor wife can find freedom. Many couples today fail to realize that they need a Redeemer. They can never "ransom" their marriage by themselves. They never were meant to be the redeemer. All of their good intentions will never be enough. The price is too high. King David understood redemption. He learned through hardships, trials, and mistakes that only God can redeem. He expresses his understanding of this truth in Psalm 103:2–5: "Bless the LORD, O my soul, and forget not all His benefits: Who forgives all your iniquities, Who heals all your diseases, *Who redeems your life from destruction,* Who crowns you with lovingkindness and tender mercies, Who satisfies your mouth with good things, So that your youth is renewed like the eagle's." God desires to redeem our marriages from destruction as well. As we consider the first action God undertook for Adam and Eve in the wake of their sin, we will learn what He does for us today.

GOD GIVES HOPE

It is important to understand hope. Hope is not based on what you already have obtained. If you already have a million dollars in your bank account, then you aren't hoping to receive it; you already have it. In contrast, hope is rooted in faith. "For we were saved in this hope, but hope

Cry out to the Redeemer... who has the power to save.

that is seen is not hope; for why does one still hope for what he sees? But if we hope for what we do not see, we eagerly wait for it with perseverance" (Romans 8:24–25). We have heard husbands and wives say, "I don't see the possibility of this marriage ever working. It is too late. My spouse will never change. I have given up. There is no hope for this marriage." Their hope was lost

because they were basing their hope on their partner, on their own determination, or on some other faulty basis. These individuals were focused on their bleak situation, not on God. *Our hope must be based on God.* Cry out to the Redeemer—not your partner or your circumstance—to restore your hope. Hope in God, who has the power to save.

Allow the Redeemer to speak words of hope to you. Psalm 42:5 says, "Why are you cast down, O my soul? And why are you disquieted within me? Hope in God, for I shall yet praise Him for the help of His countenance." Jeremiah 29:11 assures us, "'For I know the thoughts that I think toward you,' says the LORD, 'thoughts of peace and not of evil, to give you a future and a hope.'" Paul provides still more encouragement: "Now hope does not disappoint, because the love of God has been poured out in our hearts by the Holy Spirit who was given to us" (Romans 5:5). In his letter to the Romans, he writes, "Now may the God of hope fill you with all joy and peace in believing, that you may abound in hope by the power of the Holy Spirit" (Romans 15:13).

We desperately need to embrace this truth today. The chains of hopelessness are deadly. Once they have wrapped themselves around a marriage, it is hard to break free. If hopelessness has captured you, you are trapped in a pit of despair. In Jeremiah 18:12, we read the result of hopelessness: "And they said, 'That is hopeless! So we will walk according to our own plans, and we will every one obey the dictates of his evil heart.'" This is exactly what happens in marriages today. Couples give up on their marriages and choose to ignore God's ways and do whatever seems right in their own eyes. The result? Disaster! We have met individuals who are so blinded by hopelessness that even when their spouse is truly repentant and willing to work to restore the marriage, they refuse to believe it. These individuals need a Redeemer. Job 33:28 says, "He will redeem his soul from going down to the pit, and his life shall see the light."

A STORY OF HOPE

Neil and Emily had been married for seven years. Both were believers and were actively involved in ministry. However, they had allowed the Serpent access to their "garden," and he had slowly and deceitfully sowed weeds of lust, sin, and, eventually, despair. Because of Neil's struggle with pornography, his wife often felt used. Emily felt that Neil only valued her for sex. She didn't believe that Neil respected her or appreciated her abilities. Emily was a young mother who longed to feel special. Foolishly, she allowed a friendship to develop with another man from their church. They began to spend hours talking together on the phone. It seemed innocent enough: they were just talking. But their conversations grew deeper and more intimate, and they found they had a lot in common. Emily began to deceive her husband in order to find more time to spend with this other man. She deluded herself into believing that her friendship with him was not wrong. After all, they really encouraged each other.

Neil was overloaded with work and ministry, and although he noticed that his wife was acting distant, he dismissed it as simply the result of their busy schedules. Emily's relationship with this other man grew, until finally, their emotional intimacy became physical. Emily was deeply conflicted with feelings of love for this man, who treated her like a queen; yet as a believer, she knew this was sin. This adulterous affair continued for several years. Emily was in bondage. She saw no hope of her husband ever changing and no possible way to stop loving this other man.

But the Lord had not given up on Emily or Neil. Emily finally confessed her affair to her husband; he was deeply hurt, but he was willing to forgive her. But this would not be the "happy ending" to their story. Neil and Emily moved to another city, and Emily broke off contact with the man. But the chains remained. Emily was still in love with the other man and felt no love for her husband. She knew it would be wrong to divorce Neil, but she had given up hope of ever being happy in her loveless marriage.

By this time, God had begun to convict Neil of the way in which his sin and indifference had led to the breakdown in his marriage. Neil repented of his sinful actions and was determined to win his wife back, but she was cold and unresponsive. Any other man would have walked away and divorced his wife. In the first few months after moving to the new city, Emily treated Neil horribly. She could see the hurt etched on her husband's face, but she couldn't break free of the love she felt for the other man. But God whispered hope to Neil. Although he saw no visible signs of life left in his marriage, Neil prayed and placed his hope in the Redeemer. He worked at showing love to his wife even though she rarely acknowledged his attempts.

Eventually the day came when—miraculously—Emily heard a whisper of hope as well. It started as a thought. Emily was praying, and it occurred to her that God didn't intend for her to be miserable. She cried out to the Redeemer: "God, You know I still love this other man. I don't see how I can change. But God, I believe You are able to do miracles. Help me *want* to change." That was the beginning for Emily. She was honest with God. She asked God to help her *want* to change. Slowly that prayer expanded. One day Emily realized she was begging God to change her. She wasn't asking Him to make her want to change; she *did* want to change! Her hope in God grew, and so did her prayer life. "God," Emily prayed, "help me love my husband again." Little had changed externally—certainly nothing that could be seen—but internally, a miracle was taking place. Emily eventually was able to turn away emotionally from her sinful relationship, and her heart turned back toward her husband. It took time, but the day came when Emily prayed, "God, thank you! You have changed me! I really do love my husband again."

Neil and Emily are still married today. God redeemed their marriage from the bondage of sin. Neil held on to hope—not in Emily or in his circumstances—but in God. Emily's hope grew as God changed her heart and brought healing to her marriage. If you were to ask Emily today, she would tell you without hesitation that she loves Neil with all her heart. Both Neil and Emily would also tell you that their marriage has never been better. God is the God of hope.

ANOTHER STORY OF HOPE

Let us share another story of hope. We have known this couple for many years and have been amazed at how God has redeemed their marriage. We asked the wife to share their story with you, from her perspective.

"My heart's desire was for my husband to take over the spiritual leadership in our family. I had been raised in a Christian home where my father was the spiritual head of our family. Growing up I saw the role my mom had and thought I would one day have the same. When I got married, I quickly found out that my husband had had a different role model. He was not taught what it meant to be the spiritual leader of a family. So at first, I took over. It didn't take long for me to realize this was not the way it should be. I tried to push my husband into "his" role but the more I pushed, the more I drove him away.

This was not our only issue. We had different ideas, longings, hopes, and dreams in other areas as well. We came to the point where we knew we needed help from outside. Mary Lou and Tim took time to share, listen, cry, and laugh with us. I learned to actively look for and find the good sides of my husband as well as the special things he would do. Whenever I would talk with friends and work colleagues about my husband, I would only share positive things about my loved one. I knew God had given me a very special partner, and we both needed to learn to be who God wanted us to be in our relationship.

I needed to STOP and wait for my husband to catch up with me spiritually and not to run on without him. I also committed to pray for him, for myself, for us as a couple and for our children.

Others also prayed intensely for us. In the meantime, I had to learn to recognize my partner's way of showing his love for me.

It didn't happen overnight, but as I let go, I started to see God working in his life. It was as if God was just waiting for me to get out of HIS way! As I recommitted to working on our relationship, I noticed how my attitude toward my husband changed. Now my love for my honey is deeper than I ever thought possible.

When I look back over the past 25 years of marriage, I see how far we have come. Both of us have changed. My husband is taking over the spiritual leadership of our family, and I have learned what it means to be a supportive wife and mother. Never again do I want to push my husband or be pushed by him into something or someone that we aren't. I do enjoy challenging him and to be challenged, to support and to be supported, to love and to be loved. Together we want to learn to love God and each other more and more each day."

GOD GIVES COVERING

God provided a beautiful picture of redemption when He made coverings for Adam and Eve. But the coverings weren't free; they cost the life of the animal that was slain to make them. This symbolic act was fulfilled when Jesus went to the cross. As Adam and Eve received physical covering from God, so we receive "covering"—redemption—through Jesus' blood and His forgiveness of our sins. But our "covering" wasn't free: it cost Jesus His life. But, oh, the blessings we receive when we allow ourselves to be "covered" by Jesus! "Blessed is he whose transgression is forgiven, whose sin is covered" (Psalm 32:1).

We need this same covering in our marriages. It is absolutely crucial for marriages to be "covered" by the blood of Jesus. If you truly comprehend the "width and length and depth and height…" of the love of Christ, then you will be able to live with greater love, grace, and mercy in your marriage (Ephesians 3:18). Why is it that Christians who have been ransomed by the Redeemer, whose sins have been covered by the blood of Christ, can be the most unmerciful, judgmental, harsh, and unforgiving of individuals? Where is grace? Where is mercy? Where is forgiveness? Jesus taught His disciples to pray the Lord's Prayer. A little word in that prayer is often forgotten in the context of our marriages: "as." Jesus said, "And forgive us our debts *as* we forgive our debtors" (Matthew 6:12). If we truly understood the implications of the word "as," we might not be willing to repeat the Lord's Prayer as casually as we typically do. Do you realize what you are asking God in this prayer? You are saying, "God, I want you to forgive me *in the same way in which* ("as") I forgive others." Lest you miss the importance of the little word, keep reading: "For if you forgive men their trespasses, your heavenly Father will also forgive you. But if you do not forgive men their trespasses, neither will your Father forgive your trespasses" (Matthew 6:14–15). Jesus couldn't be clearer: Our marriages must be covered by the blood of Christ, but if we are to experience His forgiveness, we must also learn to forgive each other.

> *"God, I want you to forgive me in the same way which I forgive others."*

Isaiah 61:10a says, "I will greatly rejoice in the LORD, my soul shall be joyful in my God; for He has clothed me with the garments of salvation, He has covered me with the robe of righteousness." Do you rejoice in God's forgiveness of your sins? If so, why do you withhold forgiveness from your spouse? If you have truly been covered with the robe of righteousness, then you should know that that robe is big enough to cover two! Proverbs 10:12 reminds us, "Hatred stirs up strife, but love *covers* all sins." And Proverbs 17:9 teaches, "He who covers a transgression seeks love, but he who repeats a matter separates friends."

A STORY OF COVERING

Ross and Christina exemplify one of the most amazing stories of forgiveness we know. Whereas some hurts can be dealt with easily, others take substantially more time to heal. Ross hurt Christina so deeply, no one would have blamed her for walking away and never forgiving him. Christina had opened their home to help Donna, a close relative. Christina and Donna had a very close relationship. Christina was always ready to reach out in practical ways. There had never been any question that Donna should come live with them for as long as she needed. Months passed, and the joy Christina had felt at having her favorite relative so near turned to anguish when Ross told her that he had feelings for

Donna. Christina was devastated. She insisted that Ross leave their home until he could decide with whom he wanted to be. He moved out, and Donna moved in with him. Not only had her husband betrayed her, but Donna had as well. Soon afterward, their divorce was finalized.

But God was not finished. Ross repented of his actions and sought to be reconciled with his wife. I remember thinking at the time how unlikely it was that such a wound could ever be healed. Slowly and cautiously, Ross and Christina began a counseling process. Donna moved out of the area, and Ross and Christina began to date each other again, taking tiny steps forward. Trust had been broken, and it would take time to restore. But God is the Redeemer. Because Christina understood the forgiveness of Christ, she was able to forgive her husband.

Time passed, and Ross and Christina were remarried; and they are still married today! What a miraculous story of grace and mercy! But another act of redemption was yet to come. God had more "covering" to do. Some years later, Christina was attending a family gathering that Donna had asked if she could attend. It took courage for Donna to go to the reunion, especially because she didn't know how Christina would react. But Donna took the initiative and approached Christina with a sincere and humble apology. That's when another miracle occurred, something only God could do: God gave Christina the ability to forgive Donna and to forget the past. The two women were reconciled, and they are closer today than they were before. They never mention the past. They both "stepped under" the covering of Christ's blood and found redemption.

Whenever we meet couples who tell us they can't forgive the hurts they have suffered, we tell them this story. God's power to forgive is far greater than we can imagine. As we experience His power to forgive, we also receive healing and restoration. God is the God of covering.

GOD GIVES PROTECTION

At first glance, it may seem cruel that God kicked Adam and Eve out of the Garden of Eden. It had been the only home they had known. They must have had sweet memories of wandering with God in the cool of the evening. The Garden was exquisite beyond description! Was God just punishing them for their disobedience? We don't think so. He already had pronounced curses on both of them. But God is not only the Judge,

He is also the Redeemer. By expelling Adam and Eve from the Garden, God showed His hand of protection. His removal of Adam and Eve from the Garden protected them from eating from the Tree of Life. Had they eaten of the tree, they would have lived forever in their fallen state. Even though God seemed to make a terrible situation worse, His action was for Adam and Eve's—and all of mankind's—ultimate good.

Romans 8:28 reminds us, "And we know that all things work together for good to those who love God, to those who are the called according to His purpose." Notice that it doesn't say that "all things are good;" rather, it says "all things work together" for good. Have you felt that your marriage is in the wilderness? Perhaps you have felt like Adam and Eve after they got kicked out of the Garden. You may be going through tough times in your marriage, but this may be just the thing that God is using to "work together for good." Just because bad things are happening doesn't mean God has lost control. Remember: Although it seemed like a bad thing for Adam and Eve to be expelled from the Garden, it was for their ultimate good.

In the Old Testament, we read that the Israelites wandered in the wilderness for forty years under the leadership of Moses. At the end of this period, Moses reminded the Israelites of God's provision: "For the LORD your God has blessed you in all the work of your hand. He knows your trudging through this great wilderness. These forty years the LORD your God has been with you; you have lacked nothing" (Deuteronomy 2:7). A few chapters later, Moses states,

"And you shall remember that the LORD your God led you all the way these forty years in the wilderness, to humble you and test you, to know what was in your heart, whether you would keep His commandments or not. So He humbled you, allowed you to hunger, and fed you with manna which you did not know nor did your fathers know, that He might make you know that man shall not live by bread alone; but man lives by every word that proceeds from the mouth of the LORD" (Deuteronomy 8:2–3).

Does that seem like a contradiction? Deuteronomy 2:7 says, "…you lacked nothing," but Deuteronomy 8:23 says, "So He humbled you, allowed you to hunger…" How could Moses say that the Israelites lacked for nothing if the truth was that God allowed them to go hungry? The point is that God always gives us what we need, not always what we want. God knew that the Israelites needed to learn that "man shall not live by

God always gives us what we need, not always what we want.

bread alone," and He used their hunger to teach them. The Israelites never lacked for what was important; God gave them exactly what they needed. He used physical hunger to teach them to rely on Him.

You may find yourself in a difficult time in your marriage. Have you stopped to consider that perhaps God is using this to teach you something? You may be the innocent party in a situation in which you are reaping the consequences of your partner's sin. But this doesn't mean you should run away. God can use even the sins of others to accomplish His purposes. Recall the story of Joseph in the Bible. His brothers hated him and sold him into slavery. And yet God used their sinful act to put Joseph exactly where He wanted him to be—in the land of Egypt—to fulfill His plan. Joseph acted with integrity when his master's wife tried to seduce him, yet he found himself condemned to prison. This doesn't seem fair! Joseph had done what was right! But God used prison as a training ground for Joseph and prepared him to assume leadership as the second most powerful man in the nation. Bad situations? Yes. Were they fair? No. But did they thwart God's purposes? Absolutely not! God used Joseph to save his family and the land of Egypt from a terrible famine. Years later, when Joseph was reconciled with his brothers, he testified of God's purpose: "But as for you [his brothers], you meant evil against me; but God meant it for good, in order to bring it about as it is this day, to save many people alive" (Genesis 50:20).

"My brethren, count it all joy when you fall into various trials, knowing that the testing of your faith produces patience. But let patience have its perfect work, that you may be perfect and complete, lacking nothing" (James 1:2–4).

If you are experiencing a difficult time in your marriage, you need to do three things:

1. *Stand firm; don't run away from the problem.* God has a work He wants to do in your life. "But let patience have its perfect work, that you may be perfect and complete, lacking nothing." It is easy to run away from a troubled marriage. But God has something amazing planned for you both. Allow Him to complete His work in you.

2. *Search your heart.* Be sure that this difficult situation is not the result of *your* sin or poor choices. If it is, then repent. Be prepared to accept the consequences of your sin. "But each one is tempted when he is drawn away by his own desires and enticed. Then, when desire has conceived, it gives birth to sin; and sin, when it is full-grown, brings forth death" (James 1:14–15). Don't blame God for your poor choices. "Search me, O God, and know my heart; try me, and know my anxieties; and see if there is any wicked way in me, and lead me in the way everlasting" (Psalm 139:23–24).

3. *Remember God's protection.* The children of Israel wandered in the wilderness for forty years, and it was difficult. But God was with them the entire time. He provided all they needed. We may not always understand what God is doing, but we can trust Him. Proverbs 3:5–6 reminds us, "Trust in the LORD with all your heart, and lean not on your own understanding; in all your ways acknowledge Him, and He shall direct your paths." The path we are on may take us through the wilderness, but we do not walk alone.

A STORY OF PROTECTION

Tim and I have experienced God's hand of protection in our lives many times. In fact, I am sure that at times we were completely unaware of just how close we were to a fatal accident or some serious disaster. But one experience taught us a lot about God's timing and protection. We had been called to work in Austria, and at first, everything fell beautifully into place. Within an unbelievably short time, we were accepted by the organization with which we would be working. The need for us to get to the field was urgent as we were to take over the leadership of a Christian Retreat Center. The previous director was gone, and the center was vacant. Our organization needed us there right away. But we encountered a number of roadblocks that delayed our arrival for an entire year. Numerous times during that year, we asked ourselves why things had suddenly become so difficult. We knew that God had called us to go. The organization had approved us and was eager for us to get there. We couldn't understand why we kept getting delayed.

Finally, after a year, we were able to fly to Austria. It would be months before we began to understand the reasons for the delay and years before we fully grasped what God had been doing. The first thing we learned was His protection. Unbeknownst to us, there had been a misunderstanding between our organization in the United States and the board of directors in Austria. We were new to the organization and unaware of the history. Because we were unable to arrive in Austria when we had originally planned, members of the stateside organization traveled to Austria to check on the status of the retreat center. During this trip, the stateside organization and the Austrian board were reconciled. By the time we arrived, the situation was resolved, and we were able to start fresh, without inheriting any of the problems of the past. God allowed us to be delayed in order to provide for reconciliation and as a protection for us.

Years later we discovered another purpose in God's timing. During our year of "waiting," we had lived with our four children in an old van, traveling from place to place and ministering in numerous churches. It was a year during which Tim and I learned much about trusting God and allowing Him to lead us. Many times our finances were depleted, yet we saw God perform miracle after miracle in providing for us. We grew closer as a family, and it proved one of the best years in our life together. But it wasn't until much later that we became aware of the impact of this experience on our children. Our oldest daughter grew in her faith in amazing ways. She would scold us whenever we seemed to waver in our trust of the Lord! In fact, this year of waiting prepared our daughter for her future: She and her husband have served in full-time ministry ever since they were married. Many times, God has brought them through the wilderness and yet they have remained strong. Julianne often points to this "year of waiting" as having been pivotal in her spiritual life.

God used that year of "wilderness training" to prepare each of our children for a life in ministry. It wasn't a mistake that our arrival in

Austria was delayed. God was at work! He protected us through the wilderness and continues to do so today. God is the God of protection.

THE REDEEMER IN THE GARDEN

As we bring the instructional portion of this book to a close, we want to emphasize the importance of inviting the Gardener into the garden of your marriage. Perhaps you have already given up. Please listen: God is speaking to you. He hasn't given up on you or your marriage! He is the Redeemer. Carefully read the verses that follow, and allow God to speak to your heart. As you read, you may want to write down any specific promises, assurances, encouragements, or reflections that God may reveal to you. Do this exercise together with your spouse, or do it individually and then share your notes with each other afterward.

"But now, thus says the LORD, who created you, O Jacob, and He who formed you, O Israel: 'Fear not, for I have redeemed you; I have called you by your name; you are Mine. When you pass through the waters, I will be with you; and through the rivers, they shall not overflow you. When you walk through the fire, you shall not be burned, nor shall the flame scorch you'" (Isaiah 43:1–3).

"This I recall to my mind, therefore I have hope. Through the LORD's mercies we are not consumed, because His compassions fail not. They are new every morning; great is Your faithfulness. 'The LORD is my portion,' says my soul, 'Therefore I hope in Him!' The LORD is good to those who wait for Him, to the soul who seeks Him. It is good that one should hope and wait quietly for the salvation of the LORD" (Lamentations 3:21–26).

"I called on Your name, O LORD, from the lowest pit. You have heard my voice: 'Do not hide Your ear from my sighing, from my cry for help.' You drew near on the day I called on You, and said, 'Do not fear!' O Lord, You have pleaded the case for my soul; You have redeemed my life" (Lamentations 3:55–58).

"God is our refuge and strength, a very present help in trouble. Therefore we will not fear, even though the earth be removed, and though the mountains be carried into the midst of the sea; though its waters roar and be troubled, though the mountains shake with its swelling. Selah. There is a river whose streams shall make glad the city of God, the holy place of the tabernacle of the Most High. God is in the midst of her, she shall not be moved; God shall help her, just at the break of dawn" (Psalm 46:1–5).

"The LORD is my light and my salvation; whom shall I fear? The LORD is the strength of my life; of whom shall I be afraid" (Psalm 27:1).

"Have you not known? Have you not heard? The everlasting God, the LORD, the Creator of the ends of the earth, neither faints nor is weary. His understanding is unsearchable. He gives power to the weak, and to those who have no might He increases strength. Even the youths shall faint and be weary, and the young men shall utterly fall, but those who wait on the LORD shall renew their strength; they shall mount up with wings like eagles, they shall run and not be weary, they shall walk and not faint" (Isaiah 40:28–31).

"And He said to me, 'My grace is sufficient for you, for My strength is made perfect in weakness.' Therefore most gladly I will rather boast in my infirmities, that the power of Christ may rest upon me. Therefore I take pleasure in infirmities, in reproaches, in needs, in persecutions, in distresses, for Christ's sake. For when I am weak, then I am strong" (2 Corinthians 12:9–10).

"I have blotted out, like a thick cloud, your transgressions, and like a cloud, your sins. Return to Me, for I have redeemed you" (Isaiah 44:22).

"Thus says the LORD, your Redeemer, The Holy One of Israel: 'I am the LORD your God, Who teaches you to profit, Who leads you by the way you should go'" (Isaiah 48:17).

"The LORD is good, a stronghold in the day of trouble; and He knows those who trust in Him" (Nahum 1:7).

"For the LORD has redeemed Jacob, and ransomed him from the hand of one stronger than he. Therefore they shall come and sing in the height of Zion, streaming to the goodness of the LORD— for wheat and new wine and oil, for the young of the flock and the herd; their souls shall be like a well-watered garden, and they shall sorrow no more at all" (Jeremiah 31:11–12).

"Blessed be the God and Father of our Lord Jesus Christ, who has blessed us with every spiritual blessing in the heavenly places in Christ, just as He chose us in Him before the foundation of the world, that we should be holy and without blame before Him in love, having predestined us to adoption as sons by Jesus Christ to Himself, according to the good pleasure of His will, to the praise of the glory of His grace, by which He made us accepted in the Beloved. In Him we have redemption through His blood, the forgiveness of sins, according to the riches of His grace" (Ephesians 1:3–7).

"But also for this very reason, giving all diligence, add to your faith virtue, to virtue knowledge, to knowledge self-control, to self-control perseverance, to perseverance godliness, to godliness brotherly kindness, and to brotherly kindness love. For if these things are yours and abound, you will be neither barren nor unfruitful in the knowledge of our Lord Jesus Christ" (2 Peter 1:5–8).

"Therefore, if anyone is in Christ, he is a new creation; old things have passed away; behold, all things have become new. Now all things are of God, who has reconciled us to Himself through Jesus Christ, and has given us the ministry of reconciliation, that is, that God was in Christ reconciling the world to Himself, not imputing their trespasses to them, and has committed to us the word of reconciliation. Now then, we are ambassadors for Christ, as though God were pleading through us: we implore you on Christ's behalf, be reconciled to God. For He made Him who knew no sin to be sin

for us, that we might become the righteousness of God in Him" (2 Corinthians 5:17–21).

God desires to redeem your marriage. Marriage is His idea. But even more important, marriage is to be a picture of Christ's love for His Bride, the Church. This is the main reason Satan fights so hard to destroy marriages today. By destroying marriage, he seeks to destroy the picture of Jesus' love for us. Marriage should be a living example of the relationship Jesus longs to share with us. Jesus wants to have open and intimate communication with us. He desires for us to truly know Him. Jesus wants us to love Him passionately, above all else. Satan doesn't want your marriage to be a reflection of Jesus' love. But God does! God wants to bring healing, restoration, and renewal to your marriage. Will you let Him? Will you invite the Gardener into your marriage? Will you start following the rules He established in the Garden? Will you allow Him to "dig around" and eliminate those enemies that don't belong there? Will you look to Him and only to Him to be the Redeemer? He is ready; are you?

"The Spirit of the Lord GOD is upon Me, because the LORD has anointed Me to preach good tidings to the poor; He has sent Me to heal the brokenhearted, to proclaim liberty to the captives, and the opening of the prison to those who are bound; to proclaim the acceptable year of the LORD, and the day of vengeance of our God; to comfort all who mourn, to console those who mourn in Zion, to give them beauty for ashes, the oil of joy for mourning, the garment of praise for the spirit of heaviness; that they may be called trees of righteousness, the planting of the LORD, that He may be glorified. And they shall rebuild the old ruins, they shall raise up the former desolations, and they shall repair the ruined cities, the desolations of many generations" (Isaiah 61:1–4).

These verses prophesy the coming of Jesus, our Redeemer. Jesus quoted this passage, indicating that He was its fulfillment (see Luke 4:17–21).

Jesus came to heal the brokenhearted. Has your heart been broken in your marriage? Jesus came to proclaim liberty to the captives. Are you a slave to sin or in bondage to bitterness and a lack of forgiveness? Jesus came to open the prison doors and release those who are bound; are you ready to be set free? Jesus came to comfort all who mourn. He has come to comfort you, no matter what you have been through. Jesus longs to anoint your marriage with the oil of joy (for healing) and to clothe you with new garments of praise (for restoration). Jesus wants to produce fruit in your marriage. Why? **That HE may be glorified!** And His promise is that through Him we shall rebuild the ruins, raise the former desolations, and repair the ruined generations. Marriage today is in ruins. Will you allow God to rebuild your marriage and use you to help others? NOW is the acceptable year; NOW is the time.

We offer this prayer in closing:

"Jesus, You know how we have prayed throughout the process of writing this book. We commit this book into Your hands and ask that You use it as You deem fit. Jesus, You have led the person holding this book to read it. It is not a mistake or a coincidence that this book has come into his or her hands. You love him (her), and You long to redeem his (her) marriage. Simply reading a book can never heal a broken marriage. But You can! Speak to the heart of all who read these pages. Allow them, by Your Holy Spirit, to hear Your voice. Break through hard hearts and rebellious spirits. Bring conviction of sin. Let Your truth shine through, and deliver them from making excuses or believing lies. Flood their marriages with love, forgiveness, and grace. Disintegrate their darkness with hope. Jesus, we long to see marriages that are a clear reflection of Your love. Our heart's desire is to see couples arise who will choose to follow You and do whatever it takes to serve You through their marriage. Thank You, Jesus, for redeeming our marriage. Thank You for what you started in the Garden of Eden. Amen."

STUDY GUIDE

Read Genesis 3:15–23; Romans 8:24–25;
Matthew 6:12; Isaiah 61:1–4

Our prayer is that you have discovered many truths about God's plan and design for marriage throughout this journey back to the Garden of Eden. We have not shared "new truths" but rather have sought to help you see what has been there all along. God is the Redeemer. Hopelessness is a fatal disease, infecting marriages today as never before. In generations past, couples didn't give up on their marriages, even when times were tough. But this is not the case today. Far too many marriages fall prey to the destructive power of Satan. But God is still the Redeemer: We need Him to "give us beauty for ashes." He can create something new from the rubble of shattered marriages.

God gave hope to Adam and Eve in the Garden when He promised the coming of the Redeemer. We live today in the fulfillment of that Promise: Jesus came to redeem us and to cover us by His blood. If you know God's forgiveness, why do you withhold it from your spouse? You can never truly experience God's forgiveness if you refuse to forgive others—including your spouse.

We learned in this chapter that God protected Adam and Eve. Even in the midst of terrible circumstances that were the result of Adam and Eve's sin, God worked for their good. We need to remember that even trials and tribulations in our marriages can be used by God to purify, protect, and redeem us. You may be the innocent party dealing with the consequences of your spouse's sin. Remember that God is with you. He will protect you, even in the midst of disaster. Let's dig a little deeper.

DIGGING DEEPER

1. What are the three things God did for Adam and Eve in the Garden after they sinned?

   a.

   b.

   c.

2. Write your own definition of 'redeem':

3. What do we learn about hope from Romans 8:24–25?

4. On what must we base our hope? How can this change of attitude help us in our marriages?

5. God clothed Adam and Eve after they sinned. The coverings He made for them were symbolic of what?

6. How can we apply this "covering" to our marriages?

7. What is the significance of the word "as" in the Lord's Prayer?

8. In considering God's protection, we discussed how "all things work together for good." What examples can you think of from your personal life or marriage that prove this truth?

9. When facing a difficult situation, what three things are important to remember?

a.

b.

c.

10. Choose one or two of the verses we quoted at the end of this chapter and use them to develop a prayer for your marriage.

11. In what areas of your marriage do you need the work of the Redeemer?

12. With Isaiah 61:1–4 as the basis of the following phrases, check any that describe your marriage today.
    - ☐ My heart is broken because of our marriage.
    - ☐ Our marriage is being held captive to sin.
    - ☐ Despair and hopelessness have imprisoned us.
    - ☐ I need comforting.
    - ☐ Our marriage is in ashes.
    - ☐ We want God to create something of beauty.
    - ☐ Our marriage needs the oil of healing.
    - ☐ There is no joy in our marriage.
    - ☐ Our relationship is dark and dreary.
    - ☐ We need to clothe our relationship with praise.
    - ☐ We are not fruitful trees.
    - ☐ We want to be fruitful.
    - ☐ We have seen God produce amazing fruit through us.
    - ☐ God is glorified in our marriage.
    - ☐ God is not being glorified in our marriage.
    - ☐ God is rebuilding the ruins of our marriage.
    - ☐ We want God to use us to help restore other marriages.

CHAPTER FIFTEEN

TOOLS FOR THE GARDEN

Resources

If you are an enthusiastic gardener, then it is likely that you have your own personal collection of garden tools. Some—a shovel, rake, or hoe—may be rather basic. Others—an electric weed-eater, stainless steel garden shears, or perhaps a robotic lawn mower—may be fancy. Professional and amateur gardeners alike have their favorite tools, designed to ease their work and enhance their gardens. These tools may be as individual as the garden and the gardener, reflecting their unique style and preferences.

In this final chapter, we share some of our favorite "tools." By no means is this list comprehensive. You may find that some of our favorite "tools" don't "fit" you or meet your needs. These resources are provided merely as a starting place. We encourage you to contact your pastor, church leaders, or other friends for additional recommendations.

This chapter is arranged to correspond with the previous chapters of this book. We have also included numerous Web addresses, all of which are current as of the time of publication. (Unfortunately, we cannot guarantee that all of these links will remain active.)

Finally, we would love to hear from you! If God has used this book in your life or in your marriage, it would be a great joy for us to hear about it. Or perhaps you have questions or other concerns you would like to share with us. We also are available to conduct marriage seminars based on the material in this book.

Please contact us at:

Tim and Mary Lou Tiner

tiner@tinerfamily.com or ttiner@mac.com

We end this book as we began it: by quoting the prophet Isaiah.

"For as the rain comes down and the snow from heaven and do not return there but water the earth and make it bring forth and bud, that it may give seed to the sower and bread to the eater, so shall My Word be that goes forth from My mouth; it shall not return to Me void. But it [My Word] shall accomplish what I please, and it shall prosper in the thing for which I sent it. For you shall go out with joy and be led out with peace. The mountains and the hills shall break forth into singing before you, and all the trees of the field shall clap their hands. Instead of the thorn shall come up the cypress tree, and instead of the brier shall come up the myrtle tree; and it shall be to the Lord for a name, for an everlasting sign that shall not be cut off." (Isaiah 55:10–13)

May the Lord cause the garden of your marriage to bloom for His glory!

RESOURCES

Chapter One: Alone in the Garden
"It is not good for man to be alone."
Recognizing our need
- "How to Know God" - ccci.org/how-to-know-god

Chapter Two: Roots
"Let it go! Let it grow!"
Leaving father and mother
- familylife.com - Search "leaving father and mother." familylife.com has many excellent resources available.

Chapter Three: Grafted Together
"You're stuck with me!"
The attitude and action of commitment
- familylife.com - Search "commitment."

Chapter Four: Growing Together
"Are we there yet?"
Becoming one
- Kendrick, S., and A. Kendrick. 2008. *The Love Dare*. Nashville, TN: B&H Publishing.
- Smalley, G. 1996. *Making Love Last Forever.* Nashville, TN: Thomas Nelson.

Chapter Five: Differences in the Garden
"Why can't you be more like me?"
Gender differences: "Elevators and Internet hubs"
- Eggerichs, E. 2007. *Cracking the Communication Code: The Secret to Speaking Your Mate's Language*. Nashville, TN: Integrity Publishers
- Wright, H. N. 2000. *Communication: Key to Your Marriage.* Ventura, CA: Regal Books.

- Gungor, M. "Laugh Your Way To A Better Marriage."
  laughyourway.com
  DVD series, books, and other resources mix wonderful humor
  with powerful truth.

Chapter Six: Talking in the Garden
"What language are you speaking?"
Communication: "Pockets and purses"

- Smalley, G., and J. Trent. 2006. *The Language of Love.* Carol
  Stream, IL: Tyndale.
- Smalley, G., and J. Trent. 2006. *The Two Sides of Love.* Carol
  Stream, IL: Tyndale.
- familylife.com - Search "communication"
- Also see recommendations from Chapter Five.

Chapter Seven: Enemies in the Garden: Weeds
"I'm just looking…"
Lust of the eyes: Pornography and covetousness

- Daniels, R. 2005. *The War Within.* Wheaton, IL: Crossway
  Books.
- Harris, J. 2003. *Not Even a Hint.* Portland, OR: Multnomah
  Publishing. [Re-released in 2005 under the title *Sex Is Not the
  Problem (Lust Is).*]
- familylife.com - Search "pornography"
- befreeinchrist.com - Offers support, resources, and Bible Study
- xxxchurch.com - Offers support, resources, filtering software,
  Bible Study, and online video workshops for men, women,
  couples, and parents
- therebelution.com/modestysurvey/browse - This is a survey that
  reveals how a woman's dress and appearance can affect a man.
  We urge women to read this survey.
- Coyle, R. 2011. "Help, She's Struggling with Pornography."
  Leominster, UK: Day One Christian Ministries, Inc.
- Renaud, C. 2011. *Dirty Girls Come Clean.* Chicago, IL:
  Moody Publishers.

Chapter Eight: Enemies in the Garden: Fungus

"I want it all, and I want it now!"

Lust of the flesh: Hedonism

- Smalley, G. 2007. *Change Your Heart, Change Your Life: How Changing What You Believe Will Give You the Great Life You've Always Wanted.* Nashville, TN: Thomas Nelson.
- For great Biblical financial help, we recommend any of the materials by Larry Burkett. You can find his books, as well as other helpful resources at the Crown Financial Ministries: www.crown.org
- Burkett, L. 1996. *Money Before Marriage: A Financial Workbook for Engaged Couples.* Chicago, IL: Moody Press.

Chapter Nine: Enemies in the Garden: Rocks

"It's all about me!"

Pride of Life: Defeating "self"

- Robert, R. O. 2002. *Repentance: The First Word of the Gospel.* Wheaton, IL: Crossway Books.
- Chapman, G., and J. Thomas. 2006. *The Five Languages of Apology: How to Experience Healing in all Your Relationships.* Chicago, IL: Northfield Publishing.
- 5lovelanguages.com/assessments/love This site includes an assessment as well as additional resources.
- familylife.com - Search "forgiveness"

Chapter Ten: Enemies in the Garden: Moles and Mice

"Did God really say that?"

Doubts and Lies: Tunnels of doubt allow lies to enter

ADDITIONAL NOTES on doubt. Seven Greek words can be translated "doubt."

(1) *aporeo* –to be perplexed or at a loss; seeing no way out (John 13:22, Acts 25:20)[1]
(2) *diaporeo* –to be greatly perplexed (Acts 2:12)[2]
(3) *meteorizo* –to fluctuate (Luke 12:29)[3]
(4) *airo psuche* –to keep in suspense (John 10:24)[4]

(5) *dialogismos* –thoughts, imaginations, reasoning (Romans 14:1)[5]
(6) *diakrino* –to separate or withdraw, discriminate, oppose, waver, contend (Matthew 21:21)[6]
(7) *distazo* –to doubt, waver (Matthew 14:31)[7]

Each of these words applies to our marriages:
(1) *aporeo* – *"I don't understand what my wife needs. I doubt I'll ever understand her."*
(2) *diaporeo* – *"It is highly doubtful that we can save this marriage."*
(3) *meteorizo* – *"She can't decide whether to trust me. She keeps doubting me."*
(4) *airo psuche* – *"Why can't he tell me what he wants to do? I can't live with these doubts."*
(5) *dialogismos* – *"We keep fighting about what could have happened. She imagines the worst."*
(6) *diakrino* – *"I can't live with someone who doubts me all the time. I deserve respect!"*
(7) *distazo* – *"I thought she forgave me. Why is she doubting me now?"*
- DeMoss, N. 2002. *Lies Women Believe and the Truth That Sets Them Free.*, Chicago, IL: Moody Press.

Chapter Eleven: Man and Woman in the Garden
"Who's the boss?"
Submission
- Walker, J. 1989. *Husbands Who Won't Lead and Wives Who Won't Follow.* Minneapolis, MN: Bethany House Publishers.
- Lewis, R., and W. Hendricks. 1991. *Rocking the Roles: Building a Win-Win Marriage.* Colorado Springs, CO: NavPress Publishing.
- familylife.com - Search "submission"

Chapter Twelve: Man in the Garden
"Be the head!"
Man's role: Leading, serving, and loving
- Lewis, R., and W. Hendricks. 1991. *Rocking the Roles: Building a Win-Win Marriage.* Colorado Springs, CO: NavPress Publishing.

- Lepine, B. 2005. *The Christian Husband: God's Job Description for a Man's Most Challenging Assignment.* Ventura, CA: Regal Books.
- Smith, T. 1998. *Guy Stuff: Or It's Ok to Ask for Directions.* Chicago, IL: Moody Press.
- Chapman, G. 2010. *The Five Love Languages: The Secret to Love That Lasts.* Chicago, IL: Northfield Publishing.
- 5lovelanguages.com/assessments/love. This site includes an assessment as well as additional resources.
- familylife.com - Search "husband"
- McDonald, G. 1997. *When Men Think Private Thoughts: Exploring the Issues That Captivate the Minds of Men.* Nashville, TN: Thomas Nelson.

Chapter Thirteen: Woman in the Garden
"Let me help."
Woman's Role: Honor, Encourage, Love, Pray

- Lewis, R., and W. Hendricks. 1991. *Rocking the Roles: Building a Win-Win Marriage.* Colorado Springs, CO: NavPress Publishing.
- Omartian, S. 2007. *The Power of a Praying Wife.* Eugene, OR: Harvest House Publishers.
- Chapman, G. 2010. *The Five Love Languages: The Secret to Love That Lasts.* Chicago, IL: Northfield Publishing.
- 5lovelanguages.com/assessments/love/ This site includes an assessment as well as additional resources.
- familylife.com - Search "sexual intimacy"
- familylife.com- Search "wife"
- Cutrer, W., and S. Glahn. 2007. *Sexual Intimacy in Marriage.* Grand Rapids, MI: Kregel Publications.
- Wheat, E., and G. Wheat. 2012. *Intended for Pleasure: Sex Technique and Sexual Fulfillment in Christian Marriage.* Grand Rapids, MI: Revell.

Chapter Fourteen: God in the Garden
"Fear not, for I have redeemed you."
The Redeemer

Unguarded Love
by Mary Lou Tiner

She was a lovely princess – the fairest in the land,
And he, the brave and valiant prince, who asked her for her hand.
Happy ever after, they shared the shining dream,
But their eyes were blinded to the wicked serpent's scheme.

He was a crafty creature; deceit was his device.
With cunning wiles and shallow smiles, he offered his advice:
"Let me in your palace. I'll serve you faithfully.
Your friends all own a dragon, but there's none as good as me!"

The drawbridge slowly lowered. The dragon slithered in.
Destruction followed in his path; he gave a fiendish grin.
"Now I will rule this palace and you will both serve me!
You left your love unguarded, now you'll pay the penalty."

(refrain)
Don't leave your love unguarded. Don't leave your love alone.

The King of all the Kingdoms responded to their cries
And sent His Son with sword in hand to slay that beast of lies.
And He restored the Kingdom to its rightful heir,
And left His sword above the door, ever guarding there.

(refrain)
Don't leave your love unguarded. Don't leave your love alone.

©2012

STUDY GUIDE
ANSWER KEYS

INTRODUCTION

1. Psalm 18:30
   a. List three key words from this text:
      1. God's way is:
         PERFECT (complete, faultless, absolutely what we need)
      2. God's Word is:
         PROVEN (dependable, trustworthy, verified, established)
      3. God is a:
         SHIELD (protection, defense, shelter, buffer)
   b. What must we do?
      TRUST IN HIM! (faith, hope, confidence, expectation, reliance, dependence)
   c. How has God's Word been proven to you in the past?
      (Responses will vary.)

2. Read Isaiah 55:8–9.
   How can we apply this verse to marriage? What "ways" of man could be included here?
   (Answers will vary.) The world often sets the standards of behavior for marriages today. God's Word reminds us that God's ways are not man's ways. We should not try to fit our marriages into the world's mold; rather we need to seek the Lord's thoughts and His ways. We need to allow His ways to be our standard.
   Some examples that illustrate the ways of man versus the ways of God might include:
   (1) In certain cultures, it is considered acceptable for a husband to beat his wife. This violates God's plan for marriage, especially when we understand that marriage is a picture of how Jesus loves His Bride, the Church. Jesus would never beat His Bride.

> *(2) The ways of man are evident in the lack of commitment in marriage relationships today. Again, God's ways are the opposite of this: We are not to "break apart" what God has joined together.*

3. Read Isaiah 55:10–11.
   a. What promise do we find here about God's Word?
      God's Word will produce fruit—fruit for nourishment as well as seed for the future, which will result in an even greater harvest. God's Word has power and will not return empty (void). God is sovereign. His Word will accomplish what He desires.
   b. What do you think God wants to accomplish in your marriage?
      (Responses will vary.)
   c. Can your marriage prosper without God's Word?
      (Responses will vary.)

4. a. *(Responses will vary.)*
   b. *(Responses will vary.)*
   c. *(Responses will vary.)*

5. *(Responses will vary.)*

CHAPTER ONE
ALONE IN THE GARDEN

1. Why did God give Adam the job of naming the animals?
   God wanted Adam to discover two things: first, that he was alone, and second, that it was not good for him to be alone. God wanted Adam to truly appreciate the amazing gift He was going to give him: woman. God was preparing Adam to cherish her as well as to understand with his entire being how Eve was meant to be his completion.

2. Was it good for man to be alone? Why or why not?
   It was not—and is not—good for man to be alone. God created man with the instinctive desire to be in relationship—with God and with woman. If man could survive happily in solitude, he would tend to become totally self-sufficient, rejecting his need for God and for a relationship with Him. Unfortunately, many men have not discov-

ered this truth and so destroy their relationships with their wives and, ultimately, with God. It is through our marriage relationships that we have the opportunity to truly grow and mature. It is not good for man to be alone.

3. Name at least three things that God provided for Adam in this passage:
   (Answers may vary; possible answers include the following.)
   a. *Breath of life – a soul (vs. 7)*
   b. *Ideal home (vs. 8)*
   c. *Perfect provision (vs. 9)*
   d. *Beautiful surroundings (vs. 9)*
   e. *Riches (vs. 12)*
   f. *Purposeful work (vs. 15)*
   g. *Clear guidelines (vv. 16–17)*
   h. *Instinctive desire for relationship (vs. 18)*
   i. *The revelation of Adam's need (vv. 19–20)*
   j. *Woman, Eve*

4. Because we are created in God's image, what similar characteristics do we possess?
   (Answers may vary; possible answers include the following.)
   a. *Desire for relationship, especially with God*
   b. *Creativity*
   c. *Capacity to enjoy beauty*
   d. *Industrious/productive*
   e. *Unity in our body (body, soul, and spirit) reflects the picture of the triune God*
   f. *Ability for rational thinking: logic, desire for order*
   g. *Free will; ability to choose*
   h. *Active, vigorous*
   i. *Moral awareness*
   j. *Five senses*

5. What were the three foundational points of this chapter?
   1. *Man must realize he has a need.*

2. *Man must receive God's provision to meet this need.*
3. *Man must rejoice in the provision he has received.*

6. *(Responses will vary.)*

7. How would you summarize chapter one in one sentence?
(Responses will vary.) Man is alone, and it is not good for him to be.

8. *(Responses will vary.)*

9. *(Responses will vary.)*

10. *(Responses will vary.)*

11. *(Responses will vary.)*

12. *(Responses will vary.)*

CHAPTER TWO
ROOTS

1. Do you believe that the three rules stated in Genesis 2:24 are valid today? Why or why not?
Absolutely, yes! God, who never changes, established marriage as the first institution and gave His instruction manual for all generations. Genesis makes it clear that the instructions were not just for Adam and Eve but for all generations to come.

2. Name two individuals in the Bible who confirmed the validity of the three rules given in Genesis.
Jesus, in Matthew 19:5 and Mark 10:2-7, quoted this passage from Genesis, and the Apostle Paul, in Ephesians 5:31, also confirmed these rules.

3. Why are rules important for life generally?
Rules are given for our protection and well-being. Following the "rules" in the owner's manual for your car protects you and your car. Without rules we would live in chaos, hurting ourselves and others.

4. Can you think of another analogy (other than the car instruction manual) that illustrates how rules can be for our good?

   (Answers vary; some possible answers follow.)

   Traffic signs stipulate the rules of the road: what speed is safe, which direction we should travel, where we need to stop, who has the right of way, etc. These rules keep us safe and are for our good.

   Another example is the Food and Drug Administration (FDA), which promulgates rules related to food safety and ensures consistent labeling in an effort to prevent people from becoming sick or poisoned by the food they eat.

   Still other examples are the Federal Aviation Association; standard weights and measures; recipes; education accreditation; medical association standards of practice; civil government; etc.

5. Why is it important and logical to obey God's three rules for marriage?

   God is the Creator of marriage! He gave this institution first; as such, it is of first priority. What better source to go to than the One who created marriage in the first place? God's rules have been proven repeatedly by the test of time. His rules work!

6. Explain in your own words what it means to "leave father and mother."

   We "leave" the type of relationship we had with our parents, when we were under their care and responsibility, and we "go" to something new. When we marry, we need to take the responsibility and the authority for our new family under God. There needs to be a separation, leaving the old "roots" behind to start something new. Leaving pertains not only to the physical leaving but also to emotional, mental, and spiritual leaving. The new couple is independent of their parents, and together they stand, fully dependent on God.

7. Explain how the analogy of the root and the seed applies to marriage.

   Parents are the "roots" of the family. They provide stability and nourishment for their children. The goal is always for parents to "release" their children, just as a seed is released so it can start a new plant.

Grown children must realize that it is time to leave their "roots" in order to become "planted" and put down their own roots.

8. What can happen when seeds are planted too close together? How does this apply to marriage?

   As when corn is planted too close together, a couple's marriage can become "sick" or even "die" if either or both of them fail to leave their parents. The couple will not learn to "plant their roots deep" because the existing roots of the parent plant interfere. The risk of disease increases when plants are not separate. A new couple can become "diseased" by attitudes that might have been correct with regard to their parents but that are not for them. The new couple "plant" and the parent "plant" may compete for nutrients and water because they are too close. For example, a new wife may feel threatened by the constant interference of her mother-in-law and thus may be unable to care for her new family as she should.

9. The physical aspect of leaving involves two basic things. What are they?

   a. *Responsibility: who is responsible?*

   b. *Authority: who is in charge?*

10. What is even more difficult to do than to leave physically? Why is this more difficult?

    It is often more difficult to leave emotionally and psychologically. Emotional and psychological ties and roots to our family are far more subtle and often more deeply entrenched. Often, attitudes, habits, values, and priorities with which we have grown up are an intricate part of who we are. Things that seem normal to us can blind us.

Husbands and wives: Complete statements 11–16 alone, and then share your answers with your spouse. Fill in the blanks:

11. *(Responses will vary.)*

12. *(Responses will vary.)*

13. *(Responses will vary.)*

14. *(Responses will vary.)*

15. *(Responses will vary.)*

16. *(Responses will vary.)*

CHAPTER THREE
GRAFTED TOGETHER

1. Write your own definition of "cleave":
   "Cleave" means that two things are being permanently joined together. The word also indicates action and process. Because of the tense that is used, we could say it like this: "Be being continually glued together."

2. What is the importance of the Greek preposition "pros" as it relates to "cleaving?"
   The preposition 'pros' (proskollao) means 'to move toward something.' Process and action are involved: that is, we are moving toward being glued together.

3. How do all three rules fit together?
   It is not enough to leave (throw away the old) or to cleave (move toward becoming glued together); we also must incorporate the third rule: become one.

4. What are the six lessons we learned through the analogy of grafting?
   a. *Both of the two trees (i.e., husbands and wives) have strengths individually, but together, their strengths are enhanced and become even more fruitful.*
   b. *Both of the two trees (i.e., husbands and wives) have weaknesses which can lead to disease, unfruitfulness, and death if they refuse to be joined together.*
   c. *Grafting requires sacrifice—giving up—and can be painful, but it is worth the effort.*

> d. *We can't use a chainsaw to make the cuts necessary for grafting. The process of being grafted requires gentleness and care. We shouldn't destroy our partner in the process!*
> e. *Grafting takes time.*
> f. *Grafting is permanent.*

5. What two aspects of cleaving did we discuss in detail?
Cleaving involves two things: attitude and actions.

6. Summarize Proverbs 4:23, Proverbs 27:19, and Matthew 12:35, and explain what these verses teach about our attitudes.
All three verses talk about how we think and how the way we think affects how we behave. If we entertain thoughts of giving up, escaping, quitting, or failing, there is a good possibility that we will experience these outcomes.

7. *(Responses will vary.)*

8. What do Jeremiah 17:9 and Proverbs 28:26 teach us about the heart?
The heart is deceitful! Our emotions can easily become tainted and even corrupt. We are fools if we trust our hearts. There is only one source of true wisdom—wisdom that will not be tainted or corrupted—and that is God's Wisdom, as found in His Word.

9. According to Proverbs 3:5–6, how can we bring our emotions under control?
We need to stop leaning on our own ways (including our emotions); in everything we do, we must seek to put the Lord first, trusting Him completely and allowing Him to direct our ways.

10. We suggested four action steps you can take in regard to cleaving. They are: *Be a team, Be supportive, Be purposeful, Be prayerful.*

11. *(Responses will vary.)*

12. *(Responses will vary.)*

CHAPTER FOUR
GROWING TOGETHER

1. Write your own definition of "becoming one."
   Becoming one means no longer doing things "my way" or "your way" or the "world's way." Becoming one means doing things "our way," discovering a new way that is right for us, and this means doing things "God's way"! Becoming one is a process designed to last your entire life.

2. What were some of the first adjustments you had to make in your marriage? *(Responses will vary.)*

3. How is "becoming one" a process?
   The process of becoming one will take time. Conflicts will reveal areas of disunity in our marriages and will show us where we need to work together to become one. There will be pressure and discomfort. But the result will be worth it: our relationship will grow stronger.

4. Right now, what is the hardest area in which to "become one" with your spouse? *(Responses will vary.)*

5. What is one area of "oneness" that you and your partner have recently gained? *(Responses will vary.)*

6. How do you deal with conflict in your marriage? *(Responses will vary.)*

7. Read Romans 12:3–5. How can you apply this passage to marriage?
   We need to remember that no one is more important or valuable than the other. We need to see our marriage from God's point of view. God has given each of us gifts and abilities that the other needs and that help complete the other.

8. Read 1 Corinthians 12:12–25. The analogy is of *the body.*
   The key points are:
   a. *We are all one body (vs. 12).*
   b. *Each part of the body is valuable and important (vv. 14–17).*

    c. *God has ordained how the body is to fit together, as it pleases Him, not as it pleases us (vs. 18).*

    d. *We need each other (vv. 22–24)!*

    e. *God desires that there be no schism or division in the body (or in our marriages) (vs. 25).*

9. According to Mark 3:24–25, why is unity important in marriage?
We cannot have a successful, strong marriage if we are not "one." History, culture, society, business, and experience all tell us "united we stand, divided we fall."

10. *(Responses will vary.)*

11. Read Malachi 2:13–15. What does this passage say is the reason for being one?
God wants to produce godly offspring.

12. *(Responses will vary.)*

13. *(Responses will vary.)*

14. *(Responses will vary.)*

15. *(Responses will vary.)*

16. *(Responses will vary.)*

CHAPTER FIVE
DIFFERENCES IN THE GARDEN

1. Which two verses point out God's design of two unique and distinct beings? *Genesis 1:27 and Genesis 5:2*

2. What is the truth of Galatians 3:28?
God values everyone equally. In Christ, we all are one.

3. Paul contrasts three groups of people in Galatians 3:28. What are

these groups, and what point does he make by describing them?
Jew or Greek: God values all people equally.
Slave or free: God values people of every economic status equally.
Male or female: God values both genders equally.

4. In his sermon, Doug Clark shared five things that Jesus did that were counter to the culture of His day; they revealed how Jesus regarded women. List those five things:
   a. *Jesus called the woman to come forward in the place of worship reserved for men.*
   b. *Jesus spoke to the woman.*
   c. *Jesus touched the woman.*
   d. *Jesus affirmed the woman's worth.*
   e. *Jesus restored the woman's rightful position.*

5. What is the difference in the way a man's versus a woman's brain is wired?
   A man has fewer nerve connectors between the left and right hemispheres of his brain. He processes information on only one side of his brain at a time. A man cannot think, feel, and speak at the same time. A woman has 40 percent more nerve connectors between the left and right hemispheres of her brain than does a man. She is able to use both sides of her brain simultaneously to process information. A woman can think, feel, and speak all at the same time.

6. How is a man's brain like a multi-story office building and elevator?
   A man's brain is like an office building in which different processes take place on different floors. He has to "travel" from one floor to another to access the information on that floor; after processing it, he "gets back in the elevator" and "travels" to the "floor" where he can communicate.

7. How is a woman's brain like a wireless Internet hub?
   A woman's brain constantly sends and receives data simultaneously. She particularly wants to create new "connections" with those around her. Her "antenna" has a wide range.

8. 1 Peter 3:7 is a command. The two key words are:
Understand and *Honor.*

9. What two steps can you take to understand your partner?
Seek the Lord for wisdom, and become a student of your spouse.

10. What analogy did we give about gaining understanding?
The analogy was of a computer. You would read the directions and study it. You would care for it and value it.

11. How can you become a "student" of your spouse?
"Study" him or her. Ask questions. Be observant. Listen. Devote time and effort to understanding your partner.

12. *(Responses will vary.)*

13. What does it mean to "honor?"
To honor means to highly value the other person, to place the interest and well-being of the other person ahead of your own.

CHAPTER SIX
TALKING IN THE GARDEN

1. According to Proverbs 24:3 and Proverbs 3:13–14, why is understanding important (especially as it relates to your marriage)?
These passages tell us that a house is built and established with understanding. Those who invest in understanding gain happiness. If we want our marriages to be solid and firm, filled with joy, we must invest our time and effort to gain understanding, especially in the area of communication.

2. Isaiah 50:4 states the importance of:
Training our tongues to speak properly—that is, to speak right words that bring health and refreshment. We also read of the importance of having ears that are trained to listen.

3. What is a man's motivation for communication?
   A man's motivation for communication is to discover and express facts.

4. What is a woman's motivation for communication?
   A woman's motivation for communication is to build relationships and to discover and express feelings.

5. Name two methods of communication on which a man typically relies:
   Two methods of communication on which a man typically relies are the "single-focus approach" and the "direct request approach."

6. Name two methods of communication on which a woman typically relies:
   Two methods of communication on which a woman typically relies are the "panoramic approach" and the "indirect request approach."

7. How is a man's method of communication like "pockets?"
   Men have a separate pocket for everything. They reach into one pocket at a time and deal with what is in that pocket. They can ignore whatever is not in that "pocket" because they are focused on one thing at a time.

8. How is a woman's method of communication like a "purse?"
   Women have a purse filled with a variety of things. Everything in the purse touches everything else; that is, everything is connected. Women have difficulty taking just one thing out of their purse at a time because they have to dig past other objects to find it. They may dump out the contents of the purse to find one object.

9. How does Proverbs 15:1 relate to making direct or indirect requests?
   Direct requests are important and good, but it is also important to use "soft" or "gentle" words to avoid evoking anger. Men, who tend to be direct, must learn to temper their tone of voice and "directness" with a good dose of Proverbs 15:1.

10. *(Responses will vary.)*

11. *(Responses will vary.)*

12. *(Responses will vary.)*

13. *(Responses will vary.)*

CHAPTER SEVEN
ENEMIES IN THE GARDEN—WEEDS
1. What are the five weapons Satan used in the garden—and that he still uses today?
   1. *Lust of the eyes*
   2. *Lust of the flesh*
   3. *Pride of life*
   4. *Doubt*
   5. *Lies*

2. How did Satan use these five weapons against Jesus in the wilderness?
   1. *Lust of the flesh: Satan tempted Jesus to gratify His hunger by turning stones into bread.*
   2. *Pride of life: Satan tempted Jesus to prove He was really God by throwing Himself off the pinnacle of the temple and letting the angels rescue Him.*
   3. *Lust of the eyes: Satan tempted Jesus by offering to give Him all the glorious kingdoms of the world if only He would bow and worship him.*
   4. *Doubt: Coupled with Satan's first two temptations of Jesus was the phrase "If you are…"*
   5. *Lies: Satan promised to give Jesus the kingdoms of the world.*

3. The Greek word for lust *(epithumia)*, as used in 1 John 2:16, can be defined as: *A desire, craving, longing, or desire for what is forbidden.*

4. *(Responses will vary.)*

5. How is bindweed like the lust of the eyes?

   Many worldly things appear lovely on the outside. But these things can entwine themselves around us, ensnaring and eventually choking the life out of us. Just as we must remove bindweed by its roots, so must we remove the lust of the eyes from our lives. Bindweed also produces hundreds of seeds which can lead to even greater destruction; in the same way, the lust of the eyes leads to countless other sins and destruction.

6. Which two men in the Bible demonstrate the danger of "just looking?" What was the result of their lustful looks?
   1. *Lot lusted after the best land. Eventually, he lost his wife and possessions.*
   2. *King David lusted after Bathsheba. He committed adultery with her, conceived a child with her, murdered her husband, and sought to cover up his actions. Eventually the child died, and many serious problems plagued David and his family.*

7. What are five reasons that pornography should have no place in your marriage?
   1. *It is sin.*
   2. *It damages marriages.*
   3. *It creates a distorted view of sex.*
   4. *It is addictive.*
   5. *It destroys righteousness.*

8. *(Responses will vary.)*

9. What are seven ways to defeat the enemy of pornography?
   1. *Confess your sin to your spouse.*
   2. *Find an accountability partner.*
   3. *Clean house, and destroy all pornographic material within it.*
   4. *Develop new habits and interests.*
   5. *Let God become your passion.*
   6. *Take the offensive.*
   7. *Fast and pray.*

10. *(Responses will vary.)*

11. The lust of the eyes also includes:
    Covetousness

12. What does Jesus say in Luke 12:15?
    Be on your guard against covetousness. The measure and value of your life is not in the things you possess.

13. *(Responses will vary.)*

14. *(Responses will vary.)*

15. What are the five action steps you can take to defend against the enemy of covetousness?
    1. *Give thanks.*
    2. *Be content.*
    3. *Pray together.*
    4. *Clean house.*
    5. *Be a giver.*

16. *(Responses will vary.)*

17. Paraphrase Matthew 6:22–23.
    (Answers vary.) Our eyes are critical to the spiritual health of our bodies, souls, and spirits. If our eyes become accustomed to darkness, we will continue to crave darkness even more, with the result that soon, darkness will be all that we see. But if we learn to focus our vision on the good things the Lord has for us, we will be filled with His light.

18. *(Responses will vary.)*

CHAPTER EIGHT
ENEMIES IN THE GARDEN—FUNGUS

1. Some of the curses Adam and Eve received for their disobedience were related to their flesh. What were these curses?

1. *Eve would have pain in childbirth.*
2. *Adam would have to work hard.*
3. *Thorns and thistles would grow.*
4. *Adam and Eve would not be allowed to remain in the Garden of Eden.*
5. *They would die.*

2. Galatians 5:19–21 provides a good definition of the lust of the flesh. What sins are listed in this passage?
   Adultery, fornication, uncleanness, lewdness, idolatry, sorcery, hatred, contention, jealousy, outbursts of wrath, selfish ambition, dissension, heresy, envy, murder, drunkenness, revelry

3. Write your own definition of the lust of the flesh.
   (Answers vary.) Lust of the flesh can be defined as "pursuit of the pleasures of the senses."

4. What is hedonism? What is the relationship of hedonism to the lust of the flesh?
   Hedonism is the "self-indulgent pursuit of pleasure as a way of life." Hedonism says, "I want it all, and I want it now."

5. The Greek word *hedone* is translated 'pleasure' in our English Bibles. Explain how this word is used in the following passages:
   Luke 8:14: Good seed is choked out and killed by the pleasure of the flesh.
   Titus 3:3: We were foolish, disobedient, and deceived, serving pleasure.
   James 4:1–3: Wars and fighting come from our search for pleasure. We don't get what we want because we ask only to consume it for our own pleasure.
   2 Peter 2:13: There are consequences for living only for the sake of pleasure.

6. *(Responses vary.)*

7. What does 1 Corinthians 6:19–20 reveal about God's attitude toward our "rights?"
   We have been bought with a price and therefore should not live for ourselves.
   Our goal ought to be to glorify God with our bodies.

8. How has the attitude of "entitlement" caused problems in society today? How have attitudes of entitlement caused problems in marriages?
   The results are evident in lower standards of education; in the degradation of people's work ethic; in the enacting of laws that cater to individual greed; and in social welfare systems that foster attitudes of entitlement.
   Many husbands and wives are of the opinion that "my partner has to make me happy"; that "if he or she fails to totally satisfy me, then I will find someone who will"; or that "I want what I want when and how I want it." Such selfish attitudes destroy marriages.

9. King Solomon had it all. List a few of the things from which he tried to gain satisfaction. (Read Ecclesiastes 2:3–17.)
   Wine, folly, works, houses, vineyards, gardens, orchards, pools, servants, herds, flocks, silver, gold, treasures, singers, musical instruments, wives

10. What is the important lesson King Solomon shares in Ecclesiastes 12:13–14?
    All his possessions and accomplishments didn't satisfy. It was all vanity. He finally says, "Let us hear the conclusion of the whole matter: Fear God and keep His commandments, for this is man's all. For God will bring every work into judgment, including every secret thing, whether good or evil."

11. Name some of the ways in which the lust of the flesh is like black-spot fungus.
    The lust of the flesh thrives in "comfortable" surroundings: too much "water" and "mild temperatures." The lust of the flesh seeks instant gratification and detests sacrifices and discomfort. The lust of the flesh

also avoids "light," seeking instead to hide bad habits exposed by God's Word.

Even as black-spot fungus spreads and worsens, so the lust of the flesh can spread in our marriages.

Just as an infected rose bush becomes ugly, weak, and unfruitful, so our marriages become "ugly," weak, and unfruitful when the lust of the flesh takes hold.

12. We identified five ways to prevent and/or cure black-spot fungus. Each has an analogy to our marriages. What is the first tip for preventing black spot fungus?

    Plant the rose bush in full sunlight.

    a. What is the analogy to our marriages?

       God's Word is light to our marriage.

    b. Paraphrase John 3:19–21.

       Jesus is the Light of the World, but people prefer to stay in darkness and persist in their sin. Light is detestable to them. They are so full of darkness that the Light repulses them. But those who come to the Light find truth and defeat darkness.

13. What is the second tip for fighting black-spot fungus?

    Plant your roses in such a way as to allow for good air circulation.

    a. What is the analogy to our marriages?

       "Air circulation" in our marriages is like prayer.

    b. Paraphrase one of the verses cited in Section two.

       (Responses will vary.)

14. What is the third tip for preventing black-spot fungus?

    Water correctly: Do not overwater, and provide good drainage.

    a. What is the analogy to our marriages?

       "Water" in our marriages is acts of service.

    b. Paraphrase one of the verses cited in Section three.

       (Responses will vary.)

15. What is the fourth tip for fighting black-spot fungus?

    Remove infected leaves completely.

a. What is the analogy to our marriages?

"Removing infected leaves" in our marriages is confession and repentance.

b. Paraphrase one of the verses cited in Section four.

(Responses will vary.)

16. What is the fifth tip for protecting against black-spot fungus?

Keep your garden clean.

a. What is the analogy to our marriages?

"Keeping your garden clean" is being separate from the world.

b. Paraphrase one of the verses cited in Section five.

(Responses will vary.)

17. *(Responses will vary.)*

18. *(Responses will vary.)*

19. *(Responses will vary.)*

CHAPTER NINE

ENEMIES IN THE GARDEN—ROCKS

1. What is the analogy we gave for each of the five types of rocks?

a. *Self-exaltation is like an **idol**.*

b. *Self-sufficiency is like a **wall**.*

c. *Self-centeredness is like a **prison**.*

d. *Self-gratification is like a **treasure chest**.*

e. *Self-righteousness is like **weapons** and **buried rocks**.*

2. What is the definition of the Greek word for pride?

"Being full of smoke" or "of a puff of smoke, rising up," it also means to be "high-minded or lifted up." The Greek word for pride also can be defined as "a haughty attitude, appearing to be above others, or looking down on others contemptuously."

3. How do we get rid of "rocks" of self-exaltation?
   The antithesis of pride is humility. Humility is a natural by-product of drawing close to God.

4. *(Responses will vary.)*

5. Which man from the Bible did we describe as portraying self-sufficiency? Summarize the man's story and what he learned.
   King Nebuchadnezzar took credit for the glory of his kingdom. Although he was warned by God through the prophet Daniel, he continued in his pride. The result was that he lost his kingdom and his mind and lived as a wild animal. When he finally came to his senses, his kingdom was returned to him. He then testified of the sovereignty of God.

6. What are two steps in tearing down the "wall" of self-sufficiency?
   a. *Confess self-sufficiency as sin to God.*
   b. *Confess to your spouse that you need him/her.*

7. Which man from the Bible did we describe as portraying self-centeredness? Summarize his story and the result of the "rocks of self-sufficiency" in his life.
   King Saul was commanded to destroy an enemy. But he kept some of the spoil for himself and allowed himself to be influenced by his fear of the people. His self-centeredness destroyed him. Even when confronted with his sin, he thought only of himself and begged to be honored before the people. His self-centeredness led to fear, depression, defeat, broken relationships, and tragedy.

8. What are the two words we considered from Romans 15:6, and how do they help destroy the "rocks of self-centeredness?"
   a. *Mind: Renew your mind through study, memorization, and meditation on God's word. Don't allow negative thoughts into your marriage: Cast them out.*
      A key verse is: (Responses will vary.)

    b. Mouth: What kinds of words come out of your mouth? Remember the importance of being thankful.

    A key verse is: (Responses will vary.)

9. Paraphrase Galatians 6:7–10.

    (Responses will vary.)

10. Finally, we considered the "rocks of self-righteousness." How do I get rid of the "rocks" that say "I am right?"

    I must:

    Learn to control my tongue.

    Stop comparing myself with others.

    See myself from God's perspective.

    Confess my attitude of self-righteousness as sin.

    A key verse is: (Responses will vary.)

11. "Rocks of unforgiveness" are a certain type of "rock of self-righteousness." What analogies did we give?

    Holding on to past hurts is like burying rocks in the soil.

    Reminding your partner of past mistakes is like saving rocks to present as evidence of past hurt.

    Using past mistakes to hurt your partner is like throwing rocks at each other.

    Jesus is the Gardener. He is willing to work in the garden of your marriage and to help you completely remove these "rocks."

12. What does Matthew 18:21–35 teach?

    This is the parable of the unforgiving servant. Even though the servant had been forgiven a huge debt, he walked away and immediately demanded that his co-worker repay a much smaller debt. Although he had been forgiven much, he himself was unwilling to forgive even a much lesser offense. We do the same when we refuse to forgive others—including our spouse. We forget how much God has forgiven us.

13. *(Responses will vary.)*

CHAPTER TEN
ENEMIES IN THE GARDEN—MOLES AND MICE
1. Write your own definition of doubt.
   (Responses will vary.)

2. The Latin word for doubt is *dubius,* which is related to the words
   'duo' and '*two.*'
   a. What choice is referred to in 1 Kings 18:21?
      Serve God or serve Baal.
   b. What two things are referred to in James 1:6?
      Faith and doubt.
   c. Between what two things did Eve waver in the Garden of Eden?
      Believe God and obey, or believe the Serpent and disobey.

3. What is the key point in Romans 14:23?
   *The verse says, "But he who doubts is condemned if he eats...." Thus,
   the key is the action: Whatever is not from faith—or "whatever we DO
   that does not come or proceed from faith"—is sin. The person who acts
   on his or her doubts sins.*

4. Provide some examples of how Jesus addressed doubt.
   (Responses will vary.)
   *Jesus corrected but did not condemn Peter for doubting. He saved him
   from drowning. Jesus also answered John the Baptist's question without
   accusing him.*

5. What warning does Jesus give in Matthew 15:19? Apply this verse to
   marriage.
   *From the heart come evil actions. For example, if you allow yourself to
   doubt your partner's love for you, you open yourself up to looking for
   love in the wrong place. This can lead to adultery.*

6. *(Responses will vary.)*

7. What two types of tunnels do moles dig?

    a. *Feeding tunnels are near the surface.*

    b. *Living and storage tunnels are much deeper underground.*

8. How do these two tunnels relate to marriage?
   a. *"Feeding tunnels of doubt" are close to the surface. They are like filters that interpret another's action on the basis of false presumptions. These tunnels lead to frequent offenses and misunderstandings. A husband or wife may "dig around," looking for something to "feed" on—perhaps some minor fault or annoyance. Often, petty offenses and insignificant actions become significant problems.*
   b. *The "living tunnels" are similar to the doubts that are deeply rooted in our lives. These may be the result of past hurts, a dysfunctional family, false teaching, or lack of forgiveness. Doubts often surface that have nothing to do with our partner but that instead are rooted in our past.*

9. Tunnels can be dangerous because:
   a. *They can destroy foundations.*
   b. *They can injure innocent people (especially children).*
   c. *They can provide other enemies with access to our garden.*

10. What other enemies can "tunnels of doubt" allow to enter your marriage?
    Fear, distrust, rebellion, disbelief, bitterness, lack of forgiveness, despair

11. What foundations in marriage can be destroyed by "tunnels of doubt?"
    The foundation of trust and respect can be destroyed by doubt.

12. Who else can be injured by "tunnels of doubt?"
    Our children as well as other family members and friends can be injured by "tunnels of doubt."

13. What are three steps for eliminating doubt?
    a. *Face doubt head-on: speak the truth.*

b. *Dig deeper: Examine past hurts or experiences that may be the root cause.*

c. *"Capture" each thought and give it to Jesus.*

14. Paraphrase 2 Corinthians 10:5. *(Responses will vary.)*

15. *(Responses will vary.)*

16. *(Responses will vary.)*

17. *(Responses will vary.)*

18. According to Ephesians 6:10–11 and 13–18, what are the ten principles for defeating Satan?
    1. *Find your strength in the Lord and in His power.*
    2. *Use the defensive weapons He has provided for you.*
    3. *Take all the armor of God.*
    4. *Truth is like a belt.*
    5. *Righteousness is like a breastplate.*
    6. *Put on the shoes of the gospel of peace.*
    7. *Above all, take up the shield of faith.*
    8. *Put on the helmet of salvation.*
    9. *The sword of the Spirit is the Word of God.*
    10. *Pray always!*

19. *(Responses will vary.)*

20. *(Responses will vary.)*

CHAPTER ELEVEN
MAN AND WOMAN IN THE GARDEN

1. List a few of the key words that describe what submission is *not*.
    a. *Slavery*
    b. *Tyranny*
    c. *Repression*
    d. *Demeaning*

    e. *One-sided*

    f. *Abandoning godliness*

2. Paraphrase Ephesians 5:17–21. *(Responses will vary.)*

3. What are the five definitions of 'submission' provided in this chapter?
   a. *I allow you to do for me what it is your responsibility to do.*
   b. *I place myself under the command of a leader.*
   c. *I choose to voluntarily surrender my rights and self-interests.*
   d. *I freely offer my gifts, talents, abilities, and knowledge.*
   e. *I must obey God first.*

4. What is the key point related to pride in 1 Peter 5:5?
   This verse admonishes us to be clothed with humility. Often, our pride keeps us from submitting to another person. We think we don't need any help, or we think that we can do it (whatever "it" is!) better ourselves.

5. The Greek word for submission (*hupotasso*) means:
   "to arrange under, to subordinate, to subject, to obey, to submit to one's control, to yield to one's admonition or advice." "Hupotasso" is also "a Greek military term meaning 'to arrange [troop divisions] in a military fashion under the command of a leader.' In non-military use, it was 'a voluntary attitude of giving in, cooperating, assuming responsibility, and carrying a burden.'"

6. What are the three standards for leaders that God gives in Ezekiel 34:2–4?
   a. *Put the needs of others above their own.*
   b. *Are committed to strengthening, healing, and restoring those in their care.*
   c. *Do not rule with force or cruelty.*

7. What are some other standards for leaders that are articulated in the Bible? (Include the reference.)
   (Responses will vary.)

8. Why is it important to understand the reflexive tense of *hupotasso*, the Greek word for submission?
The reflexive tense indicates that we submit voluntarily. We are to do this ourselves. We are exhorted to freely surrender our rights and self-interest to others. On the other hand, we are not to force or demand submission from another.

9. How is the reflexive tense used in Philippians 2:5–8 and John 10:17–18?
Jesus humbled Himself (reflexive). He freely gave Himself for us. Jesus chose to lay down His life for us.

10. How does 1 Peter 4:10 relate to the fourth definition of submission?
You have been given certain gifts, talents, skills, knowledge, and wisdom. You are to be a good steward (caretaker) of the gifts God has given you. Submission means that you freely (and respectfully) offer these to your spouse for him to use as he sees fit.

11. What does the story of Ananias and Sapphira reveal about submission? (Reread Acts 5:1–2.)
God held Sapphira responsible for her choices. Her husband sinned willfully. Sapphira should have chosen to obey God first. Biblical submission is always to God first.

12. Of the five definitions of submission given in this chapter, which four are exhibited in the life of Abigail? Give specific examples. (Reread 1 Samuel 25:4–42.)
   a. *"I must obey God first." Abigail disobeyed her husband in order to obey God and His standards for godliness.*
   b. *"I choose to voluntarily surrender my rights and self-interests." Abigail risked her life to approach David and plead for the life of her husband. She also risked retribution from her husband when she told him what she had done.*
   c. *"I place myself under the command of a leader." Abigail placed herself under David's authority as the anointed King of Israel.*

    d. *"I freely offer my gifts, talents, abilities, and knowledge."* *Abigail used her wisdom and resources to solve the problem. She also offered her counsel to David.*

13. *(Responses will vary.)*

14. *(Responses will vary.)*

15. *(Responses will vary.)*

CHAPTER TWELVE
MAN IN THE GARDEN

1. Three meanings of "head" are:
   a. *Authority*
   b. *Source*
   c. *Top-ranking*

2. What is the first job description for husbands?
   Be the head servant: Serve your wife.

3. How did Jesus model leadership?
   Jesus was a servant leader. He sacrificed His rights, privileges, desires, and position to come to Earth and give His life for us. He set the example for His disciples—and for us all —of being a servant. He showed His love for us through His death on the cross.

4. What is the second aspect of the job description for husbands?
   Be the head source: Supply what your wife needs.

5. What are the two key words from Ephesians 5:28–29?
   a. *Nourish*
   b. *Cherish*

6. How are you to "nourish" your wife?
   Spiritually—through prayer and my example.

Physically—by being the provider for my family.
Emotionally—by honoring and cherishing her.

7. *(Responses will vary.)*

8. Paraphrase 1 Peter 3:7.
(Responses will vary.)

9. Explain the Biblical meaning of "weaker vessel."
"Weaker" does not mean less valuable or capable. Consider the eyes in comparison to other parts of the body: They are "weaker" than our feet and so require special care—but they are not less important.

10. Explain the Biblical meaning of "giving honor."
"Giving honor" means "to value, esteem highly, or to be precious."

11. What is the third aspect of the job description for husbands?
Be the best "head": Strive for mastery.

12. What is the key point of 1 Timothy 3:2?
The emphasis is on "being"—i.e., being a husband to one wife. In other words, it is not just being married to one's wife on paper but actually fulfilling the requirements of being a husband to her.

13. *(Responses will vary.)*

14. *(Responses will vary.)*

15. *(Responses will vary.)*

16. *(Responses will vary.)*

17. *(Responses will vary.)*

CHAPTER THIRTEEN
WOMAN IN THE GARDEN

1. The acronym HELP stands for:
   a. *Honor and respect*
   b. *Encourage*
   c. *Love*
   d. *Pray*

2. What is the difference between honor and respect?
   Respect is based on position; honor is based on who a person is.

3. According to 1 Peter 3:1–2, what is the best way to witness to an unsaved or disobedient husband?
   Through godly and respectful behavior

4. Summarize the eight ways in which a woman should respect her husband.
   a. *Acknowledge his God-given role to lead.*
   b. *Ask him to lead the family.*
   c. *Allow him to explain his choices.*
   d. *Avoid negative phrases.*
   e. *Accept the fact you won't always agree.*
   f. *Abstain from criticizing him in front of family and friends.*
   g. *Admit it openly and ask for forgiveness when you have been disrespectful.*
   h. *Absolutely never go behind his back or act deceitfully.*

5. Bearing in mind the analogy of ways in which we honor a priceless possession, how can you show honor to your husband?
   a. *Protect him from harm or damage.*
   b. *Brag about him.*
   c. *Place him in a position of prominence.*
   d. *Maintain your relationship.*

6. What is the significance of the meaning of Eve's name, particularly as it applies to wives?

The name 'Eve' means "mother of all living" or "life-giver." As women, we should give life to our family; we should build up our family and not tear it down.

7. Paraphrase Colossians 2:2. *(Responses will vary.)*

8. Encouragement is communicated through our *words* and *actions*.

9. Which verses speak about "encouraging words?"
   Proverbs 18:21, Proverbs 10:11, Proverbs 31:26, Ephesians 4:29 (and many others!)

10. Which verses speak about "encouraging actions?"
    Proverbs 31:27, Titus 2:5 (and many others)

11. What is the meaning of "love" in Titus 2:4, and how can we apply it to marriage?
    The word means "friendship." It is important to cultivate a healthy friendship with your spouse.

12. Generally speaking, two key aspects of a man's emotional need for sex are:
    a. *A man expresses intimacy through sex.*
    b. *A man gains self-worth through sex.*

13. Apply 1 Corinthians 7:3–4 to your marriage.
    (Responses will vary.)

14. Why is prayer such an important part of a woman's role as "help?"
    Prayer can change my perspective as a wife and correct areas of weakness and blind spots. Prayer should redirect my focus off the problem and onto the Problem Solver. Prayer is one important way I can come alongside my husband and support him when he is weak, tempted, stressed, unsure, or tired.

15. *(Responses will vary.)*

CHAPTER FOURTEEN
GOD IN THE GARDEN

1. What are the three things God did for Adam and Eve in the Garden after they sinned?

   a. *He gave them hope.*

   b. *He gave them covering.*

   c. *He gave them protection.*

2. Write your own definition of 'redeem.'
   (Responses will vary.)

3. What do we learn about hope from Romans 8:24–25?
   Hope is not based on what we see or already have obtained. Hope is based on God and on His power. We need to persevere because God is at work, even if we don't always see the results. Hope is rooted in faith.

4. On what must we base our hope? How can this change of attitude help us in our marriages?
   Too often we give up on our marriage because we don't "see" changes. We need to base our hope on God and His power, not on our circumstances. Changing our focus to God should renew our hope because God is able to do above and beyond what we can even imagine.

5. God clothed Adam and Eve after they sinned. The coverings He made for them were symbolic of what?
   This symbolic act from the Garden was of God's redemption. This act was fulfilled when Jesus went to the cross. We can receive redemption through Jesus' blood and forgiveness of our sins. We are "covered" by His blood. Just as animals were sacrificed to make coverings for Adam and Eve, so Jesus sacrificed His life for us.

6. How can we apply this "covering" to our marriages?
   If we have been covered by the blood of Christ, we understand what it is to be forgiven and thus are able to offer forgiveness to our spouse. We must learn to be merciful and gracious because God is merciful and gracious to us.

7. What is the significance of the word "as" in the Lord's Prayer?
   God will forgive us as we forgive each other. We cannot expect to receive God's forgiveness if we refuse to forgive each other.
8. *(Responses will vary.)*

9. When facing a difficult situation, what three things are important to remember?
   a. *Don't run away.*
   b. *Search your heart.*
   c. *Remember God's protection.*

10. *(Responses will vary.)*

11. *(Responses will vary.)*

12. *(Responses will vary.)*

END NOTES

CHAPTER ONE
[1] Henry, M. Commentary on Genesis 2. Accessed at http://www.ccel. org/ccel/henry/mhc1.Gen.i.html

CHAPTER TWO
[1] Wikipedia. Accessed at en.wikipedia.org/w/indexphp?title=Root&old id=294416536; search 'root.'

CHAPTER FOUR
[1] Dickinson, J. 1768. "The Liberty Song."

[2] Growing Up in Canada: National Longitudinal Survey of Children and Youth. Human Resources Development Canada, Statistics Canada, Catalogue no. 89-550-MPE, no.1, November 1996, p. 91.

[3] "Fatherless Homes Breed Violence." Accessed at http://www. fathermag.com/news/2778-stats.shtml

CHAPTER FIVE
[1] Clark, D. 1980. "Jesus and Women." In *Through Peasant Eyes* by Kenneth Bailey. Grand Rapids, MI: William B. Eerdmans Publishing Company.

[2] Hensley, A. "10 Big Differences between Men's and Women's Brains." Accessed June 16, 2009, at mastersofhealthcare.com/blog/2009/10-big-differences-between-mens-and-womens-brains

[3] Wright, H. Norman. 2000. *Communication: Key To Your Marriage*, Ventura, CA: Regal Books. pp. 126–31 (adapted).

[4]Hensley, A. op cit.

[5] Ibid.

[6] Wright, H. Norman. 2000. *Communication: Key To Your Marriage*, Ventura, CA: Regal Books. pp. 126–31 (adapted).

[7]ibid.

[8] Strong, J. 1979. *Strong's Exhaustive Concordance of the Bible.* Nashville, TN: Thomas Nelson Publishers. p. 54.

[9] Ibid., p. 72.

CHAPTER SEVEN
[1] Strong, J. 1979. *Strong's Exhaustive Concordance of the Bible.* Nashville, TN: Thomas Nelson Publishers, p. 31.

[2] Kastleman, M. B. 2007. *The Drug of the New Millunnium–The Brain Science behind Internet Pornography.* Provo, UT: PowerThink Publishing.

[3] Ibid.

[4] Ibid

[5]Accessed at money-zine.com/Financial-Planning/Debt-Consolidation/ Consumer-Debt-Statistics

[6]Murray, A. 1981. *With Christ in the School of Prayer.* New Kensington, PA: Whitaker House.

CHAPTER EIGHT
[1]Attributed to John Calvin.

[2] *Websters New World Dictionary,* 2nd ed. 1986. New York: Prentice Hall Press, p. 649.

[3] Strong, J. 1979. *Strong's Exhaustive Concordance of the Bible.* Nashville, TN: Thomas Nelson Publishers, p. 35.

[4] Ibid., p. 32.

[5] Strong, J. 1979. *Strong's Exhaustive Concordance of the Bible.* Nashville, TN: Thomas Nelson Publishers, p. 47.

[6] Strong, J. 1979. *Strong's Exhaustive Concordance of the Bible.* Nashville, TN: Thomas Nelson Publishers, p. 30.

[7] Elliot, J. Accessed at wheaton.edu/bgc/archives/faq/20.htm

[8] Attributed to Martin Luther.

CHAPTER NINE
[1] Strong, J. 1979. *Strong's Exhaustive Concordance of the Bible.* Nashville, TN: Thomas Nelson Publishers, p. 73.

[2] Ibid., p. 74.

[3] Robbins, D. A. Accessed at http://www.victorious.org/attitude.htm.

CHAPTER TEN
[1] *Webster's New World Dictionary, 2nd ed.* 1986. New York: Prentice Hall Press, p. 421.

[2] Shakespeare, W. *Measure for Measure*, Act I, scene 4, line 77.

CHAPTER ELEVEN
[1] Greek Lexicon entry for *hupotasso*. Accessed at http://www. biblestudytools.com/lexicons/greek/kjv/.

[2] Ibid.

CHAPTER TWELVE
[1] Amplified' Bible. 1987.La Habra, CA: The Lockman Foundation. Used by permission.

[2] Army Field Manual 21–20.

[3] Strong, J. 1979. *Strong's Exhaustive Concordance of the Bible.* Nashville, TN: Thomas Nelson Publishers, p. 72.

[4] Greek Lexicon entry for *thalpo.* Accessed at http://www. biblestudytools.com/lexicons/greek/kjv/.

[5] Chapman, G. 2004. *The Five Love Languages.* Chicago, IL: Northfield Publishing.

[6] Wright, H. N. 2000. *Communication: Key to Your Marriage.* Ventura, CA: Regal Books, pp. 126–131, adapted.

CHAPTER THIRTEEN
[1] Strong, J. 1979. *Strong's Exhaustive Concordance of the Bible.* Nashville, TN: Thomas Nelson Publishers, p. 87.

[2] *Websters New World Dictionary,* 2nd ed. 1986. New York: Prentice Hall Press, p. 674.

[3] David B. Guralinik. (1986). *Websters New World Dictionary* (pp. 1211, 2nd ed) New York: Prentice Hall Press

[4] Greek Lexicon entry for *phobeo.* Accessed at http://www. biblestudytools.com/lexicons/greek/kjv/.

[5] Strong, J. 1979. *Strong's Exhaustive Concordance of the Bible.* Nashville, TN: Thomas Nelson Publishers, p. 72.

[6] Feldhahn, S. 2004. *"For Women Only."* Colorado Springs, CO: Multnomah Publishers, Inc.

[7] Strong, J. 1979. *Strong's Exhaustive Concordance of the Bible.* Nashville, TN: Thomas Nelson Publishers, p. 37.

[8] *Websters New World Dictionary,* 2nd ed. 1986. New York: Prentice Hall Press, p. 460.

[9] Greek Lexicon entry for *kaleo.* Accessed at http://www.biblestudytools. com/lexicons/greek/kjv/..

[10] Greek Lexicon entry for *para.* Accessed at http://www.biblestudytools. com/lexicons/greek/kjv/.

[11] Greek Lexicon entry for *parakleo.* Accessed at http://www. biblestudytools.com/lexicons/greek/kjv/.

[12] Greek Lexicon entry for *parakletos.* Accessed at http://www. biblestudytools.com/lexicons/greek/kjv/.

[13] Greek Lexicon entry for *philos.* Accessed at http://www. biblestudytools.com/lexicons/greek/kjv/.

CHAPTER FOURTEEN
[1] Strong, J. 1979. *Strong's Exhaustive Concordance of the Bible.* Nashville, TN: Thomas Nelson Publishers, p. 37.

[2] *Websters New World Dictionary,* 2nd ed. 1986. New York: Prentice Hall Press, p. 1189.

[3] Strong, J. 1979. *Strong's Exhaustive Concordance of the Bible.* Nashville, TN: Thomas Nelson Publishers, p. 25.

[4] Strong, J. 1979. *Strong's Exhaustive Concordance of the Bible.* Nashville, TN: Thomas Nelson Publishers, p. 93.

[5] Strong, J. 1979. *Strong's Exhaustive Concordance of the Bible.* Nashville, TN: Thomas Nelson Publishers, p. 45.

[6] Strong, J. 1979. *Strong's Exhaustive Concordance of the Bible.* Nashville, TN: Thomas Nelson Publishers, p. 29.

CHAPTER FIFTEEN
[1] Strong, J. 1979. *Strong's Exhaustive Concordance of the Bible.* Nashville, TN: Thomas Nelson Publishers, p. 15.

[2] Strong, J. 1979. *Strong's Exhaustive Concordance of the Bible.* Nashville, TN: Thomas Nelson Publishers, p. 22.

[3] Strong, J. 1979. *Strong's Exhaustive Concordance of the Bible.* Nashville, TN: Thomas Nelson Publishers, p. 47.

[4] Strong, J. 1979. *Strong's Exhaustive Concordance of the Bible.* Nashville, TN: Thomas Nelson Publishers, pp. 8, 79.

[5] Strong, J. 1979. *Strong's Exhaustive Concordance of the Bible.* Nashville, TN: Thomas Nelson Publishers, p. 22.

[6] Ibid.

[7] Strong, J. 1979. *Strong's Exhaustive Concordance of the Bible.* Nashville, TN: Thomas Nelson Publishers, p. 24.

www.ingramcontent.com/pod-product-compliance
Lightning Source LLC
Chambersburg PA
CBHW032032080426
42733CB00006B/58